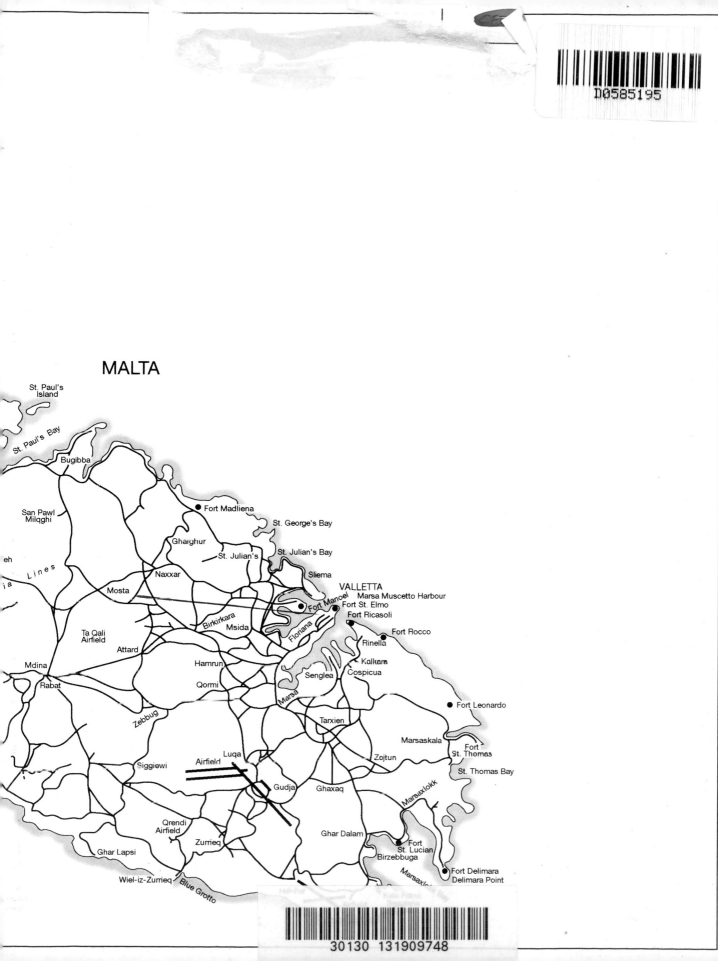

MALTA

St. Paul's Island

St. Paul's Bay

Bugibba

San Pawl Milqghi

● Fort Madliena

St. George's Bay

eh

ia Lines

Gharghur

St. Julian's

St. Julian's Bay

Naxxar

Sliema

Mosta

VALLETTA

Marsa Muscetto Harbour

Fort Manoel

Fort St. Elmo

Fort Ricasoli

Ta Qali Airfield

Birkirkara

Msida

Floriana

Fort Rocco

Attard

Rinella

Mdina

Hamrun

Kalkara

Rabat

Qormi

Senglea

Cospicua

Marsa

Fort Leonardo

Zebbug

Tarxien

Marsaskala

Fort St. Thomas

Luqa Airfield

Zojtun

St. Thomas Bay

Siggiewi

Gudja

Ghaxaq

Marsaxlokk

Qrendi Airfield

Zurrieq

Ghar Dalam

Ghar Lapsi

Fort St. Lucian
Birzebbuga

Fort Delimara
Delimara Point

Wiel-iz-Zurrieq

Blue Grotto

Marsaxlo

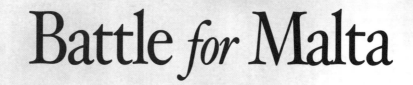

Battle *for* Malta

Battle *for* Malta

George Forty

Ian Allan
PUBLISHING

First published 2003

ISBN 0 7110 2940 7

Published by Ian Allan Publishing

an imprint of Ian Allan Publishing Ltd, Hersham, Surrey KT12 4RG.
Printed by Ian Allan Printing Ltd, Hersham, Surrey KT12 4RG.

Code:0310/xxB2

Contents

Chronology

1940

May	Reservists called up to man ARP Centres. Special Constabulary formed.
	Blackout regulations enforced from 3 May.
24 May	Lieutenant-General Sir William Dobbie KCB, CMG, DSO appointed as Acting Governor.
27 May	Curfew regulations in force.
3 June	Malta Volunteer Defence Force (Home Guard) formed.
10 June	Italy declares war on Great Britain and France, so Malta is at war.
11 June	First Italian air raid on Malta; hits Grand Harbour, Hal Far and Kalafrana. Fighter Flight (Sea Gladiators 'Faith', 'Hope' and 'Charity') in action.
18 June	First night raid on Malta.
22 June	First Italian bomber shot down by Flight Lieutenant Burges in 'Faith'.
2 August	Operation 'Hurry' — first delivery of 12 Hurricanes from carrier *Argus*; all arrive safely.
August/September	Operation 'Hats' — first convoy of three merchant ships with RN escort arrives from Alexandria carrying 40,000 tons of supplies.
November	Operation 'Collar' — convoy from Gibraltar carrying 20,000 tons of supplies delivered without loss.
11 November	The Fleet Air Arm makes a successful attack on Italian naval base at Taranto.
17 November	Operation 'White' — second delivery of 12 Hurricanes from *Argus*. Eight run out of fuel; only four arrive.
10 December	X Fliegerkorps arrives in Sicily.

1941

January	Operation 'Excess' — convoy from Gibraltar. Operation 'MW 5½' — convoy from Alexandria. HMS *Illustrious* manages to reach Malta after continual enemy air attacks, which go on when the ship is under repair in Grand Harbour. However, work continues and the carrier is made seaworthy. Manages to reach Alexandria on 23 January.
3 April	Operation 'Winch' — 12 Hurricanes sent from *Ark Royal*, all arrive safely.
8 April	Orders issued for formation of Malta Striking Force.
27 April	Operation 'Dunlop' — 24 Hurricanes sent from *Ark Royal*; 23 arrive Malta.
19 May	Lieutenant-General Sir William Dobbie GCMG, KCB, DSO, appointed as Governor and Commander-in-Chief.
21 May	Operation 'Splice' — 48 Hurricanes sent from *Ark Royal* and *Furious*, 45 arrive safely.
June	X Fliegerkorps withdrawn from Sicily to assist with Operation 'Barbarossa'.
1 June	Air Vice-Marshal Hugh Lloyd takes over as Air Officer Commanding, vice AVM Maynard.
6 June	Operation 'Rocket' — 44 Hurricanes sent from *Ark Royal* and *Furious*, 43 arrive safely.
14 June	Operation 'Tracer' — 48 Hurricanes despatched from aircraft carriers *Ark Royal* and *Victorious*; three are lost, rest arrive safely.
27 June	Operation 'Railway I' — 22 Hurricanes sent from *Ark Royal*, 21 arrive safely.
30 June	Operation 'Railway II' — 42 Hurricanes sent from *Ark Royal* and *Furious*, 34 arrive safely.
24 July	Operation 'Substance' — convoy from Gibraltar arrives with 65,000 tons of supplies.
26 July	Italian E-boat raid on Grand Harbour and Marsamxett. Brave attack, but force wiped out by shore batteries and fighter aircraft.
September	Operation 'Halberd' — convoy from Gibraltar delivers 85,000 tons of supplies.
9 and 13 September	Operation 'Status I' and 'Status II' — 60 Hurricanes from *Ark Royal* and *Furious*, 59 arrive safely
October	Force K formed to operate against Italian convoys supplying Axis troops in North Africa. Uses Malta as its base, destroying at least two enemy convoys until three of its cruisers and a destroyer are disabled by a minefield off Tripoli.
18 October	Operation 'Callboy II' — 11 Albacores and 2 Swordfish, all except one Swordfish arrive.
November	II Fliegerkorps transferred to Sicily for all-out attack on Malta.
	FM Albert Kesselring arrives in the Middle East.
12 November	Operation 'Perpetual' — 37 Hurricanes from *Argus* and *Ark Royal*, 34 arrive.
13/14 November	*Ark Royal* sunk by U-boat after aircraft delivered to Malta.
2 December	Hitler issues Directive No 38 outlining operations in the Central Mediterranean.
22 December	II Fliegerkorps begins second major German assault on Malta.

1942

February	Operation 'MF 5' — unsuccessful convoy from Alexandria, forced to turn back on 14 February.
28 February	Operation 'Spotter' — failed attempt to fly Spitfires off *Eagle*, thwarted by untested fuel tanks.
7, 21 and 29 March	Operations 'Exile', 'Picket I' and 'Picket II': 31 Spitfires safely delivered from *Eagle*.
	Operation 'MW 10' — convoy from Alexandria, serious losses, only 5,000 tons of stores saved.
April	Climax of Blitz with many buildings destroyed and only a few serviceable aircraft left.
14 April	10th Submarine Flotilla forced to leave Malta due to enemy bombing.
15 April	Malta awarded the George Cross.
20 April	Operation 'Calendar' — USN carrier *Wasp* carries 47 Spitfires (601 and 603 Squadrons); 46 arrive but followed by massive enemy retaliation so that only 7 are left serviceable 48 hours later.
21 April	Photo reconnaissance over Sicily reveals glider strips at Gerbini ready for Operation 'Herkules' (Axis attack on Malta).
23 April	39 General Hospital at St Andrew's destroyed by German dive-bombers.
26 April	Ultra intercepts show that Germans have plans to move *Luftwaffe* units of II Fliegerkorps from Sicily to other locations such as North Africa.
29–30 April	Meeting between Hitler and Mussolini at which invasion of Malta (Operation 'Herkules') is approved.
2 May	More intercepts from Ultra confirm *Luftwaffe* withdrawal from Sicily; London tells Malta to discount Axis invasion plans.
7 May	Field Marshal Viscount Gort VC, arrives to take over as Governor from General Dobbie.
9 May	Operation 'Bowery' — aircraft carriers *Wasp* and *Eagle* deliver 60 Spitfires safely to Malta.
9 May	Water economy measures, because of the effects of the recent heavy bombing on the water supply, mean that standpipes are closed down all night.
10 May	Heavy air battles over Malta, during which 36 enemy aircraft destroyed by fighters and ground AA fire. Smoke screens used for the first time.
	Kesselring states that his task of neutralising Malta is complete.
19 May	Operation 'LB' — HMS *Eagle* delivers 17 Spitfires all safely. 77 safe arrivals in the last nine days and resulting air victories over Malta mark a turning point in air war over the island.
19 May	Axis spy (Carmelo Borg Pisani) lands by MTB, captured and hanged 28 November.
June–October	Aircraft carriers *Eagle* and *Furious* despatch a total of 226 more Spitfires of which 213 arrive safely. Severe food rationing now necessary.
3 June	Operation 'Style' — 31 Spitfires sent from *Eagle*, 27 arrive.
9 June	Operation 'Salient' — 32 Spitfires sent from *Eagle*, all 32 arrive.
11–16 June	Operation 'Vigorous' — large convoy from Alexandria, forced to turn back — so no supplies are delivered and Malta is running out of food. Operation 'Harpoon' — large convoy from Gibraltar, also heavy losses, but 25,000 tons of food get through (enough for 2–3 months). Rationing now reaches a peak.
2–14 July	Renewed Blitz on island is then followed by shelving of Operation 'Herkules' because of the fall of Tobruk and advance of DAK in North Africa.
July–October	Successful raids from Malta by bombers and torpedo planes on enemy convoys bound for North Africa materially assist Eighth Army in halting Rommel's advance and then preparing for Battle of El Alamein.
15 July	Operation 'Pinpoint' — 32 Spitfires sent from *Eagle*, 31 arrive.
21 July	Operation 'Insect' — 30 Spitfires sent from *Eagle*, 28 arrive.
10–15 August	Operation 'Pedestal' — convoy from Gibraltar, hit by enemy continuously for five days — only five merchant ships reach Malta, but land 53,000 tons of supplies, saving island.
11 August	HMS *Eagle* sunk by U-boat.
11 August	Operation 'Bellows' — 38 Spitfires sent from *Furious*, 37 arrive.
17 August	Operation 'Baritone' — 32 Spitfires sent from *Furious*, 29 arrive.
10–20 October	Final Axis Blitz, then *Luftwaffe* units transferred from Sicily to North Africa to support DAK — raids on Malta lessen considerably.
13 November	Final cancellation of Operation 'Herkules'.
15–20 November	Operation 'Stoneage' — convoy from Alexandria, brings 35,000 tons of stores, which finally lifts siege.
18 November	RAF from Malta attack Sicily.
December	Operation 'Portcullis' lands some 55,000 tons of supplies with no losses.
31 December	Siege virtually over.

1943

January	Force K reconstituted (see April 1941).
20 January	Operation 'Childhood' — attack by British MTBs based on Malta, against German and Italian craft attempting to close on Valletta harbour.
23 February	Last significant air raid.
12 March	Lord Gort is presented with a Sword of Honour.
4 April	Malta Special Service Troops leave Malta on operations.
13 April	Attack on Kerkenna Islands.
8–22 June	US engineers build new airstrip on Gozo.
20 June	The King visits Malta.
7 July	British Government declaration of intent to hand back power to the Maltese people after the'war.
10 July	Operation 'Husky' — Allied invasion of Sicily.
5 August	General Eisenhower holds meetings in Malta.
3 September	Sole surviving Sea Gladiator 'Faith' presented to Malta.
10–11 September	Surrender of Italian Fleet at Malta.
15–18 September	234 (Malta) Infantry Brigade operations in Dodecanese.
29 September	Badoglio signs Italian surrender at Malta.
17–19 November	Churchill visits Malta.
8 December	Roosevelt visits Malta.

1944

5 August	Lord Gort leaves Malta and hands over to Lieutenant-General Schreiber.
15 August	Forces from Malta support Operation 'Dragoon' — Allied amphibious invasion of Southern France.
28 August	Last 'Alert' sounded at 8.43pm and 'All Clear' at 9pm.
10 December	Home Guard stands down.

1945

30 January–1 February	British and American Chiefs of Staff hold pre-Yalta meetings in Floriana.
30 January	Churchill arrives by air.
2 February	Roosevelt arrives by sea.
2/3 February	All visitors, including VIPs, leave Luqa for Yalta.
4 February	Special Constabulary stands down.
7 May	End of war in Europe.
15 August	End of World War 2.
19 August	Victory and Thanksgiving service at Valletta.

Below: The Great Dictator speaks. Benito Mussolini, *Il Duce,* declared war over the Italian radio, at 7pm on the evening of 10 June 1940. He would be killed in the last days of the war, Italy having already surrendered in 1943.
IWM — FLM 1506

Introduction

'My mission of securing and protecting Axis supply in the Mediterranean was of paramount importance. It was to be accomplished by putting enemy naval and air installations on the island of Malta out of action.' These were the words of the most important wartime German commander in the Middle East, namely, the Commander-in-Chief South, Generalfeldmarschall Albert Kesselring. They were written under the heading 'The Situation at the end of November 1941' as part of a detailed history of the war in the Mediterranean area, which Kesselring compiled for the Allies whilst in prison camp soon after the end of the war. Whilst he makes the point that he wrote his history without any reference material — including, initially, even any maps — he does say that others 'in the know', for example, *Luftwaffe* Generals Seidemann and Deichmann, both of whom had at one time been chief of staff to Kesselring, did carry out an objective review of his work, so he must have been fairly happy with its accuracy. Therefore it is most relevant that he gives such importance to the task of dealing with this tiny archipelago — especially as the Axis failed to achieve their mission to neutralise it, which undoubtedly had a disastrous effect on all future Axis campaigns in the theatre.

We will be examining the reasons for this failure in some detail in this book, but clearly Malta was always at the very top of the German field marshal's agenda. As we will see, he blames inaction by Adolf Hitler as being the root cause of the problem, in particular that the Führer did not do enough to stir up Germany's inept ally, Italy, to more positive action. On the face of it, from the outset the Italians easily had the land, sea and air power to deal with the overstretched British, yet, despite some individual acts of extreme bravery, they completely failed even to begin to do anything constructive anywhere in the Mediterranean. Their failure over Malta — and that of the Germans too — was due in no small measure to the bravery, determination and tenacity of the entire population — military and civilian — of Malta, whose story I have tried to tell in this book.

Malta, having the only British-controlled harbour between Gibraltar and Alexandria, was crucial to the success of Allied operations in the Middle East. However, its proximity to enemy territory, in particular to Sicily, which was only some 60 miles away, meant it was difficult both to defend and to resupply. The Axis appreciated the need to capture Malta, but, after making plans to do so (Operation '*Herkules*'), they 'bottled out', preferring to try to neutralise the tiny archipelago by air bombardment and sea blockade. One can draw an almost exact parallel with the Germans' failure to deal with Great Britain in 1940, after they had lost the Battle of Britain, then continually postponing and finally cancelling, their intended invasion of Great Britain (Operation '*Seelöwe*' ['Sealion']), deciding that they could starve the British into submission. They did not succeed for much the same reasons as they failed over Malta.

The Italians began their air assault on Malta on 11 June 1940, and, despite the island's chronic shortage of both anti-aircraft artillery and fighter planes to defend against the hordes of Italian bombers, the Italians did not succeed in denting the defences. Then the Germans also arrived on Sicily to lend their support and tried with the might of the *Luftwaffe* between January and April 1941, again without lasting success. 'Barbarossa' and the increasing German involvement on the Eastern Front was bound to affect German participation in the Mediterranean. Nevertheless in 1941 and 1942,

massive amounts of bombs were dropped; indeed between 1 January and 24 July 1942, there was only one 24-hour period during which no bombs were dropped on Malta. As in the London Blitz, air raids became a part of daily life, for civilians and military alike, over 5,000 people being killed and wounded, whilst the general health of the population declined drastically due to inadequate food. On 15 April 1942 King George VI bestowed the award of the George Cross on the islands, which thereafter became known as 'Malta GC' — a well-deserved and unique achievement.

Clearly the Axis thought that Malta GC had suffered more than was humanly possible to withstand, because, on 10 May 1942, Kesselring announced that Malta had been neutralised, which was of course far from the truth. The convoys still managed to get through despite horrendous casualties, the critical 'Pedestal' convoy of August 1942 making all the difference between starvation on the one hand and survival on the other. The Axis powers were forced to launch yet another series of intensive raids in October 1942, but by then it was far too late, Malta had weathered the storm and was now slowly building up its strength so as to be able to take on offensive operations.

The remarkable change that had been achieved can be gauged from what General Dwight D. Eisenhower had to say about Malta (in his memoir *Crusade in Europe*), when he, plus General Alexander and Admiral Cunningham, visited the island as guests of the Governor, Lord Gort:

> '*Malta presented a picture far different from one of a few months earlier, when it was still the target for a hostile air force that had little effective opposition. Malta had taken a fearful beating but the spirit of the defenders had never been shaken. As Allied air and naval support approached them through the conquest of North Africa, they rose magnificently to the occasion. By the time we found need of Malta's facilities its airfields were in excellent condition and its garrison was burning to get into the fight.*'

Sadly, my only visit to Malta was in 1953, when I stopped there overnight whilst returning to the UK by air from the Far East, having been 'medevaced' from Korea, after losing an argument with a Chinese mortar bomb. Unfortunately illness last year, whilst I was researching for this book, prevented me from renewing my all too brief acquaintance with the island so I have had to do everything at long range.

Many books have been written about Malta and the significant role it played in World War 2, so what makes this book different from all the rest? I would like to think that it is the tried and tested formula by which I have now written 12 books in Ian Allan Publishing's 'At War' series, starting with the *Desert Rats at War — North Africa* way back in 1975. The formula was new in those days, very different to the normal style of staid Regimental Histories, being based instead on what I called 'pictorial evocations', that is to say, telling the story by means of a suitable mix of first-hand 'I was there' battle accounts, together with relevant, exciting photographs, some provided by individuals, the rest chosen with care from relevant collections — in this case those of the National War Museum Association (NWMA) of Malta, the Imperial War Museum (IWM) and the Bundesarchiv. I always tried to tell the story from both sides, so, just as I did in the *Battle for Crete*, this book has a fair amount of information about the Axis and, in particular, about Operation '*Herkules*', the planned invasion of Malta which, thanks to Hitler's decision, was never put into practice.

Acknowledgements

As usual I have many people to thank for their help and kindness. In particular, Frederick Galea, Maltese historian, author and the Honorary Secretary of the NWMA, who has been my constant link with the island. Having been prevented by illness from visiting Malta, I had the great good fortune to establish contact with him and to meet him in London when he made a brief visit there in 2002. Since then he has continually provided me with photographs, information and advice, so I could definitely not have managed without his expert help. The same goes as far as Frank Rixon BEM and Peter Rothwell are concerned, both being senior members of the George Cross Island Association. They have been a constant source of information and 'I was there' stories from both the six volumes of Frank Rixon's *Malta Remembered*, which contain a wealth of information on events and stories as told by veterans of Malta GC, and equally importantly, the regular GCIA newsletters which Peter Rothwell has edited. Again I must thank them both for their most valuable assistance.

Some years ago, after many visits to the IWM Department of Photographs, I decided also to explore their Sound Archives and ever since have found them to be a continual source of valuable information, so my thanks go to both these departments and their staff for all their help. In addition, my thanks go as always to the MOD Whitehall Library and to the Public Record Office, also to the RAF Historical Branch, the Commonwealth War Graves Commission and the Malta Tourist Office. The same applies to the Regimental Museums of the Devons and Dorsets, the Durham Light Infantry, the Queen's Own Royal West Kent Regiment, the Royal Hampshire Regiment, the Cheshire Regiment, the Manchester Regiment, the Royal Irish Fusiliers, and to the Corps museums of the RAMC, the RMP, the REME and the Royal Engineers Library, all of which have kindly assisted me. My thanks must also go to all those who have allowed me to quote from their reminiscences, be they to be found in the GCIA documents already mentioned or elsewhere. I hope the following is a complete list, but I apologise if I have missed out anyone: Mrs Daphne Barnes, R. Bleasdale, Douglas Geer, Nat Gold, Harry Gratland, Bill Green, Mrs H. Langford, Mrs P. B. Lucas, Harry Moses, Mrs R. Rivett, Mrs Philippa Szymusik, Mrs T. R. Tutt and Dr Vivian Wyatt, together with numerous others whose names appear with their reminiscences but who have sadly passed on. Mrs H. Langford of Cattistock, Dorset, deserves special mention as it was her uncle, Eddie Beater from Dorset, who took some of the very evocative naval photographs of convoys in the Med. Born and raised to farming (which he hated!), he was lightweight boxing champion of the West of England and put himself down as professional boxer to 'escape' into the navy from his reserved occupation. He survived at least one sinking and postwar joined the Merchant Navy, then worked in ship-building, so the sea was in his blood. I was particularly pleased to have his photographs as they have not been seen before in any other books.

George Forty
Bryantspuddle
May 2003

Opposite below: Malta by night. Air raids continued day and night, so the searchlight units had a busy time lighting up the night skies for the AA gunners. Streams of tracer are also visible at the far end of Grand Harbour, Valletta.
IWM — GM 1542

Left: Air Raid Warning! Raising the red flag on the Palace lookout tower in Valletta was a warning to all of an impending air raid. It was accompanied by the sounding of the siren. Some days it flew for six hours at a stretch. IWM — GM 460

Below: Bombing Malta. It is the afternoon of 24 April 1942 and the suburbs of Floriana, southwest of Valletta, are hidden behind a thick curtain of dust from exploding bombs. On the left of the photograph is the Phoenicia Hotel and, on the right, the famous twin towers of St Publius Church. NWMA Malta — 6200)

Right: Keep Smiling! The imperturbable grin of RQMS (later Major) F. R. A. 'Nobby' Read of the Hampshires says it all. *IWM — GM 2805*

Below: 'I read the news today.' Everyone on the island, both civilians and garrison members, kept abreast of the news by reading the *Times of Malta*. Here Gunner D. V. Heritage of Mapton, Leicester, reads his copy. *IWM — GM 1630*

Opposite above: Malta under attack. Bombs fall in Grand Harbour as the Germans try to sink the carrier *Illustrious* (hidden by the clouds of dust behind the largest crane on the right of the picture), 10 January 1941. *Bruce Robertson*

Opposite below: Malta Convoys, September 1941. HMS *Hermione* seen from HMS *Sheffield* (its pom-poms are just visible); both were part of the escort for convoy Operation 'Halberd', which got through to Malta with just one of its nine merchantmen being sunk and landed 85,000 tons of stores. *IWM — A 5742*

Chapter 1
Malta and its People

Faithful British Sentinel

'Since the days of Nelson Malta has stood a faithful British sentinel guarding the narrow and vital sea corridor through the Central Mediterranean. Its strategic importance was never higher than in this latest war.'
Winston Churchill[1]

'Malta, my dear Sir, is in my thoughts sleeping and waking.'
Horatio Nelson

The ancient archipelago of Malta, which has been an independent republic since 1974, is located in the central Mediterranean and comprises six rocky islands/islets — three inhabited: Malta, Gozo and Comino, and three uninhabited: Cominotto, Filfla and St Paul's. It lies some 60 miles (100km) to the south of Sicily, whilst the distance to Cape Bon in Tunisia, North Africa, is 200 miles. Gibraltar is about 1,000 miles away and Alexandria some 820 miles. The islands have a total area of 121.9 square miles (315.6sq km). The main island of Malta is 94.8sq miles in area, Gozo 25.9sq miles, Comino 0.97sq miles and the other small islets a total of 0.19sq miles. Malta is 16.8 miles long by 9.3 miles at its widest point, with a coastline some 85 miles long. Gozo, which is 9 miles long by 4.3 miles across, with a coastline of 27 miles, is separated from Malta by the 3.4-mile wide Comino Channel in which lies Comino.

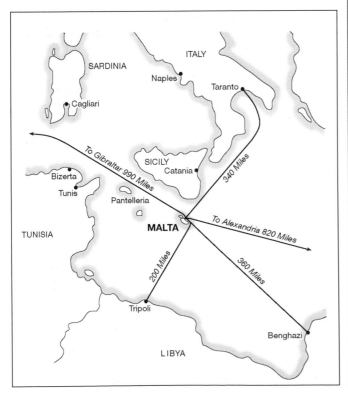

Ever since earliest times Malta has been looked upon as 'the navel of the inland sea', long providing a natural bridge between Europe and Africa. Its strategic location and wonderful natural harbours have ensured that it has, throughout the centuries, played a vital role in the continuing struggles of a succession of great powers vying for dominance in the Mediterranean. Long ago, between 4000 and 2500BC there was an advanced culture flourishing on the islands and, although many of its ancient mysteries are even now still unsolved, it is credited with building some of the earliest free-standing religious architecture in the world. There is also evidence of there being both Phoenician and Carthaginian rulers of Malta — the name of the islands is itself of Phoenician origin ('Mlt' pronounced 'Malet' and meaning 'place of refuge' or 'safe harbour') — then, in 218BC it came under the Roman empire (known as 'Melita') and remained so until AD870 when the Arabs conquered the islands. Somewhat earlier, St Paul had been shipwrecked on Malta in AD59 and, it is said, had converted the population to Christianity. The Arabs were defeated in 1091 by the Norman ruler of Sicily and the Roman Catholic religion was re-established.

During the Middle Ages the islands gained fresh importance and this was especially true at the time of the Knights of St John, who held Malta for almost 270 years, successfully withstanding the first great siege of Malta by the Ottoman Empire in the 16th century. On that occasion they held off the Turkish fleet from May to September 1565, with heavy losses being suffered on both sides. They would continue to hold the islands until surrendering them to Napoleon and the French in 1798. Malta would next be blockaded by Britain and then occupied by British forces in 1800. However, in 1802 the Treaty of Amiens restored the islands to the Knights, but they did not return to their rule because the people protested and instead agreed to acknowledge the monarchs of Great Britain as the rightful future sovereigns of Malta, always provided the British maintained the Roman Catholic Church and honoured the Maltese Declaration of Rights. These conditions were accepted and ratified by Britain in the Treaty of Paris in 1814, after which Malta became a British colonial possession, ruled by a British governor, with English as its official language.

For the next two centuries Malta, with an ever-increasing economy and population, was indivisibly bound to the United Kingdom and the British Commonwealth, becoming a most important naval base, built and developed to safeguard the most vital 'Imperial Lifeline' between the UK, India, the Far East and Australasia, via the Suez Canal, which was opened in 1869. To quote from Ian Allan Publishing's *Sea Battles in Close-up No 11*:

'The base was fully equipped with docking and repair facilities capable of dealing with the heaviest ships in service in the Royal Navy. It also had ample reserves and resources, sufficient to maintain the British Mediterranean Fleet which was based at Malta and which, between World Wars 1 and 2, was second in strength only to the Home Fleet. The security of the base, symbolised by the presence of up to four battleships and their attendant cruisers and destroyers anchored in Grand Harbour, seemed unshakeable.'[2]

And of course, as the dockyard developed, so it became the economic mainstay of the islands.

During the Crimean War and the Great War, Malta provided not only a military and naval base for Britain, but many Maltese also joined the Royal Navy and the Merchant Navy. At the time of the ill-fated Gallipoli landings in April 1915, it also became 'The Nurse of the Mediterranean', thousands of casualties being brought to the islands for treatment in one of the 27 large hospitals that were established there. Its nearest neighbour, Italy, was a partner on the Allied side during the Great War, so presented no threat. Malta became self-governing in 1921, although power and responsibility was still shared between Maltese and British ministers. Then, in 1933, when it became clear that the now-Fascist Italy would have to be looked upon in future as a potential enemy, Malta reverted to a colonial regime. Its heroic story during the second great siege in World War 2 is the subject of this book so there is no need for further explanation at this time, but one of the high spots was naturally the award of the George Cross to the islands on 15 April 1942. Later in the war, on 7 July 1943, the British Government made a declaration of intent to hand back power to the Maltese people after the war, explaining how:

> 'For more than 10 years, between 1921 and 1933, the people of Malta enjoyed full legislative and administrative responsibility under the Crown in the conduct of their national affairs, the control of naval and military Services and of all matters appertaining to the position of Malta as an imperial fortress, or otherwise affecting imperial interests or policy being reserved to the Imperial Government. It is the policy of His Majesty's Government that responsible government in the same sphere should again be granted to Malta after the war.'

At the end of hostilities no time was lost in taking the first steps to implement this undertaking. Nevertheless such matters take time, especially as the idea of full integration into the United Kingdom had first to be thoroughly explored. Thus it was nearly another two decades before Malta achieved its independence within the British Commonwealth, on 21 September 1964. Then another decade later, it became a republic in its own right — Repubblika ta'Malta. Its alliance with Great Britain officially ended in 1979, since when it has sought, and obtained in most cases, agreement from the major world powers to pledge their support for Malta's continuing neutrality in all future conflicts.

Malta now has a population of some 375,000 people, most of whom live on the main island of Malta. Although the state-owned Malta Drydocks is still Malta's largest industrial employer, tourism has become its major industry, with some 1.1 million visitors coming to the islands' sunny shores for holidays. In 1997, tourists provided about 40% of Malta's national income, over half of them coming from the UK and Ireland.

Topography

At first glance the main island may seem to comprise just a featureless rocky plateau, but in fact there are a number of topographical regions. In the west there is a high limestone plateau, falling away in steps on all sides and providing only for some sparse grazing for sheep and goats; seawards is a cliff-fringed coastline with sheer drops. To the north, the plateau is edged by an escarpment, whilst in the east it is cut by a number of small valleys. In these lower-lying areas, the soil is good and, by making full use of irrigation, crops are intensively cultivated. North of the plateau there are ridges and depressions, which are continued in the islands of Comino and Gozo. In the south and southeast of Malta there are gently undulating uplands which is where many of the people live. The coastline has high cliffs in the southwest, gentle bays in the northwest, and wide beaches in the north. The Grand Harbour of Valletta is a natural deep-water harbour with a depth of some 25 metres, which has ensured its economic and strategic importance over the centuries.

One of Malta's major problems is that it is badly supplied with drinking water. There are no rivers or lakes, so it depends very much on its winter rainfall. This has over the years provided underground stores of fresh water, despite the porous nature of the limestone rocks that causes some to run away into the sea. However, nowadays there is an ever-growing need for water because of over-use, especially by the tourist trade, so seawater desalination plants are being built. The hot, dry summers and mild, wet winters are influenced by the trade winds, the mistral and, less pleasant, the xlokk that brings sultry, warm and humid air from North Africa, particularly in the late summer/early autumn.

A Diverse Population

As already mentioned, over the past 6,000 years the islands have had many foreign invasions, the result being that the population is now very mixed. The present inhabitants are mainly the descendants of southern European (Italy/Sicily) and North African/Arab peoples. In addition, during the 20th century there was an increasingly large number of Anglo-Maltese marriages, so there is a sizeable British minority, as well as smaller numbers of Greeks, Syrians and Indians. Malta has two official languages — Maltese and English. As the latter is taught at school from an early age almost every Maltese speaks English. The Maltese language is a 'fusion' of a Sicilian form of Italian and North African Arabic; in fact it is the only Semitic language written in Latin script, with 24 consonants and five vowels in its alphabet.

'A Land of Honey and Roses'

Sir Harry Luke KCMG, LLD, who was Lieutenant-Governor of Malta, 1930–8, wrote an 'account and an appreciation' of his days in Malta in which he says:

> 'If anything shaped as differently from a circle as the Mediterranean can be said to have a centre, that centre is Malta . . . equidistant from the Mediterranean's western and eastern extremities; it is half-way house between the Occident and Orient, historically no less than geographically; it has been its nerve-centre — and more than its nerve-centre, its magnet — from the 'time whereof the memory of man runneth not to the contrary.' All the people of the Middle Sea have possessed, influenced or coveted Malta at one time or another.'

Sir Harry also wrote this about the countryside of Malta, which I think gives the reader a delightful — and still largely true — picture of the small group of islands which Cicero called 'a land of honey and roses', and which its inhabitants still know as 'the flower of the world'. He writes:

> 'A word has been said already as to the grandeur of the cliff scenery of Malta. Inland on the other hand, the countryside can scarcely be called either grand or impressive, and during the summer months there is little colour to set against the brown aridity of the fields other than the sage of the olive, the carob and the fig-trees, and the pinks and whites of the oleanders beside the roads. But after the autumn rains have begun to refresh the parched earth the land rapidly assumes a mantle of young green, and the wild flowers appear shyly above ground, beginning with two lovely miniature blooms — the brilliantly blue Iris minuta and the even more ethereal, strongly scented satarina. This, the

Right: The unsinkable aircraft carrier. An aerial view of the Maltese islands from the south, looking like 'a silver leaf in an azure sea'. The islands of Malta and Gozo can be seen clearly, with the tiny island of Comino in between.
NWMA Malta — 12335

Below: A view across part of the countryside of Malta, looking north from the statue of St Joseph, Victoria Lines. The small fields and stone walls were a major feature of the countryside.
IWM — A 11331

tiniest narcissi, looks as if it had been called into being by a touch of a fairy's wand in Walt Disney's Fantasia. Later, in March and April, Malta and Gozo alike seem to glow with the crimson, deepening into purple, of the sulla, the clover or sainfoin with which thousands of acres are sown for fodder. Among the most striking blends of colour are those produced by many varieties of Bougainvillea (which flourishes exceedingly in Malta), and the purple — and — cream flowers of the wild caper, against the background of rich gold fortifications.' [3]

Another historian, Robert A. Bonner, also wrote about the special landscape of Malta in his fascinating, small, illustrated book about the 8th (Ardwick) Battalion of the Manchester Regiment (TA) which served in Malta throughout the siege. The book is naturally mainly about the men of the battalion and their experiences — 'The Ardwick Boys' as they were called, after the district of Manchester from which so many of them came. He has this to say about Malta:

'Clinging to the rock are an infinity of terraced fields, some hardly bigger than a suburban back garden but all surrounded by stone walls built from the flints cleared from the earth by hand. On all sides a multitude of wind pumps to raise the water for irrigating the crops. From the coast, looking up the slopes, Malta appeared to be solid stone as only the terraced walls could be seen; but from the tops looking down the whole landscape was one of luscious growth or in winter rich red brown earth. All this against a continual background of brilliant blue sea, blue sky and burning sun.' [4]

Although, like everywhere else in Europe, the built-up areas on the islands have increased dramatically (recently rising from 6 per cent to 17 per cent of the total area) with the increased housing sadly destroying much of the countryside, Malta is still a profusion of coloured blossoms during the rainy months. Certainly that is how it must have looked in the 1930s as global war came ever nearer. At that time much of the countryside was under intensive cultivation and an immediately recognisable feature were the stone walls that the farmers built around their fields in order to prevent the shallow soil from being blown away at certain times of the year. The whole island was a patchwork of stone walls and narrow lanes, dotted in places with watchtowers — left over from piratical days and now used as grain stores. Although it was a somewhat featureless landscape, about an hour before sunset the whole island took on a soft radiance that:

'. . . deepens to rose, so that it is transformed as the shadows lengthen, into a loveliness as unreal as a fairy story. The immense fortifications with their deep ditches and airy bridges, the palaces, the churches and reflection-painted harbours are no longer reminders of a turbulent and blood-stained history, but part of the fabric of enchantment while the light lasts.' [5]

On the small farms the main crops were potatoes, maize, wheat and animal fodder, together with grapes, figs, peaches and oranges. In some more sheltered valleys even bananas and dates could flourish. The secret of success was irrigation, and long-established wells determined the sites of the farms, whilst herds of goats had long provided milk for the poorer people. The main form of transport was the motor bus, which ran between the towns, whilst for shorter, local journeys everyone used the *carrozzi* — a four-wheeled cart drawn by a small horse (barbs from North Africa) whose harness was splendidly decorated with brasses, tassels and even a pheasant tail feather to top off the horses' headdress. On water, in the har-

bours, they used the gondola-like dghaisa, in which the rower stood facing the bows. Such was Malta as the war clouds approached.

A Soldier Remembers

'March 1939 saw me arrive to join the 16th Company (Searchlights) having been trained at Haslar, Gosport' — that is how ex-Royal Engineer, Joseph C. Bushell, began his reminiscences of life on Malta prewar. He continued:

'Much of our time was spent on training at night with the help of the Fleet Air Arm, flying Swordfish from Hal Far. On occasions we were given the opportunity to fly at night in the "target" planes to see what searchlights looked like from the other end. Of course these were the halcyon days and I do not think that many young people could see the possibility of war. It was the day of "The Gut" and the "Gharry", with "Housey-Housey" at the Vernon and La Valette clubs, grand opera at the Opera House in Strada Reale, chicken and chips for half a crown and "Blue Label" at threepence a bottle. When the declaration of war against Germany came I was in fact manning a searchlight at Hal Far "drome". The pace of life did not change very much, there was still plenty of everything and the war seemed a long way away.

'Early in 1940, it was decided to move the detachment from Hal Far, to a coastal position about a mile from the Grand Harbour in the direction of Kalafrana. It was in fact an old Victorian [?] coastal fort. In the walls of the main emplacement there were still embedded huge steel rings, which one supposes were used to move the single gun. Our war really started on the 10th June 1940, when Italy declared war that evening. The following day the bombing started.' [6]

Security

In the middle of 1936 the Italian Consul-General was expelled for organising espionage and subversion and thereafter Italy appears to have abandoned any further attempts at spying or sabotage. On Italy's entry into the war Italian residents and some pro-Italian Maltese were interned and there was no sign of any Fifth Column activity or resumed espionage. This was the situation until 19 May 1942, when Carmelo Borg Pisani, a Maltese, landed at first light on the southeast coast from an E-boat, with a wireless set, maps, money and instructions to report to Italian naval intelligence on operational movements, morale and food supplies. Fortunately, he was immediately captured by an alert patrol from the 1st Dorsets and handed over to military intelligence. He was executed in November 1942 and there were no further attempts to land spies.

War Approaches

In the 1940s Malta had a population of about 275,000 people, most of whom lived on the main island, which meant that there were some 2,250 people per square mile, making it one of the most densely populated places in the world. However, the population was probably in a better situation than it had been for the past hundred years, despite the general standard of living being low. Most people had sufficient food and the basic essentials of life, but luxuries were only for the rich. A few thousands of the people were unemployed and there was some poverty in the more depressed areas of the three main cities of Valletta, Marsa and Hamrun. As Dr Charles Boffa wrote about the days just before the war in his book on the second great siege of Malta:

'Radiant spring was reigning over our islands. In the country, the idyllic sight of farmers following a plough pulled by a horse or

*donkey was still common. Sunshine wrought its magic on
everything. The crowded streets of Valletta were a kaleidoscope of
life and colour. By day the city buzzed with vigour, the market
resounded to the hubbub of housewives haggling and hawkers
crying out their wares. Valletta had many stately old palaces,
auberges and mansions, many of which were later destroyed
through enemy action . . . Contrasted with the animation of
Valletta was the peaceful atmosphere of Rabat, Mdina, Dingli,
Naxxar, Mgarr and Mellieha, all situated on high ground. From
here could be viewed a lovely expanse of terraced and walled
fields, valleys, groves, spires and other picturesque villages.
Sunshine bathed the countryside and farms . . . From the air,
Malta looked beautiful, covered with the freshness of spring. After
dark, most of the villages retained their aura of mystery. The
quaint and narrow blacked-out streets were still and silent. The
good things in life went unappreciated. Soon the landscape would
be darkened by exploding shells and death.'* [7]*

Notes
1. Winston Churchill: *The Second World War*, Volume III, 'The Grand
   Alliance'.
2. Peter C. Smith and Edwin Walker: *The Battles of the Malta Striking Force*.
3. Sir Harry Luke: *Malta, An Account and an Appreciation*.
4. Robert A. Bonner: *The Ardwick Boys went to Malta*.
5. Charles J. Boffa: *The Second Great Siege — Malta 1940–43*.
6. Taken from *Malta Remembered*, Volume 1.
7. Charles J. Boffa: *The Second Great Siege — Malta 1940–43*.

Opposite top:
Most country people kept chickens, but like the goats and rabbits, many were
killed off when food became short. Eggs also went up in price — from a few
pence to at least 15 shillings a dozen.
IWM — A 11341

Opposite bottom:
A peaceful scene in a back street of Balzan. Together with Attard and Lija, it
became known as one of the 'Three Villages'. All three were flooded with
refugees when Valletta and the other larger towns were evacuated early on in
the war. Seven out of every ten of the island's goats had had to be killed
before the siege was over.
IWM — A 11333

Below:
Valletta harbour. Maltese workers unloading fruit and other supplies from the
neighbouring island of Gozo. This tranquil scene was actually photographed
after over two years of bombing on 17 August 1942.
IWM — A 11326

Above: Still for hire. Prewar, the main form of transport for most people was the motor bus, but when petrol supplies became almost non-existent, it was back to a donkey cart or 'Shanks' pony'. In town, for short journeys, the *carrozzi* (a Maltese cab) was used; some were still plying for hire in the bombed streets of Valletta. They were drawn by small horses (barbs from North Africa).
IWM — GM 1182

Right: 'Keep smiling!' A cheerful group of Maltese mothers and children sit on the pavement in Valletta, undaunted by the enemy air raids.
IWM — GM 2058

Chapter 2

Setting the Scene

To Defend or not to Defend?

The prewar defensive situation that existed in Malta was unfortunately no different from that which pertained over most of the British Empire, namely that the elastic was being stretched almost to breaking point as far as the soldiers on the ground and the airmen in the skies were concerned and even some of the sailors were not entirely certain that Britannia still ruled the waves. However, most ordinary people seemed to have an unshakeable optimism that they could always rely upon the Senior Service to produce whatever miracles were needed to retrieve any situation, no matter how dire, before it was too late. This did not, however, make for a happy situation, although it is doubtful whether many of the civilian population of this vital link in Britain's worldwide defences, actually knew how bad things really were. The figures make sobering reading. For example, when Air Chief Marshal Sir Arthur Longmore assumed command of the RAF in the Mediterranean and Middle East in May 1939, he found that his parish was some 4.5 million square miles in size, and that to protect this vast area he had just 29 squadrons — a total of about 300 aircraft — half of which were based in Egypt, the rest being spread between Palestine, the Sudan, Kenya, Aden and Gibraltar. Malta didn't even figure in the list. He had no modern fighters or long-range bombers; he was short of aircraft spares and other equipment; and the strength of his squadrons in Egypt and Palestine was only 96 bombers and bomber transports, most of which were Bristol Blenheim Mark I light bombers and Bombay transport aircraft.

Longmore's tiny force was dwarfed by the Italian *Regia Aeronautica*, which had some 2,600 first-line aircraft, Mussolini having taken great pains to create a large, modern air force when he came

Below: Air Chief Marshal Sir Arthur Longmore commanded the RAF in the Mediterranean and Middle East at the start of the war. He usually piloted his own aircraft when visiting the large number of RAF stations in his far-flung command. On his right is Squadron Leader A. R. W. Curtis, his personal staff officer. *IWM — CM 571*

into power — he once boasted that he would black out the sun with his planes! To be fair, it had probably reached its peak in 1936, since when its war potential had been reduced through lack of reserves and equipment. Nevertheless, in general terms the units of the Italian Air Force were still better armed and more easily reinforced than any of their RAF counterparts. However, as Philip Guedalla points out in his book on Middle East air power in the early 1940s:

> *'Since air warfare is less dependent on machines than on the men who fly them, it was felt that the RAF was likely to excel the Italians in tactical efficiency. Their pilots were expected to be more temperamental than our own; and although they might perform with credit in air combat, it was doubtful how they would be able to sustain reverses.'* [1]

The upshot of this situation, especially because of Malta being so close to Sicily and the Italian airfields there, was the considered view of the British Air Ministry that the island was far too vulnerable to air attack to be defensible, especially because it was far too easily cut off from the basic supplies it needed to maintain its garrison and civilian population. Therefore there were no RAF aircraft permanently stationed on Malta.

Fortunately the problems were not all on the British side. The Italian Air Force had for some years studiously followed the doctrines of General Giulio Douhet, Italy's foremost air power theorist of the inter-war period, who had advocated the use of strategic bombers to attack enemy cities and their industrial plants, at the expense of co-operation with the other two services. Thus the Italians lacked an adequate torpedo bombing force, whilst their bombs were generally too small to be effective against ships. It would appear that one reason why the Italians neglected torpedo bombers was because torpedoes cost considerably more than bombs. The inadequacy of the Italian-made bombs led *Il Duce* (literally 'The Commander' — a title that Benito Mussolini had conferred upon himself) to adopt a highly devious plan. He pretended to order the 15th Bomber Wing, which was equipped with old, obsolete biplanes, to become a suicide unit – the pilots would crash their planes into British warships. Mussolini then took steps to ensure that the British became aware of this order and was delighted when it was accepted by them as being true.

We will come back to the topic of whether or not Britain's leaders considered Malta to be worth defending in a moment, but first let us look at the situation in the other two armed services. Though the Army elastic was just as stretched as that of the RAF, at least the defence of Malta was included in its plans. C-in-C Middle East at the time was General Sir Archibald Wavell, a soldier of considerable experience who had fought in both the Boer and Great Wars. 'The Chief' as he was affectionately called, was a brilliant commander, much admired and respected, although well known for his general inarticulacy. His total ground forces in the area were 36,000 British and Commonwealth troops in Egypt, together with a further 14 infantry battalions scattered around the rest of the Middle East, Malta having a regular garrison of four of the British battalions. As with the RAF, what Wavell's men lacked in quantity — the Italian

Above: Longmore had only 96 obsolescent bombers and bomber transports, most of the former being Bristol Blenheim Mark Is as seen here, which had an effective range of only 678 miles. Later they were joined by the longer-nosed Mark IV, which had almost double that range. *IWM — CM 27*

Regio Esercito then numbered about 86 divisions, with over 220,000 Italian and colonial troops in North Africa alone — they made up for in quality. Wavell's tiny force would soon prove its superb fighting ability despite the enormous odds. Quality would once again win over quantity, the British regulars and the men from Australia, India, New Zealand, South Africa and the rest of the Commonwealth, quickly establishing their superiority everywhere.

On the Mediterranean Sea, the Royal Navy, under its C-in-C, Admiral Sir Andrew Browne Cunningham (known by one and all as 'ABC' after his initials), had from the outset to be prepared to deal with the large and powerful *Regia Marina* which, by July 1940, had six battleships including two new 35,000-ton 'fast' battleships (*Littorio* and *Vittorio Veneto*), plus 19 cruisers, about 50 destroyers, 100 submarines and numerous smaller vessels. Their main bases at Taranto and Naples were handily placed to control the Eastern Mediterranean — which Mussolini considered to be an 'Italian lake'! Nevertheless, despite the Royal Navy now being on its own, without French support from late June 1940, and increasingly vulnerable to attack from the air as well as the sea, ABC's Mediterranean Fleet would prove capable of fulfilling the tasks of supplying and protecting Malta, safeguarding convoys through the Mediterranean and the Red Sea, whilst constantly attacking enemy convoys and their supply lines to North Africa. The grievous losses that were inevitable were accepted without flinching. As Cunningham famously remarked: 'It takes the Navy three years to build a ship; it takes three hundred to rebuild a reputation.' Therefore, from the outset, they would take the fight to the enemy no matter what the odds might be.

Cunningham recognised from the beginning the vital part that Malta had to play in the battle and the Admiralty took an entirely different view from that of the Air Ministry. Notwithstanding this, soon after war was declared, the majority of the fleet was quietly withdrawn from places like Malta (apart from a few submarines), to the comparative safety of Alexandria. The following table gives an interesting comparison between the British fleet, based at Alexandria and Gibraltar, and the Italian Navy with its multiplicity of available bases such as Augusta, Brindisi, Messina, Palermo, Syracuse and Taranto. As will be seen, there was a definite British inferiority in numbers, especially as far as escort vessels and submarines were concerned.

Type of Ship	Britain		Italy
	Alexandria	*Gibraltar*	
Battleships	4	1	6
Aircraft carriers	1	1	none*
Cruisers 8in	none	none	7
Cruisers 6in	8	1	12
Destroyers	20	9	51
Misc *(incl escort vessels and MTBs)*	none	none	71
Submarines	12	none	115

* but many shore-based aircraft were available

The Other Axis Partner

Of course I have deliberately left the other relevant Axis partner, Germany, out of the argument, because at this stage Hitler was satisfied that the Italians had everything under control and would soon be able to see off the tiny British forces in the area of Mussolini's lake. What would happen when he realised the incompetence of the Italians and their inability to cope will be dealt with in due course.

The Arguments

Whilst it may seem strange that there should have been such a divergence of views, especially when one considers Malta's unique position, its wonderful harbour and port facilities, the Air Ministry's pragmatic view was based upon hard-headed, difficult to fault, logical arguments, even though it may have sounded defeatist. For example:

Population

The tiny, rocky archipelago held a massive population, making it one of the most densely packed corners of Europe, so there were many civilian mouths to feed, in addition to the sailors, soldiers and airmen who would make up the large garrison that would be needed for its defence.

Food and Other Commodities

Despite the fact that, prewar, Malta had exported some potatoes and fruit, the archipelago could only produce about a third of its own requirements of foodstuffs and less than 5 per cent of such staple needs as iron and steel, coal, and other essential raw materials. It had to import everything else, mostly from its nearest neighbours, who were, unfortunately, about to become the immediate aggressors, despite any hopes to the contrary.

Vulnerability

It would take Italian bombers just 20 short minutes to fly the 60 miles of airspace that separated the airfields on Sicily and their intended targets on the islands. Mass bombing of civilian targets, as had been evidenced in the Spanish Civil War, could swiftly reduce cities, towns, aerodromes, dockyards, harbours and other vulnerable areas to uninhabitable rubble — Italian and German pilots had done just this in Spain.

Defences

As we have seen, Malta, like so many other parts of the British Empire at that time, was short of all the basic items needed to defend

Below: 'The Chief'. General Sir Archibald Wavell was a brilliant, highly respected soldier, whose total ground forces in the Middle East were some 36,000 men in Egypt, plus just 14 other infantry battalions spread over the rest of his vast command. *IWM TR 841*

itself properly, such as troops, guns, naval vessels, aeroplanes, reserve stocks of food, ammunition and other supplies. So far as anyone knew, the British fleet had all but withdrawn some years before, whilst there were no fighter aircraft on the island to defend it.

To quote Philip Guedalla again:

'Whilst it is almost inconceivable that Great Britain could find itself without allies, embarrassed in the East and at war with both France and Italy, or even with one of these two powers alone . . . If, however, we did find ourselves at war against such a combination, there is no doubt that we should be compelled, temporarily at least, to close the Mediterranean to all British sea and air traffic, to abandon Malta and to withdraw the fleet.'

There were many senior officers, especially in the Army and RAF, who felt this was the correct answer to the problem, having been persuaded by the force of the logical arguments as outlined. In addition, there was the inescapable fact that Great Britain might well need all its resources to look after its own islands, especially when standing alone in 1940.

The Key

However, despite all these negative arguments, those who were passionate about retaining Malta through thick and thin, had on their side probably the most important single advantage, one that would see the islands and the islanders not thrown to the wolves. This was the unshakeable opinion of the incoming Prime Minister, Winston Churchill, who, ever since his days in the Admiralty during the Great War, had always considered that Malta held the key to the Eastern Mediterranean and with it the security of Egypt and the Suez Canal. And he was not alone, being supported to the hilt by 'ABC', who had already shown considerable moral courage and breadth of view in his diplomacy in the light of the destruction by the British of the French Fleet at Oran.[2] Cunningham now stressed the importance of Malta and emphasised the catastrophic effect on Britain's prestige that complete withdrawal would bring. Fortunately, Churchill and Cunningham were able to sway the War Cabinet and the proposal to vacate Malta was abandoned. 'I do not know how near we came to abandoning the Eastern Mediterranean', said Cunningham, 'but if it had come to pass it would have been a major disaster, nothing less.' Nevertheless, he and Churchill did not have an easy task, there being continual opposition from high-ranking Army and RAF officers.

The Italians Declare War

At 7pm on the evening of 10 June 1940, an enthusiastic crowd of Roman citizens gathered in the Piazza Venezia and dutifully listened to Il Duce making yet another of his bombastic speeches. The speech was also broadcast over Rome Radio. Unfortunately, as it would turn out for Italy, this time Mussolini was not declaring war on some impoverished African country like Abyssinia, but rather against Italy's erstwhile Great War allies, Great Britain and France. Granted, France was within days of surrendering to the Germans and the British had withdrawn their Expeditionary Force from the Continent back to their island fortress. Nevertheless, they were still a force to be reckoned with, especially whilst the Royal Navy still ruled the waves. The dictator had been agonising for days, trying to decide whether or not to join the war or stay neutral. However, now he had made up his mind, and was determined to act whilst there were still some rich pickings to be had. 'If we have decided to face the risks and sacrifices of war,' he told his audience, 'it is because the honour and interest of Italy requires it of us.' He was nevertheless careful even in such a bellicose speech to try to reassure his imme-

diate neighbours of his 'honourable intentions'. 'I solemnly declare,' he assured them, 'that Italy does not intend to drag into the conflict its neighbours, Switzerland, Yugoslavia, Greece, Turkey and Egypt.' Then he added rather ominously that the strict application of his words depended upon them rather than on Italy, which did nothing to calm the frayed nerves in diplomatic circles.

Malta 'The Rock'

The success in taking an aggressive stance and the justification for all the suffering that the islands had to face, can best be measured by an admission made by both German and Italian historians, who postwar said that Malta was: 'the rock on which our hopes in the Mediterranean foundered'. An early vindication that this policy was the correct one came a few days after Mussolini had declared war when, on 9 July 1940, Cunningham took his whole fleet to within sight of the Italian coast and engaged a strong force of the enemy, which made a hasty exit. This was followed 10 days later, when HMAS *Sydney* encountered two Italian cruisers near Crete and sank one of them. These two actions set the pattern which saw the Italian Navy go out of its way to avoid battle, heralding a new optimism. Plans to abandon Malta were scrapped and a decision made in their place that whatever the costs, convoys to Malta must get through. The Italian Navy appeared to believe that they would suffer a terrible defeat at the hands of the British, so that the Royal Navy would then be able to 'ramble about the Mediterranean inflicting whatever damage it wants to our scarcely defended coast'.[3]

Notes
1. Philip Guedalla: *Middle East 1940–1942, A Study in Air Power.*
2. On 3 July 1940 Force H under Admiral Somerville bombarded the French fleet in the French naval base of Oran, when they refused his ultimatum: either to join the British; or disarm and sail to a neutral port; or to scuttle their ships where they lay. Force H sunk the battleship *Provence* and damaged numerous other vessels. Only the fast battleship *Strasbourg* and six destroyers escaped to Toulon.
3. Jack Greene and Alessandro Massignani: *The Naval War in the Mediterranean 1940–1943.*

Left: Later, the British battalions would be joined by Maltese men of the 1st Battalion, The King's Own Malta Regiment, who were embodied in August 1939. Here one of the battalion stands guard on Valletta harbour. *IWM — GM 290*

Below: ABC's flagship was the battleship *Warspite*, seen here entering Grand Harbour. The photograph was in fact taken in September 1943, after the siege had ended. Note the Seafire fighter on the flight deck of the carrier. *IWM — A 20652*

Right: All the RN vessels initially based on Malta were just a few submarines, the rest of the fleet having been quietly withdrawn to Alexandria. This is HMS *Taku*, an early T Class submarine, pictured here at the Lazzaretto Submarine Base, Manoel Island.
NWMA Malta — 1796

Below: War Headquarters, Malta. This was the entrance to Lascaris Barracks in the Great Ditch below the Duke of York entrance to Valletta. Innumerable tunnels connected various operations rooms and departments, including the GOC's office.
IWM — GM 2270

Chapter 3
The Garrison Assembles

A Slow Military Build-up

The military build-up of the islands' defences was still slow, even when it had been decided that Malta would be defended. Some pillboxes and other beach defences had been built during the Abyssinian crisis in 1935 and more were now constructed in 1939–40. Each was manned at best by a weak infantry section, comprised usually of an NCO and six men, armed with rifles, hand grenades and, where possible, a light machine gun. They were meant to be able to prevent enemy landings; however, numbers of available troops were initially pitifully small so, for example, none could be spared to defend Gozo, which inevitably left a large gap in the defences.

To defend Malta when war was declared against Germany in September 1939, there was a garrison of some 4,000 men, which included four regular British infantry battalions: 2nd Battalion, The Devonshire Regiment (2 Devon); 1st Battalion, The Dorsetshire Regiment (1 Dorset); 2nd Battalion, The Royal Irish Fusiliers (2 R Ir F); 2nd Battalion, The Queen's Own Royal West Kents (2 RWK). Together they formed the infantry element of 231st Infantry Brigade under the command of Brigadier L.H. Cox. At that time the brigade was simply known as 'The Malta Infantry Brigade'. They were reinforced by a battalion of local Territorials — 1st Battalion, The 1st King's Own Malta Regiment (1 KOMR) — who were embodied at St George's Barracks, St George's Bay, in August 1939.

Above: These soldiers are unloading food and other supplies that had arrived on a convoy early in the war. *NWMA MALTA — 6929*

Above:
Reinforcements arrive. British troops land in Malta to reinforce the garrison. Initially there was a steady stream of reinforcements to build up the garrison, but of course movement by sea became more and more difficult as the air offensive increased.
IWM — GM 346

Opposite top:
Lieutenant-General Sir William Dobbie KCB, CMG, DSO, was appointed as Acting Governor on 24 May 1940 and then, on 19 May 1941, became Governor and Commander-in-Chief. Churchill described him as being 'a Cromwellian figure at the key point'.
IWM — GM 786

Right:
General Dobbie inaugurates the third session of the Council of Government in the Tapestry Chamber of the Palace, Valletta. The beautiful Gobelin tapestries have already been taken down and stored for safe keeping.
IWM — GM 175

Opposite bottom and right:
Special Order of the Day, as written by General Dobbie on 18 June 1940.
NWMA Malta — 12488 and 12489

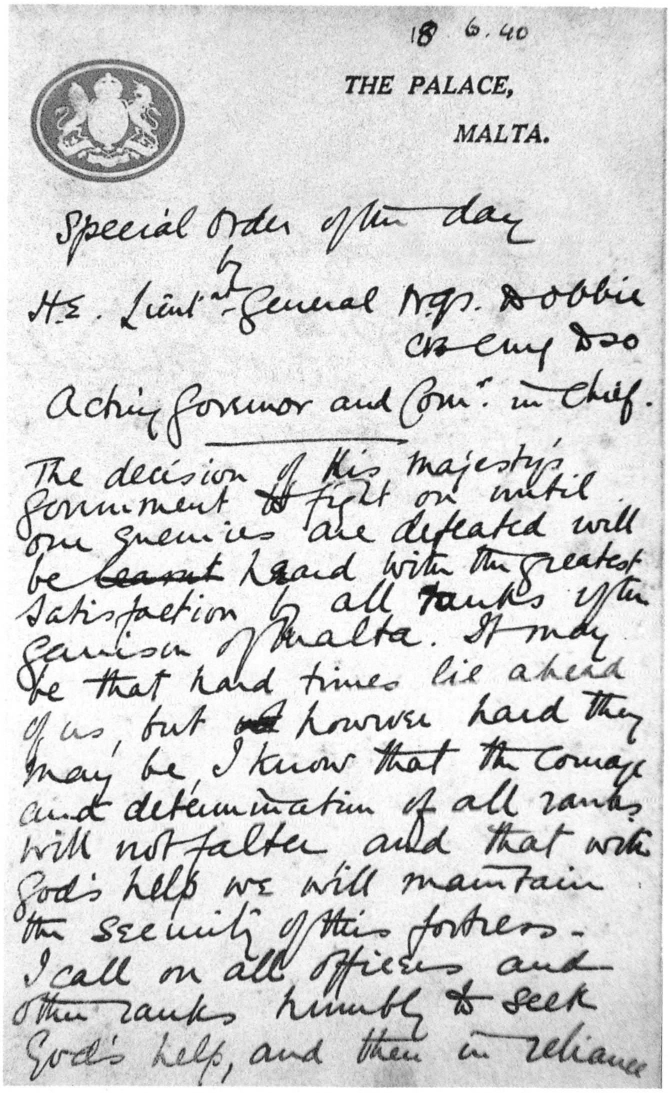

18 6. 40

THE PALACE,
MALTA.

Special Order of the day
by
H.E. Lieut.-General W.G.S. Dobbie
CB CMG DSO
Acting Governor and Com. in Chief.

The decision of His Majesty's Government to fight on until our enemies are defeated will be ~~learnt~~ heard with the greatest satisfaction by all ranks of the Garrison of Malta. It may be that hard times lie ahead of us, but ~~at~~ however hard they may be, I know that the courage and determination of all ranks will not falter and that with God's help we will maintain the security of this fortress. I call on all officers and other ranks humbly to seek God's help, and then in reliance

Initial Defence Plan

The defence plan was designed to protect against a surprise seaborne invasion, so it concentrated mainly on coastal defences, especially to protect the Grand and Marsamxett Harbours, the east coast and the Marsaxlokk (Marsa Scirocco) Bay. It was considered that the rest of the coast was reasonably secure as the cliffs made access difficult. The open northern beaches, such as Mellieha Bay, St Paul's Bay and Ghajn Tuffieha Bay were all suitable for assault landings; however, only some five miles inland there was a formidable natural obstacle — an escarpment, known locally as the 'Victoria Lines'. The escarpment had been reinforced with fortifications, while carefully sited artillery battery positions on this line, could, it was considered, deal with any incursions from the north. These included any enemy tank attacks through the passes in the escarpment.

Deployment

1 KOMR was allocated the northern end of the island and on 28 August 1939 moved to Mellieha, whilst the battalions of the Malta Infantry Brigade were spread out as follows:

East coast north of Valletta — 2 R Ir F
East coast south of Valletta — 1 Dorset
Most of Marsaxlokk Bay, plus various possible landing places on the south coast, including Wiel-iz-Zurrieq and Ghar Lapsi — 2 RWK
In reserve at Attard — 2 Devon

Beach defence posts were hurriedly constructed. To quote, for example, from the RWK history:

> *'The section posts were made of reinforced concrete. The beach posts were normally one storey and camouflaged to merge with the coastal background, while the depth posts were of two storeys and constructed so as to resemble the numerous small sandstone buildings that were dotted about the island. The armament of the back posts usually included a Vickers medium machine gun or a Bren light machine gun and an anti-tank rifle. And the fire-plan was to shoot along the coast wire so as to stop the enemy on the beaches. The depth posts were supplied with a small searchlight called a Lyon Light, for which a concrete emplacement was provided on or near the post. The power for this light was provided by a small petrol engine, which was often difficult to start and tricky to keep running. The depth posts were numbered L.1, L.2, etc., throughout the south of the island. The beach posts were referred to by distinctive letters and a number according to their position, such as 'C.5' (Calafrana [Kalafrana] 5), 'B.Z.4' (Birzebbuga 4) and 'S.O. 2' (Marsa Scirocco [Marsaxlokk] 2). Later on a number of reserve posts were constructed; these were numbered from R.1 to R.34 throughout the island.'* [1]

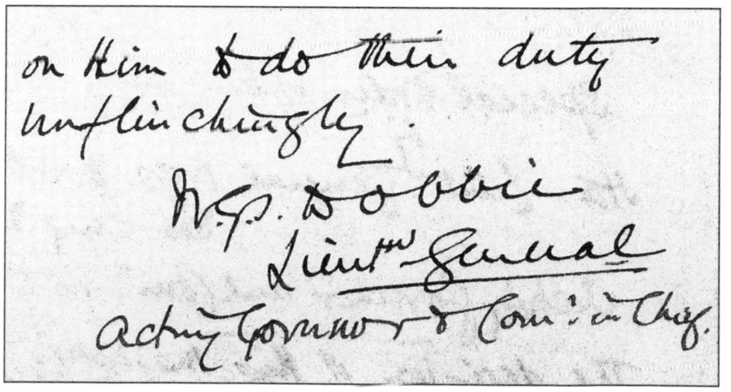

on Him to do their duty unflinchingly.

W.G.S. Dobbie
Lieut.-General
Acting Governor & Com. in Chief.

In addition to the posts, barbed-wire entanglements had to be erected, and this took a number of days of, as one RWK soldier recalled, 'back-breaking work in the extreme heat'.

By early October 1939 it had become apparent that Italy had no immediate intention of entering the war, so the threat of invasion faded and precautions could be relaxed. Billets were requisitioned near to battle positions and defence posts were manned only at first and last light 'stand to'. 2 RWK, for example, moved their Battalion Headquarters into a school at Tarxien, with their HQ Company in various nearby houses. Their reserve company moved into billets at Bir id Deheb with its HQ in the Australian Bar. Near to the beaches they occupied a block of flats, a large house called Belle Rive and a bar at Birzebbuga called The Smiling Prince. Rifle companies did likewise, setting up their messes in similar requisitioned houses, restaurants and bars. At the same time a percentage of the troops were able to leave the defence sector each evening for recreation — to play sport, visit the local cinemas, theatres and opera house. And, of course, those married men with families on the island could visit them. Those officers who owned cars could still use them, just so long as they complied with blackout regulations and were able to obtain petrol, which was now rationed.

Contraband Control

A pleasant change in routine came with the establishment of a system by which ships suspected of carrying contraband of war were intercepted and searched. Part of the search team was a detachment of soldiers who were taken on board a naval destroyer or small craft, ready to be put onto the suspect vessel, which was then taken to Alexandria or Malta. These detachments were often away from the island for some six to seven weeks, which made a very pleasant change from the boring routine of guard duty and manning beach defences. Battalions, of course, were changed around as well. For example, 2 RWK moved back to St George's Barracks in the New Year (1940) and took over the role of Fortress Reserve Battalion from 2nd Devons, who went out to the beach sector at Marsaxlokk. 'This was generally looked upon as a good move,' comments the RWK history, 'because Malta can be very uncomfortable with its cold winds in the winter, and fires were available in barracks but not in many billets near the beaches.'

Bren Carriers with the Fortress Reserve

The reserve battalion battle position was at Ta Qali aerodrome, near the centre of the island, from which roads radiated in all directions. These roads were frequently narrow and considerable knowledge of the island and map-reading skill was necessary to guide the whole reserve battalion, in lorries, along some of the possible counter-attack routes. Sergeant Stanley Haywood was in charge of the carrier platoon of the 2nd Devons. He had arrived in Malta in early September 1939 and had had to get to know every part of the island as quickly as possible — including every goat track!

'It was at Ta Qali we tried out the carriers to see what they were capable of,' he recalled later.

'Mosta lay to the north up a nice straight road with no houses, only shacks on either side of the road. Here we tested them for speed and got up to 60mph, but if they had got out of control there would have been not much we could have done about it.

Above: Men of the Devons on patrol, pass a defence post. Shortage of petrol did not hamper the mobility of the garrison, who used bicycles to great effect.
IWM — GM 2794

Above: Bren carriers were a valuable part of the fortress reserve and, like all AFVs, were camouflaged using this unique 'stone-wall' camouflage pattern, so that they would blend in with the hundreds of stone walls on the islands. This one has some added natural camouflage as well. *IWM — GM 834*

Cobbles were the worst things for tracked vehicles — it was just like having ball-bearings under one's feet! On the Mosta side of the aerodrome there was a steep downward slope. Here we drove the carriers along sideways to see what angle they could be driven at before slipping or losing a track. To the southeast towards Rabat, there were peaks where we made them climb until they failed or were on the point of slipping backwards. In this way we found out exactly what we could expect of them in case the need arose at any time . . . On the edge of the airfield we found drainage ditches had been dug. These made good gun positions. We also had gun positions on Mellieha Ridge.' [2]

Other Coastal Defences

In addition to the infantry defence posts there were coastal artillery guns. Initially there were just 32 coastal artillery guns — seven 9.2-inch, 10 6-inch, six 12-pounders and nine double-barrelled 6-pounders. All these guns were manned by the Royal Malta Artillery [4], except for the largest which belonged to the 4th Heavy Regiment, Royal Artillery. The guns were located at Forts Benghajsa, Bingemma, Campbell, Delimara, Madliena, Ricasoli, St Elmo, St Leonardo, St Rocco and Tigne. There were also a few old guns that had been retrieved from the naval dockyard and put back into commission.

Anti-Aircraft Defences

Despite the fact that it had been agreed to build up Malta's defences to a total of 122 heavy anti-aircraft (AA) guns, 60 light AA guns and 24 searchlights, by June 1940 only the searchlight numbers were up to scratch, there still being only 34 HAA and eight LAA guns on the

islands. Air raid shelters for both military and civilians alike were also in short supply, various go-ahead, prewar schemes having been turned down by the British Government as being too expensive. Despite these setbacks, and thanks in no small way to the Royal Malta Artillery and the King's Own Malta Regiment, who played a major part in manning the defences, Malta would eventually have all the firepower it needed and the men to man them. The arrival of the monitor HMS *Terror* from the Far East also helped to provide more firepower.[3]

And every gun was vital, there being over 3,200 alerts sounded for raids on the island during the siege, in which over 14,000 tons of bombs would be dropped between December 1941 and May 1942, damaging over 24,000 buildings and killing some 1,468 civilians — that is to say, one in every 200 of the population. Anti-aircraft guns would account for 236 enemy aircraft.

Sergeant Tom Ashby was a member of 16th Fortress Company, Royal Engineers, who manned the anti-aircraft searchlights. There was another Sapper Fortress Company on Malta, the 24th, which had coastal defence duties, including searchlights and later on provided the Bomb Disposal Unit — a job they learned as they went along! We have already met Joseph Bushell in Chapter 1; now some reminiscences from Tom Ashby:

'We disembarked from our ship to take our first steps on Malta at 3.30pm on 15 March 1940, then we marched from the quay across Floriana Square to Floriana Barracks which was to be our headquarters. The barracks was part of the old fortification, built in the time of the Grand Master of the Knights of St John, our barrack rooms were long and beneath the ramparts the doors opened onto the courtyard.

'After settling in a meal was laid on, then we were free to go to the local bars and so find our way around. Off we went, across the square, through the arch and down Strada Reale past the Opera House with the Police Station underneath. What a lovely place it was and very old. Someone mentioned the Gut, so we decided to find it, to see what the famous place looked like. Having found it, we visited the bars, the 'Golden Eagle', the 'Silver Horse', 'Tony's Bar', the 'George the Fifth', plus some cafes for 'Big Eats'.

'Twice a week we were taken to Fort Ricasoli by dghaisa rowed by a Maltese boatman employed by the services; sometimes the swell in the harbour was so high we thought we would never make it — but he always got us there and back. About April 23rd, we were sent to our site at Marsascala [Marsaskala], a little fishing village, the site was under the St Thomas tower. Soon we were friends with the folk in the village. The local bar, which was only a short distance away, befriended us and we could get bottles of Blue Label beer at 2½ pence a bottle or a crate of 24 bottles for half a crown. Whoever went down to the bar usually brought back a crate for the detachment who were on duty, so they could all have a drink at 'stand down', before they turned in . . . During the day we cleaned our equipment and had a practice manning of the searchlights and the sound locator, two hour guard duties and telephone manning. On June 9th at 1800 hours I received the message from HQ stating that the Government had issued an ultimatum to the Italian Government that if they had no reply, Britain would be at war with Italy from midnight. After logging the message in the book I went outside to tell the others. They would not believe me and eventually phoned HQ for confirmation. Having recovered from the surprise news we set about finishing the defences of our position. The machine-gun post was completed, barbed wire around the site was inspected and a coil of barbed wire placed ready to pull across the entrance. It was now 2300 hours so we sat around waiting for the news. We turned in at 0200 hours on 10th June. Rising again at 0600, the phone rang at 0651 with the order to "Stand By", as we were now at war with Italy and war could be expected. That was the start of "Great Expectations", knowing that Sicily was only 60 miles distant — equal to a journey from Portsmouth to London. It was a lovely day, the sky was clear and blue, the sea calm — we went for a swim but still expected to hear the drone of aircraft, but the day passed peacefully.'[5]

Above left: Basic low-level AA defence was provided by machine-gun posts like this one in a small stone sangar. The weapon is the Savage-Lewis machine gun that was widely used as a low-level AA gun in single, double and quadruple mounts by the Army, RAF and Home Guard. *NWMA Malta — 1828*

Above: AA searchlights like this one were an integral part of the air defence of Malta. The agreed build-up of AA defences included 24 searchlights, and they were all in position by June 1940, although the island was still short of AA guns. *RE Library*

Left: A Bofors 40mm LAA gun in action. Without doubt the most widely used, and most important, light anti-aircraft gun of the war was the Swedish-designed Bofors, which had been delivered to 18 countries before war started. It was built under licence by 10 of these, whilst many were captured/taken over for use by the Germans. *IWM — GM 744*

Above: Loading a QF 4.5in AA gun. This started life as a naval weapon, on trials in 1936. However, it was then decided to use some for land mountings around dockyards and naval installations, crewed by the Army. Its shell weight was 54.43lb and it had a maximum ceiling of 42,600 feet. *IWM — GM 941*

An Even Slower Build-up In The Air

AA guns alone could not defend against attacking enemy bombers so fighter aircraft were also urgently needed. The prewar estimate had been that at least four fighter squadrons would be required to defend Malta properly. However, all that the RAF initially had on Malta was a small number of obsolete London II flying boats, whose pilots had never flown a fighter aircraft in their lives. There were also, quite by chance, a number of Fleet Air Arm Gloster Sea Gladiators crated up and stored at the FAA depot at Kalafrana, awaiting shipment to Alexandria. They had been left behind by the aircraft carrier HMS *Glorious* when she left to take part in the Norwegian campaign. Four of these aircraft were uncrated and assembled. They would form the one and only fighter flight and, as we shall see, write their own special chapter in Malta's history.

Though we shall deal with the air defence of Malta more fully in a separate chapter, for the moment we will only note that, just as

with the ground troops, the build-up of aircraft, both for defence and attack, was a slow business. First to arrive was a handful of Hawker Hurricane fighters to help the Sea Gladiators defend against the Italian bombing raids, forcing them to start sending fighter escorts. They were followed by Fleet Air Arm Fairey Swordfish torpedo bombers, then more Hurricanes. Next came photographic reconnaissance aircraft such as the American-built Martin Marylands; then attack aircraft — light Bristol Beaufighters and heavy Vickers Wellingtons — to take the fight to the enemy, who of course included, from early 1941, the German *Luftwaffe* as well as the Italians. A full list of RAF, FAA and Commonwealth squadrons that served on Malta is attached at Appendix II to this chapter. Probably the most significant arrivals were the Supermarine Spitfires which began to arrive in March 1942, being flown in off aircraft carriers. With the RAF were men from all over the British Commonwealth and from other Allies, such as the United States of America and France. Conspicuous amongst them were Australians, New Zealanders and Rhodesians, and, in particular, Canadians, who made up more than a quarter of the air crews in 1942. A total of 568 aircraft would be lost in the defence of Malta, but nearly double that number of enemy aeroplanes (1,129 to be exact) would be shot down.

Airfields

In October 1939 work had started on laying three tarmac strips at the new aerodrome of Luqa. Fortuitously, it was completed six months later, two months before Italy declared war. Obstructions were then hurriedly placed at the ends of the three runways to prevent enemy aircraft from landing. Luqa became operational on 28 June 1940, when the Gladiator flight moved there. Eventually facilities included taxi-tracks, dispersal areas and aircraft pens. The other two operational RAF airfields were at Hal Far and Ta Qali, both of which were grass, the latter being regularly used before the war by the Italian civil airline. The FAA depot at Kalafrana was used by RAF seaplanes whilst there were more seaplane facilities at Marsaxlokk and St Paul's Bay; these were also regularly used by the Italians. Later, there were airstrips at Safi and Qrendi.

Stanley Haywood of the Devons reported in his diary for Friday, 19 April 1940 that, in addition to carrying out maintenance on their Bren carriers, they were also given the job of:

'. . . building aircraft pens or sangars as we called them. This was to protect the planes from bomb splinters, etc when they were dispersed round the perimeter of the aerodrome. These were built of four gallon fuel tins (for aircraft) and sandbags filled with earth or sand. The sangar was built in the shape of a "U", but the entrance of each faced a different direction. We started building the pens on the eastern side of Luqa aerodrome, working towards Hal Far aerodrome.'

This building of aircraft pens was, at that time, ahead of having any aircraft to put into them, but it was clearly a sensible precaution to take and one that would pay dividends in the months to come.

Malta Command Expands

On land, 231 Infantry Brigade would be joined by 232, 233 and 234 Infantry Brigades as Malta Command expanded and new units arrived. The size of the Army garrison would thus rise to some 30,000 men, two-thirds of whom were British and one-third Maltese. Details of these formations are shown in Appendix I to this chapter. It will be seen that a total of 17 infantry battalions, four of which were battalions of the KOMR, served on Malta during the war, although two of these (30 Northumberland Fusiliers and 1 King's Own) would not arrive until after the siege proper had ended. Some battalions came from Egypt so were acclimatised to the Middle East already, whilst others had to face the longer sea voyage from the United Kingdom. The Hampshires (1 Hamps) were in the former category, having left Egypt for Malta on 21 February 1941, on board the cruisers Orion and Ajax, bound for, as their history puts it, 'an unknown destination'. Two days later they disembarked in the Grand Harbour at Valletta. Their initial primary roles would be the defence of the airstrip at Safi and the southern dispersal areas of Luqa airfield. In addition they had to defend a considerable area against airborne invasion and also act as brigade reserve. Their history sets the scene:

'At first, after the bare desert, life in Malta gave the appearance of being very comfortable; food was plentiful, everyone made themselves comfortable as they could and there was a lively and cheerful social life.

'It was not altogether as it seemed,' their history goes on: 'for air raids would soon become frequent and violent . . . the enemy was determined to "neutralise" Malta and they seemed to have all the cards, and all the aircraft. But the Malta Garrison settled

down to stick it out, to hit back as hard as they could and to see that, come what may, Malta was not "neutralised".'

The Ardwick Boys, that is to say, the 8th Battalion of the Manchester Regiment[6], had a longer journey to Malta, namely from Cherbourg (where they had been serving as part of the BEF in France) to Gibraltar, leaving France before the German Blitzkrieg struck, on board a prewar luxury liner the SS Oronsay, as their history happily relates:

'Never surely did soldiers have a better sea trip, for the whole ship catered for the Ardwicks and them alone. With stewards serving all meals, all decks available for exercise, plenty to drink and plenty to smoke at naval prices, the battalion would have liked to have cruised on for a long time on the Oronsay, but four days later they arrived at Gibraltar.'

They stayed in Gibraltar for a week, and then on 17 May 1940 were told to report back to the ship. They handed in their battledress and drew up khaki drill and were soon off on the next leg of their journey to Malta, this time with a destroyer escort.

'On the fourth day Malta and Gozo appeared on the horizon and later that day the battalion disembarked in Grand Harbour. Their berths on the Oronsay were immediately filled by the wives and children of the mainly naval garrison who were being evacuated to England. The Oronsay sailed later that night.'[7]

To start off, the battalion was moved by lorry to Ghajn Tuffieha camp in the northwest of the island. It was a well-appointed camp of wooden huts, with plenty of administrative buildings, good cooking facilities, and so on, and, best of all, was just one minute away from the inviting-looking blue sea. However, although the camp would remain in their possession until it was badly bombed by the Luftwaffe some two years later, only a small proportion of the Manchesters' soldiers would ever be there for very long. This was because, like most other battalions on Malta, they had a wide range of duties to perform, with companies often miles away from their battalion headquarters. Their initial deployment gives a good indication of this: Battalion HQ and part of HQ Company — Ta Saliba crossroads; HQ Company headquarters — Ghajn Tuffieha; A Company — Hal Far aerodrome; B Company — Luqa aerodrome; C Company — St Paul's Bay; D Company at Il Fawara. Coastal companies were even further dispersed, being broken down to the inevitable section defence posts. So, to visit all the posts in a company area might well take three hours of walking up and down the precipitous coastal tracks. It is no wonder that, as their history explains:

'The occupants of these posts were well satisfied with their lot, with little to do but maintenance, the warm Mediterranean within yards of their post and above all no chance of being surprised by anyone from higher authority who had to have the gap in the wire opened for them, by which time everything would be under control!'

That was of course the up side; the down side was the necessity to find one sentry by day and two by night out of the small section of 6-8 men. Take away the sick, those on courses, and other absentees and invariably the men in the sections ended up doing two hours on and two off continually, with no chance of improvement. Once the air raids began, of course, things were a great deal worse.

The Manchesters' history also makes the point that the aerodrome companies had to watch the:

'. . . shiny Italian airliners come and go, their swarthy side-whiskered pilots looking contemptuously at the toiling Ardwicks as they dispersed their air raid shelters and thickened their head cover.'

These same pilots were all members of the Italian Air Force Reserve, so must have had a good idea of the state of the islands' defences before they came to bomb them.

The 1st Battalion of the Durham Light Infantry (DLI) was one of the later battalions to arrive, embarking at Alexandria for Malta on 24 January 1942. By then enemy action to try to sink the convoy, including HMS *Breconshire*, a naval storeship, and the destroyer HMS *Kingston* in which they were somewhat unwilling passengers, was almost continuous, as their history explains:

'On the 26th the weather deteriorated and air attacks increased. The worse it became, the greater grew the prospects of evading the Luftwaffe; but by late afternoon the ship's roll was so great that many cared little what happened! Torpedo bombers which appeared about 6pm tried to hit one of the escorting destroyers but without success. The convoy steamed ahead for Valletta and sailed into the Grand Harbour at 10am on the 27th. The Battalion disembarked to the accompaniment of an enemy air raid on the dockyard — a taste of things to come.'

The complete battalion had not embarked, A Company and the rear party having been left behind in Egypt. Their journey was to be considerably more hazardous:

'The journey began in February in the merchantman *Clan Campbell* which was hit in a heavy air attack and had to put into Tobruk before limping back to Alexandria. The ship containing the Battalion's equipment was sunk. Another attempt was made in March, when the men were distributed among four vessels — the *Breconshire, Clan Campbell, Pampas* and *"An Other"*. They were escorted by four cruisers and fifteen destroyers and there was a naval officer in each merchantman. As before, all went well for the first two days after which the convoy was attacked with increasing tempo. The climax was reached when it was reported that the Italian fleet had been sighted. Destroyers immediately laid a smokescreen, the cruisers steamed flat out straight through the convoy and the naval officers took over their respective ships. As Malta drew nearer, the attacks increased in intensity until it was clear that only Providence could save the convoy. *Clan Campbell* was sunk, though most of those in her were picked up. A destroyer raced to pick up survivors only to be badly holed herself. The crew, undaunted, lined the decks, raised their caps, gave three cheers for the King and all jumped together, an example of morale and discipline that none who saw it will ever forget. In a few minutes they too were picked up by another destroyer. *Pampas* was hit by two bombs which fortunately were deflected by her superstructure into the sea. As she was carrying a thousand tons of octane spirit as well as a cargo of ammunition those on board were more than relieved! *Breconshire* and the remaining vessel were both damaged and could not reach the harbour; and the former was ultimately beached at the southern tip of the island.'

As their history fittingly comments:

'Through all these hazards, and indeed despite them, "A" Company and the rest of the rear party in due course rejoined their comrades. They considered themselves fortunate, for the convoy was the last to reach the island for many months to come.'

1 DLI then settled into its new role and soon became accustomed to its new surroundings, though the rocky island with its many walls and terraces was very different to the Western Desert. However, their positions in the Verdala–Rabat–Dingli area gave them a magnificent view over the whole island. Their task was mobile reserve for the garrison and, in order to enable them to get around quickly, the battalion was issued with 400 bicycles. From then on routine was divided between tactical exercises and the building of anti-blast pens for aircraft on Ta Qali and Luqa aerodromes — hard work, especially on short rations. There was an extensive radar system on the island that enabled them to obtain accurate early warning of enemy air raids which increased in tempo as the days passed. So effective was this system that, as their history explains:

'Col Arderne [the CO] would await a "plot" of over 100 aircraft before mounting his bicycle and freewheeling down to the airfield where the Battalion was working. There he would stand, completely imperturbable, awaiting the enemy's arrival; and he would be deeply disappointed if he were forced to take cover or — as frequently happened — the "plot" wheeled suddenly and made for another airfield.'

Work hard! Train hard! Play hard! Undoubtedly this could have been the motto of the army garrison in those early months, as one of their GOCs (Major-General D. M. W. Beak VC, DSO, MC, put it when he took over command of the Army in Malta in January 1942: 'You will do PT every morning before breakfast; you will cycle in full equipment for 20 miles; you will run and walk alternately for 15 miles in full equipment!' That was the tune and everyone became proud of their task and proud of themselves, despite the monotony of such unspectacular, yet vital jobs, like post-manning. Even when the extra troops had arrived, the tasks for each brigade were still considerable. For example, 231 Brigade was responsible for 30 miles of coastline of which two-thirds were suitable for amphibious landings; the brigade area also contained an aerodrome used by both RAF fighters and Fleet Air Arm torpedo bombers, two emergency landing strips, one of which was used as a decoy, a seaplane base and a dispersal area for aircraft, all of which needed protecting.

The King's Own Malta Regiment
The KOMR was embodied at St George's Barracks, St George's Bay, and then, on 28 August 1939, moved north to Mellieha. Volunteers continued to flock in and so, on 21 September, a second KOMR battalion was formed. This was followed a few months later by a third, and a Static Group KOMR that later became another battalion (10 KOMR). In addition, the Malta Auxiliary Corps (MAC) was formed, which consisted of despatch riders (DRs), motor mechanics, drivers, hospital orderlies and mess orderlies. Numbers were attached to British infantry battalions, some even reporting with their own transport — both cars and lorries — which were then requisitioned to bring motor transport (MT) sections up to establishment! In February 1941 the Council of Government of Malta introduced conscription, which made all men between 16 and 65 liable for national service, whilst those between 18 and 41 were also liable for service in the armed forces.

Working on the Docks
The 1st Battalion, The Cheshire Regiment, was responsible for defending the dockyards from 15 April 1941 until 23 January 1943 and during this period received 119 bombing attacks concentrated solely on the dockyard, during which some 700 tons of bombs were dropped. B Company of the Cheshires who were billeted in the

Above: A wide range of weapons and equipment was unloaded in Malta, including a small number of tanks — like this Cruiser Tank Mark I (A9). It had a maximum speed of 25mph, but only thin armour. It mounted a 2-pounder and three machine guns (two in the small round turrets on either side of the driver). It was part of a detachment of A Squadron, 6 RTR, sent to reinforce the Malta Independent Tank Troop in early 1942. *IWM — GM 455*

dockyard had their accommodation destroyed no fewer than four times by direct hits. They also helped to unload the merchant ships, under continuous bombing, and to assist warships to get to sea, by helping to supply ammunition for their anti-aircraft weapons. The happy association between HM Dockyard Malta and the battalion was recognised in February 1943 when the Regimental Crest was unveiled by Mrs MacKenzie, wife of the Admiral Superintendent of the Dockyard (see photograph on page 80).

Dangerous Cargo

Other infantry battalions also worked as dockers, winchmen and dockside workers, in order to get valuable cargoes off and out to

the dumps in the country as quickly as possible, whatever the circumstances, as S. J. Chalk of the Hampshires recalled, in *Malta Remembered*:

'Everything was organised to get the cargo off and out to the dumps in the country, work would go on non-stop, and in the event of enemy aircraft approaching, the whole of the docks and the Valletta area would be covered by a smokescreen. This happened a few times, but work continued despite the coughing and watery eyes. Despite the fact that we were very hungry at the time, the way we tackled the job was a revelation. It may surprise some to know that most days we ate the day's ration in one meal and had to wait 24 hours until the next one. When the merchant ships Orari *and* Troilus *berthed at Valletta in June 1942, 3,200 tons were discharged in the first 24 hours, 4,800 in the second 24 hours and the whole 15,000 tons were moved from the holds to the dumps in 108 hours. When the* Melbourne Star *arrived with the remnants of the 'Pedestal' convoy [see Chapter 12], she*

was unloaded by 231 Brigade — Hampshires, Devons and Dorsets — in record time. There was friendly rivalry between the units to see who could shift the most cargo. Signs such as: "A ton a minute — Nothing in it!" would be chalked up on the quayside. My battalion, the Hampshires, later had to unload the Robin Locksley and we shifted 7,785 tons of cargo between dawn on 20th November and the evening of the 25th. All the hard work is clearly fixed in my mind, but the names of the ships and the tonnages I gleaned from our Regimental history. Troilus was bombed into a complete wreck whilst it was in dry dock I remember. Also, one episode that really sticks in my mind is not in the history books and I cannot even remember which ship it was. Owing to tankers being the prime target for enemy aircraft and submarines, it was decided to transport some high octane petrol in the holds of ordinary merchantmen. This fuel, in 4-gallon containers of very thin metal, was packed, two containers to a cardboard carton, then stacked into the bottom deck in one of the holds.

'We were standing by ready to unload as soon as the ship was ready, dressed in PT kit. We had been warned that one spark could send us all to oblivion. That was an understatement, because when the hatches were removed we could see the air disturbance caused by the fumes and smell them. The first group, consisting of an officer and about 12 men, including myself, went down the ladder into the hold and down came the loading platform from the hoist. We all started off all right. I can remember putting some boxes onto the platform, but then feeling very queer, just as though I had drunk too much booze. I then remember the officer and some of the men lying or sitting on the deck, then nothing more until coming out on the top deck, and being violently sick. People were fussing around us and told us that the petrol fumes had got the better of us and that another group had had to go down to put us on the platform and hoist us up on the derrick.

'Sitting up on deck recovering, we could watch the next attempt to get the fuel unloaded. The Navy was called in to rig up air chutes, from which came long flexible tubes ending in face masks. The next group of men went down, donned the masks and proceeded to unload. All went well until men turned from the platform to get another container and the tubes crossed, resulting in the whole lot becoming hopelessly entangled — that idea was then abandoned! It was then decided that the only solution was for one group to go down the ladder, work like mad until a whistle blew, then, whilst the group came up the port ladder, a fresh group would go down the starboard ladder and take over. The system worked and we were able to get thousands of gallons of high octane fuel out to the aerodromes where it was sorely needed. Whether this idea was repeated on any other ship I have no idea.'

Summary

To close the Army part of this chapter let us summarise the main tasks which the infantry battalions had to perform. These were:

Island Defence The defence of Malta in the event of an invasion was the primary role of the Army. Equally important was its role as part of the air defences and, until the RAF had arrived in sufficient strength, the Royal Artillery anti-aircraft units — both light and heavy — together with those of the Royal Malta Artillery, played a major part. Equally important were the searchlights of the 16th Fortress Company, Royal Engineers.

Coastal Defence Coastal artillery played its part, as did the infantry-manned blockhouses along the coastline.

Mobile Reserves Each brigade maintained at least one battalion as

a mobile reserve. Due to transport and fuel shortages, bicycles were issued — on a scale of 650 to battalions on mobile reserve duty. Methods were devised so weapons and equipment could be carried on these machines. With these and their other transport the troops carried out regular patrols within their brigade areas.

Airfield Defence This task not only covered the close defence of the airfield with infantry weapons but also, as the siege progressed, actually helping the gunners to man their LAA guns. As we have seen, other tasks included the building of shelters, both for men and for aircraft; creating some 28 miles of dispersal area between Luqa and Hal Far airfields (known as the 'Safi Strip' and built almost entirely by men of the Hampshires); the constant filling in and levelling of runway craters after raids, so as to keep airfields functioning. As there was a shortage of RAF ground crews, special teams of soldiers were trained to refuel and to rearm fighter aircraft so that they would be ready to take off again immediately the call came. They also filled ammunition belts and worked on the aircraft machine guns and cannons, some becoming expert armourers; indeed, they were soon an indispensable part of the maintenance team on each airfield: 'I would have been out of business but for the soldiers,' commented Air Vice-Marshal Lloyd.

Dockwork As well as being there to provide close defence of the dock areas as and when necessary, the soldiers also helped to unload the cargoes that the convoys brought in, then took them to suitably located, safe dumps well away from the much bombed dockland areas.

Air Raid Precautions Whilst the Malta Police and the civilian ARP organisation were in the main responsible for Air Raid Precautions duties, the military were also given the tasks of dealing with and disposing of delayed action bombs (mainly an expert job for the Sappers — see later), plus rescue and rubble clearance after raids.

Miscellaneous It goes without saying that such units as the medics, the dentists, the chaplains and others, all carried on with their normal tasks.

The War at Sea

As already mentioned, the Royal Navy had all but deserted Malta when Italy joined the war; thereafter British naval forces operated from Alexandria and Gibraltar — all except for just six submarines that remained in Malta. Then, early in April 1941, Admiral Cunningham gave orders for a small strike force of four destroyers (HMS *Jervis*, *Janus*, *Nubian* and *Mohawk*, under the command of Captain P. J. Mack, who was Captain (D) 14th Destroyer Flotilla) to return to the island. All arrived safely in Malta on the 11th. Their first sortie took place a few days later, when a reconnaissance aircraft spotted an enemy convoy of four merchant ships, escorted by three torpedo boats, on its way from Palermo to Tripoli. The destroyers swiftly headed out to sea to intercept them, as did some Swordfish torpedo bombers. Unfortunately neither the destroyers nor the aircraft sighted the convoy and the ships returned to Malta on the 12th. However, they would soon have success and on the 15th, another convoy, of four German troopships plus an Italian ammunition ship, was sighted off Cape Bon, escorted by three Italian destroyers. During the engagement that followed, Mack's strike force sank all eight of the enemy vessels for the loss of the *Mohawk*, struck by two torpedoes. Undoubtedly this action vindicated the sending of the surface striking force to Malta.

From then on, the surface and submarine strike forces operated from Malta with considerable success, although, it has to be said, not without considerable casualties as well. This was, however, in line with Admiralty policy, Churchill having left them in no doubt that the Mediterranean Fleet's prime task was to stop all seaborne traffic between Italy and North Africa, and that casualties would have to be accepted if this policy was to be successful. For the rest of 1941 various strike forces were made up and operated with considerable success, until the air war reached such a crescendo that it was just too hazardous for surface forces to operate or for maintenance to be achieved in the dockyards. The surface ships were therefore once again withdrawn to Alexandria. Submarines remained initially, submerging to the bottom of the harbour when in port during the day. However, they also eventually had to go to Alexandria and Gibraltar. Once the tide of the war in North Africa began to turn in favour of the Allies, and the precious supply convoys managed to get through, then some degree of normality returned and it was possible once again to station surface forces at Malta, with the inevitable effects upon enemy convoys. Details of Royal Navy units based on Malta are given in Appendix III to this chapter.

As Vize-Admiral Weichold, head of the German naval staff in Rome, rightly commented in *Axis Policy and Operations in the Mediterranean*: 'Rommel's difficulties were due rather to the dramatic fall in the shipping tonnage plying the African route: of the 1,748,841 tons of Italian shipping of January 1940, 1,259,001 tons had been sunk by the end of 1942.' The part that the surface ships, the submarines and the aircraft based in Malta played in this achievement was considerable.

Supplying Malta

Equally vital to Malta were the almost continuous convoys that sought to bring the food, ammunition and everything else that the people on Malta — civilians and servicemen alike — needed to survive. Every merchant vessel had to be protected from enemy attack and every convoy operation — and there were scores of them — was fraught with danger. From the air, the sea and under the waves, the enemy tried to prevent the supplies from getting through, to starve Malta into submission, just as they were trying to do to Great Britain. They would fail.

Notes

1. H. D. Chaplin: *The Queen's Own Royal West Kent Regiment 1920–1950.*
2. Extract from the Malta diary of Stanley Haywood, 2nd Battalion, The Devonshire Regiment, held by their Museum and a copy provided to me by kind permission of RHQ, The Devonshire and Dorset Regiment.
3. A monitor was a shallow-draught warship with an immense beam and armed with one or two capital ship main guns, for shore bombardment purposes.
4. From 1800 onwards numerous Maltese regiments, both regular and militia, were raised as part of the British Army. These included The Royal Malta Fencible Regiment (from 1815), later redesignated The Royal Malta Fencible Artillery (from 1861) then The Royal Malta Artillery (from 1889). In 1976 it was redesignated as 1st Regiment, Armed Forces of Malta.
5. From *Malta Remembered*, Volume 1.
6. In fact 8 Manchesters were not just the boys from the Ardwick area of Manchester. In late 1939 they had received a large draft of 18- and 19-year-olds from the Royal Welch Fusiliers; then later, whilst in Malta, they would be further reinforced by a draft of 120 from the Loyal Regiment. Nevertheless, by the end of the war they were 'All 100 per cent Manchesters'.
7. Robert A. Bonner: *The Ardwick Boys went to Malta.*

Above: 'They shall grow not old as we that are left grow old.' The Burial Service of a senior officer in progress at the Pembroke Cemetery, St Andrew's Church. Representatives of all three Services were present — the RN Chief of Staff, the AOC and, on the far right, the GOC, Major-General D. M. W. Beak VC, DSO, MC. IWM — GM 735

Appendix I. Order of Battle of Ground Forces of the Malta Command

Headquarters, Malta Command
Malta Infantry Brigade/231 Infantry Brigade
In September 1939 this was a regular Infantry Brigade, known as the Malta Infantry Brigade. On 7 August 1940 it was redesignated as Southern Infantry Brigade; on 14 July 1942 redesignated as 1st (Malta) Infantry Brigade; on 1 April 1943 finally called 231st Infantry Brigade but had left Malta Command 29 March 1943.

Infantry Battalions

2 Devon	throughout
1 Dorset	throughout
2 RWK	until 27 July 1941
2 R Ir F	until 6 August 1940
1 KOMR	1 February–6 August 1940
2 KOMR	1 February–6 August 1940 and 5 January–29 March 1943
8 Manchester	20 May–6 August 1940
3 KOMR	1 July 1940–29 March 1943
1 Hampshire	21 February 1941–end
8 King's Own	2 August 1941–12 May 1942

232 Infantry Brigade
Formed Malta on 7 August 1940 as Northern Infantry Brigade; 14 July 1942 redesignated 2nd (Malta) Infantry Brigade; 1 April 1943 redesignated 232 Infantry Brigade; on Malta until 3 November 1943.

Infantry Battalions

8 Manchester	7 August 1940–27 August 1943
2 R Ir F	7 August 1940–5 April 1943
1 KOMR	7 August 1940–20 March 1943
2 KOMR	7 August 1940–4 January 1943 and 29 March–9 October 1943
4 Buffs	22 February 1941–12 May 1942
8 King's Own	8 January–10 October 1943
3 KOMR	29 March–9 October 1943

Central Infantry Brigade/233 Infantry Brigade
Formed Malta on 27 July 1941 as Central Infantry Brigade; 14 July 1942 redesignated 3rd (Malta) Infantry Brigade; 1 April 1943 redesignated as 233 Infantry Brigade.

Infantry Battalions

11 LF (Lancashire Fusiliers)	27 July 1941–20 May 1944
1 Cheshire (MG)	27 July 1941–22 January 1943
2 RWK	27 July 1941–10 April 1943
1 DLI	27 January–12 May 1942
4 Buffs	11 April–5 September 1943
1 KOMR	11 June 1943–31 August 1945
10 KOMR	4 May 1942–5 October 1943
2 KOMR	10 October 1943–31 August 1945
3 KOMR	10 October 1943–12 April 1945
30 Northumberland Fusiliers	14 May 1944–31 August 1945

Western Infantry Brigade/234 Infantry Brigade
Formed Malta on 13 May 1940 as Western Infantry Brigade; 14 July 1942 redesignated as 4th (Malta) Infantry Brigade; 1 April 1943 redesignated as 234 Infantry Brigade.

Infantry Battalions

4 Buffs	13 May 1942–10 April 1943 and 26 October–16 November 1943
8 King's Own	13 May 1942–7 January 1943
1 DLI	14 May 1942–9 September 1943
1 Cheshire (MG)	23 January–10 June 1943
2 R Ir F	6 April–16 November 1943
2 RWK	11 April–16 November 1943
1 King's Own	20 October–16 November 1943.

Supporting Arms

Royal Armoured Corps
No 1 Independent Troop, RTR

Royal Artillery on Malta
12 Field Regiment
12 Gun Operations Room Regiment
4 Coast Regiment
4, 7 and 10 HAA Regiment
32, 65, 74 and 107 LAA Regiment
26 Defence Regiment
Searchlight Batteries
Coastal Observation Detachments

Royal Malta Artillery
1st Coast Regiment
2nd HAA Regiment
3rd LAA Regiment
4th Searchlight Regiment
5th Coast Regiment
11 HAA Regiment (TA)

Royal Engineers
16 and 24 Fortress Companies
1, 171 and 173 Tunnelling Companies
1 and 2 Works Companies

Royal Corps of Signals
Malta Signal Company
4 Company, Air Formation Signals Unit
Pigeon Loft Unit

Service Units
In addition to the above there were units of the RASC, RAMC, RAOC, REME, CMP, RAPC, RADC, RPC, Intelligence Corps and the Chaplains Department.

Source: *Orders of Battle, Second World War 1939–1945*, published by HMSO.

Appendix II. RAF and FAA Squadrons with Flights Serving on Malta

Squadron	Aircraft flown	Date first arrived	Remarks
No 18	Blenheim	12 Oct 1941	Left January 1942, returned in July 1943 equipped with Bostons.
No 21	Blenheim	27 April 1941	Last sorties February 1942, left 14 March.
No 22	Beaufort		Used Malta for refuelling purposes only.
No 23	Mosquito	27 Dec 1942	Operated from Luqa.
No 37	Wellington	8 Nov 1940	Operated from Luqa, left March 1942.
No 39	Beaufort	June 1942	Initial detachment of 5 aircraft. Joined by aircraft from 86 and 217 Squadrons in Aug 1942 to become 39 Sqn.
No 40	Wellington	24 Oct 1941	Operated from Luqa, left Jan 1943.
No 46	Hurricane	6 June 1941	Operated from Hal Far (also operated Beaufighters).
No 69	Maryland/Hurricane /Spitfire etc	10 Jan 1941	Operated mainly from Luqa (also from Ta Qali).
No 82	Blenheim	21 May 1941	Left for Far East March 1942.
No 86	Beaufort	13 July 1942	
No 89	Beaufighter	7 March 1942	Left to go back to Egypt March 1943.
No 104	Wellington	16 Oct 1941	Operated from Luqa, withdrawn June 1942, but later returned until 23 Jan 1943.
No 105	Blenheim	25 July 1941	Left 11 Oct 1941 to return to UK.
No 107	Blenheim	15 Sept 1941	Operated from Luqa, withdrawn 9 Jan 1942 after several losses.
No 108	Beaufighter	June 1943	Had earlier absorbed 89 Sqn Malta flight.
No 110	Blenheim	29 June 1941	Operated from Luqa.
No 113	Blenheim	27 Sept 1941	Reinforcements arrived from Egypt Jan 1942.
No 126	Hurricane/Spitfire	28 June 1941	Operated from Hal Far and Ta Qali, also had aircraft dispersed on Safi Strip.
No 139	Blenheim	16 May 1941	
No 148	Wellington	1 Dec 1940	Formed from Malta Wellington Flight.
No 185	Hurricane/Spitfire	12 May 1941	New unit formed at Hal Far.
No 203	Blenheim/Maryland		Maritime reconnaissance based in Egypt.
No 217	Beaufort		En route for India, regrouped at Malta, June 1942.
No 221	Wellington	8 Jan 1942	Operated from Luqa, moved to Italy March 1944.
No 227	Beaufighter	20 Aug 1942	Operated from Luqa, moved to Egypt 16 Feb 1943.
No 228	Sunderland	June 1940	Operated from Kalafrana, left for Egypt in March 1941.
No 229	Hurricane/Spitfire	27 March 1942	Moved to Sicily Jan 1944.
No 233	Hudson	June 1940	First aircraft led the first Hurricanes to ME. Remained on Malta until shot down by mistake. Joined by rest of sqn July 1942.
No 235	Beaufighter	June 1942	On loan from Coastal Command for convoy protection.
No 242	Hurricane	12 Nov 1941	With 605 Sqn flew Hurricanes off HMS *Ark Royal* and *Argus* to Malta. Based Hal Far, then Luqa.
No 248	Beaufighter	10 Aug 1942	Pilots returned to UK after 'Pedestal' Convoy, leaving aircraft in Malta.
No 249	Hurricane/Spitfire	21 May 1941	Arrived Ta Qali. Claimed 1,000th enemy aircraft shot down over Malta.
No 252	Beaufighter	1 May 1941	Left 21 May 1941 and moved to Egypt.
No 256	Mosquito	4 July 1943	Night fighters for invasion of Sicily.
No 261	Sea Gladiator /Hurricane	16 Aug 1940	Re-formed by amalgamation of Fighter Flight, Malta and 12 Hurricanes from HMS *Argus*. Bore brunt of early raids.
No 272	Beaufighter	6 Nov 1942	Moved from Egypt to Ta Qali. Left for Sicily Sept 1943.
No 601	Spitfire	20 April 1942	Flown off USS *Wasp* to Luqa, immediately in action.
No 603	Spitfire	20 April 1942	As for 601, based at Ta Qali.
No 605	Hurricane	12 Nov 1941	As for 242 Sqn. Disbanded March 1942, pilots joined 185 Sqn.
No 683	Spitfire	6 Feb 1943	Formed from Spitfire PRU Flight of 69 Sqn.
No 1435	Spitfire	1941	Designated as No 1435 Flt for night-fighting duties. Became a sqn on 2 Aug 1942 (the only sqn with a four-figure number).

In addition there were: Malta Night Fighter unit of Hurricanes formed in August 1941; a Malta Wellington Flight formed in the UK in October 1940, then flew to Luqa; Special Duties Flight of Wellingtons sent to Malta in September 1941 to find enemy surface shipping.

Commonwealth Squadrons

No 3 (RAAF)	Kittyhawk	4-18 July 1943	Operated from Ta Qali in preparation for the invasion of Sicily.
No 458 (RAAF)	Wellington	7 Jan 1943	Detachment of 3 aircraft operated at Luqa initially with 69 Sqn, until more aircraft arrived.
No 12 (SAAF)	Boston	July 1943	Moved to Hal Far from Tunisia.
No 21 (SAAF)	Baltimore	July 1943	Moved to Hal Far from N Africa.
No 24 (SAAF)	Boston	July 1943	Moved to Hal Far from N Africa.
No 40 (SAAF)	Spitfire	17 June 1943	Arrived Luqa to supply tactical reconnaissance support for invasion of Sicily.

FAA Squadrons

No 800X	Hal Far	May 1941
No 806	Hal Far	Jan 1941
No 815	Hal Far	Jan 1941
No 819	Hal Far	Jan 1941
No 820	Hal Far	Aug 1943
No 821	Hal Far	Nov 1942
No 826	Hal Far	Dec 1942
No 828	Hal Far	Oct 1941
No 830	Hal Far	Jun 1940

Source: Agius and Galea: *Lest We Forget.*

Appendix III
Warships of the Malta Striking Forces

Cruisers (5)
Ajax, Aurora, Gloucester*, Penelope, Neptune*.

Destroyers (23)
Decoy, Havock*, Jackal*, Jaguar*, Janus*, Jersey*, Jervis, Juno*, Kandahar*, Kashmir*, Kelly*, Kelvin, Kimberley, Kingston, Kipling*, Lance*, Legion*, Lively*, Maori*, Mohawk*, Nubian, Sikh*, Zulu*

All ships were Royal Navy vessels. Those starred thus * were lost at sea. Therefore, out of 28 British warships involved in Strike Force actions, 19 were lost, all in the Mediterranean in 1941–2. Of these, 12 were bombed, three mined, two torpedoed, one ran aground with temporary repairs from battle damage and one was sunk by shore batteries (off Tobruk).

Right: Malta at Bay. Dramatic shot of a 40mm Bofors AA gun crew, loading a four-round clip into their LAA gun in its sandbagged position, defending the entrance to Grand Harbour, Malta. *IWM — GM 944*

Chapter 4

The Enemy

Axis Operations

German, and to a degree, Italian operations in the Central Mediterranean were largely based upon Hitler's Directive No 38, which was issued from the Führer's Headquarters on 2 December 1941. It is worth quoting in full here both because of the relevance of certain parts of it to Malta, and also to show how convoluted the chain of command was for the commander on the spot. There were clearly too many fingers in the pie and Kesselring must have constantly felt thwarted by being unable to make important decisions quickly.

> **Directive No 38**
> *'The Führer and Supreme Commander of the Armed Forces*
> *Führer Headquarters*
> *2 December 1941*
>
> 1. In order to secure and extend our position in the Mediterranean, and to establish a focus of Axis strength in the Central Mediterranean, I order, in agreement with the *Duce*, that part of the German Air Force no longer required in the East, be transferred to the South Italian and North African areas, in the strength of about one air corps with the necessary anti-aircraft defences. Apart from the immediate effect of this movement on the war in the Mediterranean and North Africa, efforts will be made to ensure that it has a considerable effect upon further developments in the Mediterranean area as a whole.
> 2. I appoint Field Marshal Kesselring to command all forces employed in these operations. He is also appointed Commander-in-Chief South. His tasks are:
>   a. To secure mastery of the air and sea in the area between Southern Italy and North Africa in order to secure communications with Libya and Cyrenaica and, in particular, to keep Malta in subjection.
>   b. To co-operate with German and allied forces engaged in North Africa.
>   c. To paralyse enemy traffic through the Mediterranean and British supplies to Tobruk and Malta, in close co-operation with the German and Italian naval forces available for this task.
> 3. Commander-in-Chief South will be under the orders of the Duce, whose general instructions he will receive through the Commando Supremo. In all Air Force matters Commander-in-Chief Air Force will deal direct with Commander-in-Chief South. In important matters the High Command of the Armed Forces is to be simultaneously informed.
> 4. The following will be subordinate to the Commander-in-Chief South:
>   a. All units of the German Air Force stationed in the Mediterranean and North African areas.
>   b. The air and anti-aircraft units put at his disposal for the execution of tasks by the Italian Armed Forces.
> 5. German naval forces in the Central Mediterranean remain under command of the Commander-in-Chief Navy. 'For the execution of all tasks assigned to him, Commander-in-Chief South is authorised to issue directives to the German admiral with the Italian High Command and, if necessary, to Naval Group South (for the Eastern Mediterranean). Operation orders will be issued by the naval headquarters concerned in agreement with Commander-in-Chief South. Requests by Commander-in-Chief South for combined operations by allied naval forces will be made exclusively to the German admiral with the Italian Naval High Command.
> 6. The duties of the Commander Armed Forces South-East and of the German general at the HQ of the Italian Armed Forces remain unchanged.'
>
> Signed: *Adolf Hitler*

The Axis Forces

Whilst we have looked at the ground troops of the Malta garrison in some detail there is no need to explain the organisation of the Italian and German ground troops that were present in the Eastern Mediterranean, except for those that were potential components of the Operation 'Herkules' invasion force, which are dealt with in Chapter 6. Here we will concentrate on air and naval forces.

The Italian *Forze Armate*

The *Forze Armate* (Armed Forces) of the Italian state were regarded as a single service with three main branches: The Royal Army (*Regio Esercito*); the Royal Navy (*Regia Marina*) and the Royal Air Force (*Regia Aeronautica*). In addition there were the Royal Customs Guards (*Regia Guardia di Finanza*) and the Fascist Militia (*Milizia Volontaria per la Sicurezza Nazionale* — MVSN) who were also known as the Blackshirts (*Camice Nere* — CCNN)

As will be seen from the chart, Mussolini occupied no fewer that five posts in the Italian High Command, being Supreme Commander and Head of the Government, Minister for War, Minister for the Navy and Minister for the Air Force. He was also Minister of the Interior and President of the Fascist Grand Council, so he had a complete stranglehold on all aspects of running the Italian Armed Forces and thus was directly responsible for all that happened to Malta. Under the Supreme Commander was the Chief of the Supreme General Staff, who, when war was declared, was Marshal Pietro Badoglio. He would resign on 26 November 1940, after Italy's failures in Greece and North Africa, his place as Capo di SMG being taken by General Ugo Cavallero. Head of the Navy was Admiral Cavagnari, who was replaced at the same time as Badoglio resigned, by Admiral Arturo Riccardi.[1] Running the Air Force was General Pricolo.

Regia Marina

Apart from a few minor engagements in the Adriatic, the Italian Navy saw little action in the Great War, nor did it carry out much

Structure of the Italian High Command 1940

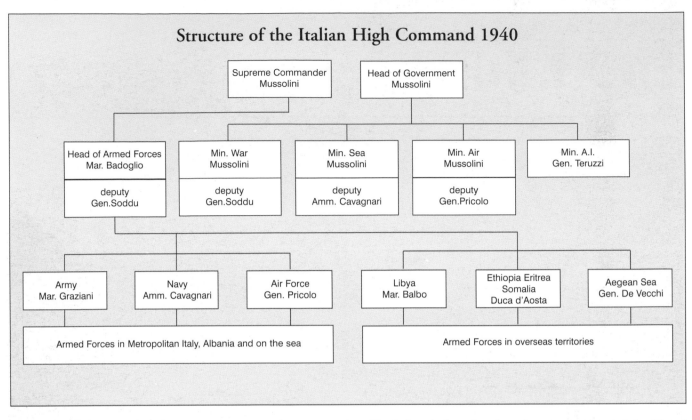

training during the inter-war years, so it lacked experience in naval strategy and tactics. However, with the arrival of the Fascists, things improved, and Italian warships were, on the whole, well built and well armed, although some still needed modernisation. In 1939, for example, they had four old World War 1 battleships in service, only two of which (*Cavour* and *Cesare*) had been modernised. In 1940 the fleet was considerably improved by the commissioning of two new 'fast' battleships, the 35,000-ton *Littorio* (name changed to *Italia* in August 1943) and the *Vittorio Veneto*. Both had a speed of 31 knots and mounted nine 15in guns. Two more of this class were planned, the *Impero*, whose launch was inexplicably delayed, and *Roma*, which was torpedoed and sunk by German aircraft on 9 September 1943, whilst en route to Malta to surrender with the rest of the Italian Fleet.

Regia Marina					
Class of Warship	Tonnage	Main Armament	Speed (kt)	Armour (in)	
Battleships					
Littorio (2)	35,000	9 x 15in	31	14	
Cavour (4)	24,000	10 x 12.6in	10	27	10
(*Cavour, Cesare, Andrea Doria, Caio Duilio*)					
Cruisers					
Heavy (7)	c10,000	8 x 8in	32–35	6–8	
(*Zara, Fiume, Gorizia, Pola, Bolzano, Trieste, Trento*)					
Light (12)	5,000–8,000	8–10 x 6in	35–37	4–8	
Destroyers					
Fleet (61)	1,060–1,630	up to 5 x 4in	34–39	n/a	
Escort (69)	up to 680	3–4 x 4in	30–32	n/a	

The Italians had no aircraft carriers, arguing that their land-based aircraft were always in range. However, this would prove to be a decided disadvantage. Some ship-borne seaplanes (Meridionali Ro43 and Ro44) were carried on larger vessels for reconnaissance purposes. Of their 19 cruisers, seven were heavy (mounting 8in guns), the rest light (6in guns). They also had 51 destroyers, 115 submarines, plus 71 escort vessels, MTBs and the like.

Initially, the Navy was divided as follows:

At Taranto: three battleships, three heavy cruisers, five light cruisers, 28 destroyers, 22 submarines

At Naples: one battleship, four light cruisers, 18 destroyers, 11 submarines

The rest were spread amongst ports in Sicily (Messina, Augusta, Syracuse, Palermo), Sardinia (Cagliari), the Adriatic (Brindisi, Bari), the Ligurian Sea (La Spezia), Libya (Tobruk, Tripoli) and the Red Sea.

Main Perceived Threat

It was the large Italian submarine fleet that seemed to pose the greatest danger when war was declared, as four-fifths of them were ready for action. However, this threat did not materialise and 38 were sunk during 1940–1, so the numbers left on patrol were greatly reduced. Amongst the bravest and most successful Italian sailors were undoubtedly the crews of the midget submarines, who did well in attacks against Alexandria and Gibraltar, but their attempt to strike at Grand Harbour, Malta, on the night of 25/26 July 1941, would end in catastrophe.

The British opinion of the Italian Navy is succinctly explained in a wartime HMSO booklet entitled *East of Suez, West of Malta* and published in 1943. In it the Admiralty says:

'Although Italian seamen have never lacked courage, her Navy has not the professional and psychological outlook of the bluewater sailor; and under Mussolini's regime, political

Above: Four Italian 8in gun cruisers, the *Zara*, *Fiume*, *Gorizia* and *Pola*, photographed here in Naples harbour. Three of them would soon be destroyed by the Royal Navy in the Battle of Matapan. *IWM — Z 2803D*

Above: Photographed returning to base is this Italian submarine. Initially, they were reasonably effective against Allied merchant ships travelling alone, as their doctrine called for them to operate individually rather than in 'wolf packs' like the U-boats. *IWM — Ger 1112W*

uncertainty must inevitably have penetrated the wardrooms and mess-decks of the fleet. When that happened, it was perhaps no longer completely reliable as a weapon of war. A suspicion of this may have decided Italy to put her faith in air power and take no undue risks with her fleet.'

Note also the remarks made by Field Marshal Kesselring. He paints a similar mixed picture of the Regia Marina in a report published postwar in the American series 'German Military Studies':

'The Italian Navy deserved the name "fair-weather fleet". The morale of the crews of the small vessels was in part outstanding. This advantage was set off by the want of seaworthiness and age of the ships. Mechanical equipment was faulty . . . The morale of the battle fleet could not compare to that of the small ships.'

Regia Aeronautica

In broad terms the Italian Air Force was numerically superior to those elements of the RAF which opposed it in the Middle East area generally and over the Mediterranean in particular. The Italians had some 2,600 first line aircraft. Like the Italian Navy, the Air Force had played only a minimal part in the Great War, but from 1922 onwards *Il Duce* had taken a personal interest in it and, by 1936, had created a large, modern air force. It was probably better armed and certainly more easily reinforced than its British counterpart in the area. Nevertheless, like the RAF in the Middle East, it also had shortages of aircraft spares, equipment and aviation fuel. In addition the maintenance organisation was poor, so aircraft service-ability rates were low. Pilots were well trained and some had 'battle' experience, having bombed civilian targets in Abyssinia and Spain, but as mentioned in an earlier chapter, morale was somewhat shaky once the battle commenced.

There were four distinct components in the Italian Air Force:

Air Army All air forces designed to carry out aerial warfare, including the air defence of Italy and of its overseas territories.

Army Air Force All air units assigned to the Army to provide air observation, communications and fire support. Pilots and equipment were from the Air Force, whilst specially trained Army officers were used as observers.

Naval Air Force Air units assigned to the Navy to provide air observation, communications and fire support. As with the Army support units, equipment and pilots were provided by the Air Force, while observers were specially trained naval officers.

Colonial Garrisons Air units stationed in the colonies to provide for garrison duties.

Italy was divided into four territorial air zones and four territorial air commands, whilst the Air Army comprised all the combat elements in the Mediterranean area. It consisted of two air fleets, organised into divisions, brigades, wings, groups and squadrons. Additional wings were located in the Dodecanese Islands, Albania, Sicily and Sardinia. An air fleet consisted of two or more homogeneous fighter or bomber air divisions, each division containing two or more air brigades, each air brigade two or more air wings, each air wing two or more groups and each group two or more squadrons. A bomber squadron contained six first line aircraft, plus three reserve, while all other squadrons had nine first line and three reserve.

Reinforcement for the Italians was very easy as a prewar exercise had shown, when some 400 bombers were moved to North Africa in a matter of a few days. Depots at Naples, Bari, Taranto and Catania were able to pass aircraft over to Tripolitania, while Italy was out of range of RAF fighters except for the area that could be reached from Malta.

Regia Aeronautica — Main Aircraft Types in Service, 1940-1						
Type	Speed (mph)	Celing (ft)	Range (miles)	First Flew	Armament	Crew
Fighters						
Fiat CR32	230	29,500	530	1932	8 x MG 1 x 220lb bomb	1
Fiat CR42 *Falco*	267	34,450	480	1936	8 x MG 2 x 220lb bombs	1
Fiat G50 *Freccia*	293	32,800	620	1937	4 x MG 1 x 20mm cannon	1
Macchia MC200 *Saetta*	312	29,200	355	1937	2/4 MG 2 x 352lb bombs	1
Bombers						
Breda 65 ground attack	255	25,910	682	nk	5 x MG 880lb bombs	1/2
Fiat BR20M	270	31,500	920	1936	4 x MG 5,511lb bombs	5/6
Savoia-Marchetti SM79 *Sparviero*	267	23,300	1,245	1934	4 x MG 2,640lb bombs	4/5
Savoia-Marchetti SM81 (obsolete at start of war but used in Africa)	211	23,000	930	nk	5 x MG various bombs	
Caprioni Ca133 (also earlier Ca101 and Ca111 used as bombers, troop carriers, ground attack and resupply forward troops)	174	14,330	840	1935	up to 4 x MG 2,200lb bombs	
Cant Z1007	280	26,500	3,100	1937	4,410lb (internal) or 2 x 1,000lb torpedoes 4 x 551lb bombs underwing	
Army Co-operation						
Meriodionali Ro37 bis (Ro1 also — similar characteristics)	200	30,000	1,190	nk		
Transport						
Savoia-Marchetti SM82	205	20,500	1,160	nk	load up to max of 8,240lb (normal 6,600lb)	
Marine						
Cant CZ501 flying boat	165	22,000	2,850	nk	bombload 1,100lb	
Cant CZ506 seaplane	240	27,500	1,310,	nk	bombload 2,200lb	

The Germans

Die Wehrmacht

The three main branches of Germany's armed forces were the Army (*Das Heer*), the Navy (*Die Kriegsmarine*), and the Air Force (*Die Luftwaffe*). They all came under the *Wehrmacht* High Command (*Oberkommando der Wehrmacht*). The OKW consisted of four main components: the *Wehrmacht* Operations Office (later called the *Wehrmacht* Operations Staff), the Office of Foreign Affairs and Intelligence, the Economics and Armaments Office, and the Office for General *Wehrmacht* Affairs. The main task of the OKW was to correlate and supervise the individual strategy of the three service headquarters: the Army High Command — *Oberkommando des Heeres* (OKH), the Navy High Command — *Oberkommando der Marine* (OKM), and the Air Force High Command — *Oberkommando der Luftwaffe* (OKL). Chief of Staff of the OKW was

Above: Known as the *Folgore* ('Thunderbolt'), the Macchi MC202 single-seat interceptor was undoubtedly the best wartime fighter to serve in large numbers in the *Regia Aeronautica*. It took part in numerous actions against Malta and Allied convoys in the Mediterranean. *IWM — IA 24306*

Above: Photographed over Hal Far aerodrome, Malta, on a bombing mission, is this Savoia-Marchetti SM79 *Sparviero* ('Sparrowhawk') medium bomber. Some 600 were in service when Italy entered the war and they were deployed in every theatre in which Italian forces operated. *Bundesarchiv — 146/80/89/13*

Feldmarschall Wilhelm Keitel, who was involved in all Hitler's strategic decisions. His fawning attitude towards the Führer earned him the contempt of many of his colleagues, who called him *Lakeit-el* in a punning reference to the German word for footman or lackey.

OB South The senior command elements of the German armed forces were of course far more preoccupied with global events — and in particular their titanic struggle with the Soviet Union — than to be continually concerned with Middle East affairs. This was the task delegated to the highly efficient, energetic and able Feldmarschall Albert Kesselring (known as 'Smiling Albert'), who was appointed OB South on 28 November 1941. From his office in Rome he commanded all German land and air forces in the Mediterranean. His relations with Rommel were somewhat stormy from time to time; however, both men respected each other and endeavoured to work harmoniously. Two of Kesselring's main tasks were to interdict British shipping in the Mediterranean and to gain air superiority in the area. He, above all others, recognised that the neutralisation of Malta was clearly top priority, but he was continually frustrated by Hitler and the OKW. His first major German air offensive on Malta was aimed literally at bombing Malta out of the war; however, it had had to be halted before its completion, because Hitler ordered *Luftwaffe* resources to be sent to support the gigantic German offensive towards Stalingrad and the Caucasus. Soon after the start of Operation 'Torch' (the Allied invasion of North Africa on 8 November 1942), Kesselring became Mussolini's military deputy and commander of Italian forces as well as Luftflotte 2

Below: Feldmarschall Albert Kesselring (with the light coloured top to his hat), photographed here talking with some *Luftwaffe* staff in North Africa. 'Smiling Albert' as he was nicknamed, was C-in-C South and thus in command of all German forces in the Mediterranean area. *Author's Collection*

and Panzerarmee Afrika. He would survive the war, having been taken prisoner on 6 May 1945, and be condemned to death but the sentence would be commuted to life imprisonment. He was released in 1952 (because of ill-health) and died in 1960.

Kesselring's views on the importance of Malta can be judged from the following extract from his memoirs:

'Meanwhile Malta had assumed decisive importance as a strategic key-point, and my primary objective at the beginning was to safeguard our supply lines by smoking out that hornets' nest. Time was required to build up the ground organisation in Sicily, to bring forward our air formations and the supplies needed to smash Malta's naval and air bases, as well as secure the co-operation of the Italian air force in our offensive. For the moment it was impossible to do more than reinforce the air umbrella over the most indispensable convoys.'

Kriegsmarine

German co-operation with the Italian Navy really began during the Spanish Civil War, when the Italians assisted German ships operating in the western Mediterranean. Before then the Italians had not openly welcomed the presence of German naval officers — those who were allowed on board Italian vessels had to wear civilian clothes. Additionally, there were no offers of giving them clandestinely the opportunity for the practical training that was prevented by the Versailles Treaty. There was also undoubtedly a certain amount of arrogance from the Germans, who saw themselves as superior, the German Fleet commander, Admiral Boehm, saying rather patronisingly that it was the Italians who wanted to learn from the Germans rather than the other way around.

U-boats and E-boats The main element of the *Kriegsmarine* operating in the Mediterranean was a significant number of U-boats. In September 1941 OKM had ordered the then Konteradmiral Karl Dönitz (later to be Grand Admiral and C-in-C of the entire *Kriegsmarine*), who was at the time C-in-C U-boats, to send one-third of his force into the Mediterranean, thus forming a new submarine division under Korvettenkapitän Victor Oehrn. Two flotillas were diverted from their normal hunting grounds in the Atlantic and sent into the Mediterranean, the 23rd being based in Greece at Salamis and the 29th at La Spezia in Italy. The latter flotilla would later change its base three more times, moving from Italy to Toulon, then to Pola (Yugoslavia) and finally to Marseilles. In September 1944, once North Africa was lost and Italy invaded, the surviving boats moved east under the command of the admiral in the Aegean.

The U-boats would have some worthwhile successes in the Mediterranean. For example, *U81* would sink the aircraft carrier *Ark Royal* and *U331* the battleship *Barham*, both in November 1941, whilst another aircraft carrier, HMS *Eagle*, was sunk by the *U73* in August 1942. During the war 65 U-boats were sunk or badly damaged in the Mediterranean, a fair number while running the gauntlet through the Strait of Gibraltar. Two flotillas of Fast Attack E-boats were also sent into the Mediterranean, being transported overland to Italy. The 3rd Flotilla was based near Agrigento in Sicily. One of its first operations was to lay mines off Valletta on 15 January 1942.

Kesselring had been convinced that the Italian Navy was large enough for any and all likely tasks, so there was no need for any German surface escort forces. However, towards the close of 1942 a single *Kriegsmarine* destroyer that had been completed in a Greek shipyard was commissioned.[2] It did excellent work. German submarines also took part indirectly in protecting Axis supply lines. Depending on the situation they cruised in the eastern or the western part of the Mediterranean but mostly off the chief ports of Gibraltar and Alexandria, ready to attack British convoys or ships of the fleet. Due to their small numbers, the victories chalked up by German submarines could never be considered decisive. They did, however, help to disrupt British traffic in the Mediterranean.

Luftwaffe

X Fliegerkorps Under command of Generalleutnant Hans Geissler, this was the first German air unit to be sent to gain control of the skies over the central Mediterranean, so that Rommel's newly arrived *Deutsches Afrika Korps*, could be safely transported to Libya and then kept supplied. X Fliegerkorps was sent to Sicily from Norway on 10 December 1940. At first it included only bombers and dive-bombers but the following month Messerschmitt (Bf) 109 fighters were added. Altogether there were some 400 aircraft — a tall order for the 16 Hurricanes then on Malta. Geissler's bomber pilots — both the dive-bombers and the straight and level bombers — had been specially trained in engaging naval targets, one of their first victims being the aircraft carrier *Illustrious*, which was hit six times during operations to cover the movements of a number of convoys towards Greece and Malta on 10 January 1941. Some 30–40 Junkers (Ju) 88s and Ju87 Stukas made their first appearance, making their attacks with great skill and determination, quite unlike anything the Royal Navy had experienced at the hands of the Italians.

Despite the considerable number of casualties, grievous damage and many fires on board, *Illustrious* was brought into Malta, only to be heavily bombed once again. Eventually she managed to escape to Alexandria, but was out of the war for a considerable length of time. The day after this engagement the dive-bombers damaged the cruiser *Southampton* so badly that she had to be abandoned and sunk. As

John Terraine says, in his book *The Right of the Line*: 'The Germans wasted no time in casting a shadow which was going to lie over the Mediterranean for a long time to come.'

II Fliegerkorps (Luftflotte 2) Under the command of Generalleutnant Bruno Lörzer, this formation replaced Luftflotte X in the Mediterranean and comprised a mix of Ju87 Stuka and Ju88 dive-bombers, with Bf109F and Bf110 fighters. The first units to arrive in Sicily were the Nachtjagdgeschwader 2 (1/2nd Night Fighter Wing) and the Küstenfliegergruppe 106 (106th Coastal Troops), equipped with Ju88s and under the command of Air Commander Sicily Oberst Roth. Building work was in progress in Sicily, to accommodate 30,000 men, whilst additional anti-aircraft batteries were sent to Naples to defend the port. II Fliegerkorps proper began to arrive at the beginning of December 1941 and on 22 December the first massive attacks were launched against Malta, with some 200 aircraft taking part. Luftflotte II initially had some 900-plus aircraft, predominantly Bf109 and Bf110 fighters, Ju87 and Ju88 dive-bombers, Heinkel (He) 111 bombers and Ju52 transport aircraft. A year later there were over 1,000, so the numbers involved were significant.

Kesselring had this to say about the air effort of Luftflotte 2 against Malta:

> 'On the German side, the Commander-in-Chief of Luftflotte 2 did everything that could be done at the time. It was impossible to accede to all demands. Our fighter wings were tried in combat with the British. The bomber formations were flown by experienced men, who, as a result of years of action, knew how to handle planes not only over land but also over water. We planned to use Ju88s for daytime sorties chiefly. The slower high-altitude bombers were employed mainly at night. We could not count on Italian bombers and fighters. These were obsolescent. Their crews lacked the proper training in night flying. The air offensive was again under the direction of the seasoned II Fliegerkorps. The attack did not result in the desired success although tactical requirements had been met and although the human element involved did its part. I was forced to discontinue it in the beginning of October 1942 on account of excessive losses and particularly in view of the Allied invasion which was to be expected then.'

Kesselring goes on to explain his reasons for discontinuing his assault and we will cover them in detail in a later, more apposite, chapter. At this stage all that is necessary is to register the fact that Luftflotte 2 was a large, well-trained force, with up-to-date combat experience and an able leadership. However, they clearly underestimated their opponents and that would prove to be their undoing.

Dive-bombing Malta

> 'The Kommodore came to the point. "At midday tomorrow, the Geschwader will attack Malta, Luqa airfield, I'd like you and your Staffel to take part."'

That was how newly arrived Ju88 dive-bomber pilot, Hajo Herrmann, learnt about his first operation from an airfield near Gerbini in Sicily that was to be his home base from February to May 1941. Born in 1913, Hajo Herrmann, the son of a Kiel engineer, had started his service in the infantry in 1933, then became an officer in the *Luftwaffe*. He went on to serve with the Condor Legion in Spain and to become a close confidant of Reichsmarschall Hermann Göring, who promoted him to high office in the fighter defence of the Third Reich, after he had created the 'Wild Boar'[3] method of night fighting. He was also one of the *Luftwaffe's* best known pilots with over 300 operational missions to his credit and acknowledged as an expert in anti-ship operations. However, he had barely had time to get his bearings when the request to join in the attack on Luqa airfield was first broached. Now his *Staffel* was airborne and fast approaching the western tip of Gozo:

'The lead aircraft was turning slowly to the left from its southwest heading and preparing to attack. Malta lay immediately behind Gozo. In the middle we could see the airfield at Luqa. We could also see the second airfield, Hal Far, past Luqa and to the right.'

At that stage there was no sign of any British fighters and Herrmann wondered if it was the calm before the storm or if they had decided to stay on the ground. However, the flak was, as he put it:

'. . . thundering up at us full belt . . . There were hundreds of guns firing at us, as if they'd been brought here from the entire Empire to guard the artery of world power . . . it was a veritable wasps' nest . . . the tracers of the 4 cm flak were whizzing through the formation. I swallowed quickly. Closing my left eye, I looked through the bombsight with my right. The shelters were dead-ahead; right on the cross . . . We had not descended to 1,200 metres yet, and the klaxon still hadn't sounded. I hoped that because there were so many of us the flak would be scattered. The leaders were still poised steady in front of us, drifting slowly across the target area. Drop your bombs! Pull out!'

The *Geschwader* got back to Sicily without incident on that occasion, having not seen any British aircraft, which as Herrmann put it: 'made the feeling of being alive even better and made us feel friendly towards everybody!' Of course it was not going to be like that on every raid over Malta and elsewhere in the Mediterranean as Herrmann and the other *Luftwaffe* pilots sought to win the air war. They operated not only over the sea lanes but also North Africa, Greece and Crete, but Malta was still their major target, especially during April and May 1941. 'Once more,' he says, 'Malta became our prime target. The island had to be kept under constant pressure so that the German and Italian reinforcements and supplies of war materials from Palermo could safely cross the Straits of Sicily and reach Tripoli along the coast of Tunisia.' Herrmann had just been promoted to become the Kommandeur of the *Gruppe* and his first operation was again over Malta, where they had to drop bombs, in order to draw up the British fighters, so as they could be engaged in a dogfight with superior numbers of German fighters — and when one also remembers that the performance of the Bf109 was superior to most British fighters apart from the later marks of Spitfire, considerable damage to Malta's air defence was always possible, until the days when sufficient Spitfires could be flown in to even up the balance.

On the occasion he describes, all went well until they arrived at the target. Then his wingman (on his left) had his windscreen blown in by AA fire and so had no protection from the slipstream. He managed to stay in formation until he had bombed, but then lost control and pulled to the side out of formation.

'What happened then, I learned subsequently, caused great amusement, not only to our crews, but also to the British, who were monitoring our radio transmissions continuously. I shouted to Oberfeldwebel Lorra on the R/T something on the lines of, "Come here you bastard, you stupid clot! If you're not back here at once, I will give you 10 days in the glasshouse!" The good

Lorra, who had been disorientated completely by the flak attack and who had broken formation involuntarily, got such a shock that he was more afraid of being locked up than of the English fighters . . . We joined up and flew back in good order . . . As Lorra had obeyed my order promptly he did not fall victim to the Spitfires — or to his Kommandeur!' [4]

Notes

1. In his autobiography Admiral Cunningham mentions a prewar meeting with Riccardi in which he was shown around the Admiral's palatial private apartments, where Riccardi 'took some pride in pointing out a book, *The Life of Nelson*, which always lay on a table by his bedside'. As 'ABC' comments dryly: 'His subsequent actions during the war rather showed that he had not greatly profited by his nightly reading.'
2. This was probably the H Class British destroyer *Hermes* that had been built in a British yard for the Greek Navy in 1939. It was commandeered by the Germans and used for convoy protection duties.
3. 'Wild Boar' tactics called for a concentration of fighters over the target area, where massed searchlights and the Allied marker flares lit up the sky and thus silhouetted the bombers for the fighters to attack. This meant that the fighters did not need to carry radar to find the bombers and so single-engined types could be used, greatly increasing the strength of the 'night fighter' force.
4. Hajo Herrmann: *Eagle's Wings*.

ZWEI VÖLKER, EIN SIEG
DUE POPOLI, UNA VITTORIA

Above: Preparing to bomb Malta. Ground crews in Sicily, preparing bomb-loads for German aircraft to drop on Malta, 12 May 1942.
*Bundesarchiv —
146/80/90/15*

Left: Heinkel 111 medium bombers over Malta. The stone walls between the small fields can be easily seen. The He111 was widely used both as a bomber and as a transport aircraft, over 7,000 being built.
*Bundesarchiv
146/80/90/12*

Opposite: Propaganda cartoon of tough-looking German and Italian soldiers marching to victory under the stirring bilingual message of 'Two Peoples, One Victory!'
Author's Collection

Chapter 5
The First Raids

The Assault Begins

At exactly 6.49am on 11 June 1940, the day following Mussolini's declaration of war, 10 Savoia-Marchetti 79 three-engined bombers took off from their base at Catania in Sicily to attack Malta for the very first time. Known as the *Sparviero* ('Sparrowhawk'), the SM79 was one of the most successful Italian bombers built during World War 2, but it had originally been designed as a civil transport aeroplane that could carry eight passengers. Instead it now carried an internal 1,250kg bomb-load, made up mainly of small 110kg bombs. They attacked Valletta, the surrounding area and Hal Far aerodrome, causing only slight damage. The island's AA gunners were able to shoot down one of the raiders and damage another. Additionally, Malta's fighter cover saw its first action, although the Italians were able to escape from them almost unscathed thanks to their superior speed.

RSM John Kelly MBE, DCM, of the Royal Irish Fusiliers, vividly remembered that 'mad, exciting morning of the 11th June 1940'. He was then a corporal in the motor transport section of the Fusiliers, living and working at their MT garage in St Andrew's Barracks. He later wrote:

'My regiment, like the other troops in Malta, had moved out to their defence positions a month before, when it was realised that Italy was coming into the war which she did, the night before — 10th June 1940. We had "Stand To" at dawn and after "Stand Down" had returned to our garage. We were still in battle order when at 7am the sirens started howling "Air Raid Warning" as the Italian air force flew in to attack Malta. In our first ever air raid we heard the roar of AA guns and the crash of bombs, in a rolling thunder, sounding closer and closer to us. Our sergeant, Billy Strawbridge, roared out over the terrible din: "Double over to the slit trenches and stand by." As one man we raced across to the slit trenches 200 yards away, led by Fusilier "Popeye" Byrne, a small man. As he ran, he approached a piece of masonry — five feet high. Popeye paused for a second, then "Springer" AA Battery 400 yards away opened up with a shattering crash. With a startled shout, "Popeye" bounded over this high obstacle, as though it was nothing and continued his run; an amazing jump for a small man. When we reached the slit trenches and stood by, ready to dive in if the bombs came any closer, I stared at "Popeye" with admiration and prayed that he would be picked to represent Ireland in the postwar Olympics, in the high jump!

As we stood there gazing up at the Italian bombers in the distance, silver specks in the blue skies, we suddenly heard the thunder of planes behind us. Turning around, to our utter amazement we saw three old biplanes — Gloster Gladiators — racing towards us. There was a shattering roar as they dived over St Andrew's, a flash of silvery wings in the golden sunlight and they were gone. Three gallant pilots in their ancient machines, flying across Malta to challenge the Italian air force. We gazed after them, in wonder, as they dwindled into the distance. "Faith, Hope and Charity" as they flew away into history. Their fame still lives on and I remember them on that sun-drenched morning in Malta so many, many long years ago.' [1]

Above: Air raid. A symbolic picture of a Gunner sounding the alert on his whistle to summon the gun crews to their action stations, having received orders over the phone from the operations room. Thousands of alerts would sound during the siege years on Malta. *Bruce Robertson*

Malta's Fighter Cover

Before detailing the rest of the early air raids, a few words about 'Malta's fighter cover' that John Kelly had just seen in action. It had been conservatively estimated that at least four fighter squadrons would be needed to protect Malta; however, there was absolutely no chance whatsoever of them being released, because home defence of the British Isles was top priority. The then AOC Malta — Air Commodore (later Air Vice-Marshal) F. H. M. Maynard — therefore looked around for a source of any available fighters. Fortunately, his chief administrative officer, Group Captain Gardner, found out that there was an unexpected cache of suitable aircraft at Kalafrana, although they were Gloster Gladiator biplanes. The background was that, earlier in the year, the aircraft carrier *Glorious* had been serving in the Mediterranean, before being rushed back to the UK to take part in operations off Norway. On first arriving at Malta she had off-loaded 18 crated Sea Gladiators (N5518 to N5535), to be held in reserve for her 802 Squadron. Before she sailed home, the carrier stopped at Malta just long enough to embark three of the aircraft, but left the other 15 behind. As there were presently no other carriers in the Mediterranean, the aircraft were not immediately needed. However, HMS *Eagle* did join the fleet in Alexandria soon after the Italian declaration of war (after a major refit in the Far East) and she took on board four Sea Gladiators from stocks held in Egypt. Subsequently, three of the Kalafrana cache were shipped to Egypt, but the remaining dozen were still there and on 19 April four of these had been issued to the Hal Far 'Fighter Flight'. By the end of May a further two had been assembled, leaving six more to be used for spares. Thus, as Christopher Shores and his co-authors point out in *Malta: The Hurricane Years 1940–41*:

'The Fighter Flight was no last minute panic organisation, but had been in existence and equipped for nearly two months before the outbreak of hostilities. The assembled fighters were subsequently fitted with armour plate behind the pilots' seats and with variable-pitch three-blade airscrews.' [2]

As well as a shortage of planes there was a pilot shortage, there being no trained fighter pilots available. Nevertheless, there were a number of volunteers and soon a flight of seven pilots had been assembled under Squadron Leader A. C. 'Jock' Martin and including Flight Lieutenant George Burges, who had been Maynard's Personal Assistant. The other five were: Flight Lieutenants Peter Alexander and Peter Keeble, and Flying Officers Peter Hartley, John Waters and William Woods. The only other aircraft in Malta at that time were five Fairey Swordfish (useful for air-sea rescue only), a few Moths, Gordons and Magisters, and the occasional flying boat (Saro London or Short Sunderland) from 202 Squadron (Gibraltar) or 230 Squadron (Alexandria) on detachment.

These then were the tiny group of pilots and their obsolescent aircraft that would write their own special page of history in the epic story of Malta.

First victory for the Fighter Flight came when Flying Officer 'Timber' Woods shot up one of the Macchi MC 200 Saetta ('Arrow') single-seater fighters that were providing escorts to the bombers during the raids that day. Woods gave a graphic account of the dogfight:

'We sighted a formation of five S.79s approaching Valletta at a height of approximately 15,000 feet and Red Two delivered an attack from astern. The enemy had turned out to sea. I delivered an attack from astern and got in a good burst at a range of approximately 200 yards. My fire was returned. I then broke away and returned over the Island at approximately 11,000 feet south of Grand Harbour. While still climbing to gain height, I observed another formation of five enemy aircraft approaching. They were about the same height as myself. I attacked abeam at about 150 yards and got in a good burst. The enemy started firing at me long before I opened up. This formation broke slightly but left me well behind when I tried to get in an attack from astern. Just after that, when again climbing to gain more height, I suddenly heard machine-gun fire from behind me. I immediately went into a steep left-hand turn and saw a single engined fighter diving and firing at me. For quite three minutes I circled as tightly as possible and got the enemy in my sight. I got in a good burst, full deflection shot, and he went down in a steep dive with black smoke pouring from his tail. I could not follow him down, but he appeared to go into the sea.' [3]

In fact, although Woods was credited with shooting down the enemy aircraft, it was subsequently discovered that the Macchi (piloted by Tenente Giuseppe Pesola) had in fact escaped and got home safely, the black smoke coming only from a hastily opened throttle rather than any serious damage.

On 22 June it was Flight Lieutenant Burges who shot down the flight's first Italian bomber — an SM79 off Marsaxlokk Bay — and so it went on throughout the next two weeks as the flight fought almost non-stop, day after day. It was a seemingly hopeless task — just a handful of old Gladiators against hundreds of Italian bombers and fighters. It was, therefore, vital to try to give them some advantage over the enemy. One problem was the slow speed of the Gladiator (maximum was 253mph as compared with 370mph of the Macchi 202 (*Folgore*), and even the SM79 bombers were marginally faster than the old Gladiators). This lengthened the intercept

time, allowing the enemy to gain a significant advantage. One method of reducing this interval was to have the pilots sitting in their cockpits, already strapped in their harness, so that all they had to do was to start their engines and take off. This meant no proper warming up period for the engine. However, the air temperature was normally high enough anyway, so that the usual run-up could be ignored without causing damage. In this way they could gain precious minutes, which meant an increase of 2–3,000 feet by the time it came to intercept the Italians. However, the strain upon the pilots was considerable, so they had to evolve a less stressful roster, and eventually each pilot got one day off in three. This meant reorganising the flight into three sub-flights of two pilots each. This did not reduce their effectiveness, however, because it was clearly better to have two aircraft in the right place and height than three too late and too low. And with several Italian raids every day, this made a considerable difference.

Another way of improving performance, as has already been mentioned, was to fit a three-bladed propeller (see photograph on page 55) and to modify the emergency boost control. This made the air-

Below: Italian bombers over Malta. First Italian bombers over Malta were 10 SM79s, the start of over 3,300 air raids that would attempt to subdue the gallant islanders. Here the Italians bomb Hal Far aerodrome early on 11 June 1940, the day after Mussolini had declared war. *IWM — KY 7871C*

Above: From the outset civilians in Malta made use of the ancient underground excavations to protect themselves from the bombing. The Air Raid Warden (wearing an armband marked A.R.W.) was a member of the Air Raid Precautions Organisation, set up before the outbreak of war, under Mr C. H. Sansom CMG. *IWM — CM 2781*

Right: Civilians make their way into an air raid shelter in South Street, Valletta. *NWMA Malta — 1823*

Opposite bottom: 'Faith, Hope and Charity'. First air defence for Malta was provided by three Gloster Gladiator biplanes — this is N5519, (with Flight Lieutenant George Burges in the cockpit) at standby, plugged in to a starter trolley. His Gladiator has been fitted with a triple-bladed propeller for extra speed, whilst the one in the background still has the original twin-bladed, fixed-pitch prop. *NWMA Malta*

Left: As the war progressed, more sophisticated shelters were constructed by Engineer Tunnelling Companies — like the 173rd, seen here at work. Their skip could carry over a ton of rock. *IWM — GM 906*

craft fly faster, but there was then the danger of straining the Bristol Mercury IX engines. Inevitably this was exactly what happened and they blew cylinders on both Martin's and Waters' aircraft. The final solution was to convert some spare Bristol Mercury XV engines (as used by the Bristol Blenheim) which had a horsepower of 920hp as opposed to the 840hp of the Mercury IX. This was just one of the many problems that this remarkable little band of pilots and ground crew overcame. Another more physical danger was the fact that Hal Far had only one fixed flight path which increased the risk of accidents during take-offs and landings. In fact, over a period of three days (21–23 June), the flight suffered three crashes, but fortunately none of the pilots was injured and the aircraft were all soon made airworthy once again.

Faith, Hope and Charity

Malta, had been the island where St Paul was shipwrecked in AD 59–60. Thus it was fitting that the famous words from the King James translation of Chapter XIII, verse 13 of his *First Letter to the Corinthians*, should become synonymous with this brave little flight: 'And now abideth faith, hope, charity, these three', so these became the nicknames of the aircraft, no matter which of the Gladiators were actually airborne that day or which of the pilots was actually flying them.[4]

Further Raids

Following on from the first raid, another wave of 15 bombers attacked Grand Harbour, Marsamxett and the dockyard, where the workers were just clocking in to start their day's work. A third group of aircraft attacked Kalafrana, whilst bombs landed on various entirely civilian areas in Gzira, Pieta, Floriana, Marsa, Tarxien, Zabbar and Sliema. There were eleven civilians killed and over 100 injured. The first military casualties occurred at Fort St Elmo, where a bomb fell amongst personnel of the Royal Malta Artillery — six were killed, including one young boy soldier, all of whom were firing their rifles at the aircraft. In all there were seven bombing raids and one reconnaissance sortie that first day; however, none of the former did any real damage to any onshore military target, but rather caused death and destruction to innocent civilians.

There were also six Maltese naval personnel killed in rather unfortunate circumstances. An Italian merchantman had been sighted some five miles off the coast, and had been deserted by her crew who had made a bodged attempt to scuttle her. Accordingly, three launches from HMS *St Angelo* (a shore establishment) were sent out to investigate, whilst a tug was detailed to tow the vessel into Marsaxlokk. They got as far as Zonqor Point, then found the ship was sinking, so decided to beach her at Marsaskala. Then Italian aircraft were spotted and the salvage operation was aborted. They reached Xghajra, where several bombs were dropped near the launches, whilst the coastal batteries at Fort Ricasoli and Fort St Elmo, who mistook the launches for enemy, opened fire. Two launches were sunk and the third badly holed — hence the unfortunate deaths.

Raids Continue

The daylight raids would soon become the pattern over the next few days, causing more and more families from the harbour area to leave their homes and seek shelter in towns and villages further inland, the villagers showing great generosity and kindness to the new arrivals. King George VI wrote some days later:

'I have already heard of the gallant spirit and fine bearing of the Maltese people since they have been brought within the battle zone and I have no doubt that they will be worthy of upholding their great traditions in this struggle in which they are now actively engaged.'

His message was published in all the island's newspapers on 19 June. On the 21st, Malta experienced its first night raids, there being four attacks between midnight and 3am, when Gozo was also bombed.

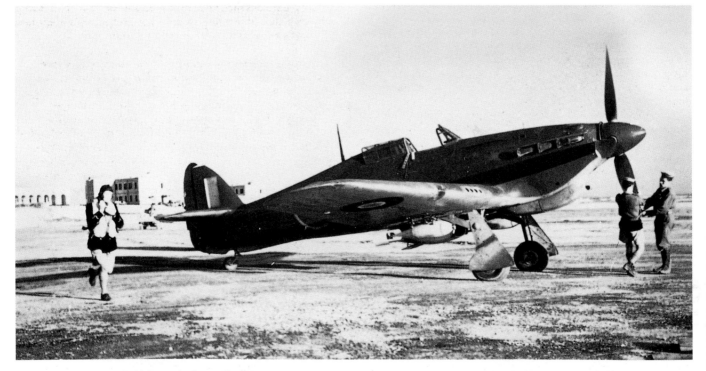

Above: Quite unexpectedly, Malta received a small number of Hurricanes, like this one at Hal Far. Until well into 1941 the Hurricane was by far the most numerous of RAF fighters in most theatres and bore the brunt of early combats against both the Germans and Italians. *NWMA Malta — 6685*

Hurricanes Begin to Arrive

Quite unexpectedly, Malta received a small number of Hawker Hurricanes, part of a batch from the UK that had been earmarked for the defence of the Fleet base at Alexandria. (Just before Italy had entered the war and France surrendered, they had flown to Alexandria via France and Tunis.) Air Commodore Maynard managed to persuade the AOC-in-C Middle East, Air Chief Marshal Sir Arthur Longmore, to let Malta have some of them, a signal from Sir William Dobbie, the Acting Governor, to the War Office, helping to clinch the deal. The intricate machinations of actually getting a share of the Hurricanes, and the pilots to fly them, to the Middle East and then on to Malta, deserve far more space than I can afford here, so suffice it to say that, by the end of June 1940, there were five Hurricanes, and pilots, plus their 'Mother' (a Lockheed Hudson with crew that had assisted in shepherding them to the Middle East). They would enter the air battles in early July at the same time as new Italian fighters (the agile but slow Fiat CR42) appeared on escort duty.

The Home Front

Air Raid Precautions

In his book *Malta: Blitzed but not Beaten*, the late Philip Vella explains how the Passive Defence Corps, which had been set up just before the outbreak of war, 'now proved its mettle'. Twelve centres were established on the island: three in Valletta, and one each in Cospicua, Floriana, Hamrun, Marsa, Mosta, Msida, Sliema, Tarxien, and Zabbar. In May 1940 reservists were called up to man the centres, both by day and by night. The staff of each centre comprised two doctors, a sergeant-major, four sergeants, some 32 men, three drivers, a telephone operator and about 10 female wardens. Each centre had an ambulance and a reconnaissance car, whilst housing a first aid post, a decontamination centre (a gas attack was the initial major bogey, which fortunately did not materialise), sleeping quarters, a canteen, a recreation room and a chapel. The entire organisation was under the eagle eye of Mr C. H. Sansom CMG. Wardens had, prewar, instructed the population in the care and use of gas masks (including special ones for babies). Now, immediately the air raid siren sounded, a roof spotter would take up his position, so that he could quickly see where any bombs landed, and once the 'All Clear' was given, direct the rescue teams to the locations as necessary to do their job.

Householders were advised to reinforce their cellars, put tape on windows to minimise flying glass and take all other sensible precautions. However, it was soon clear that this was insufficient as the bombing became more intense, and many people began to seek better shelter in old railway tunnels and even ancient underground burial chambers, whilst objects of artistic and historical importance were removed from important buildings and stored underground. Unfortunately not all such works of art were protected in this way and many were sadly destroyed.

Home Guard

The Malta Volunteer Defence Force was formed on 3 June 1940, from amongst the local hunters (kaccaturi), farmers, etc. Their main task would be to shoot at parachutists attempting to land. As with the British Local Defence Volunteers, the Malta VDF was the forerunner of the Home Guard, and it soon increased both in strength and expertise. Initially the men wore their ordinary clothes with just an armband and a steel helmet, but eventually all were issued with battledress. Their shooting skills were honed by army instructors, until they had attained a high standard of marksmanship.

Demolition and Clearance Section

This was another small organisation that would play a vital role in saving civilian lives in bombed buildings. It was part of the Public Works Department and comprised three gangs of about 40 men each, armed with picks, axes, shovels, barrows and ladders, who were ready to hurry to the rescue of those trapped under debris. Two of the gangs operated from Floriana and Cospicua, whilst the third was kept on call at HQ Passive Defence, Valletta.

Special Constabulary

This 2,000-strong all-volunteer force was established in May 1940 and patrolled the streets to enforce the blackout regulations and curfew. All lights in Malta and Gozo had to be out or suitably masked, between 7pm and sunrise, with effect from 3 May 1940. Curfew was imposed from 27 May 1940, after which date only authorised persons were allowed to be outdoors between 11pm and 5am.

The Changing Face of Malta

'The face of Malta gradually started taking a new aspect. Destroyed and dilapidated buildings became a common sight; hastily filled bomb craters added to the deterioration of local roads; barbed wire fences and other obstacles now appeared all over the Island; private cars, none too numerous these days, decreased even further; owners of motor cycles needed a special permit to use their vehicles. The oddities of war did not even spare the street names, then still written in Italian. They were anglicised.' [5]

An Army Wife Remembers

Mrs A. B. Marjoribanks-Egerton, the wife of Major Philip Marjoribanks-Egerton of the Royal Irish Fusiliers, kept a diary of her days on Malta (September 1939 - August 1942) and, like RSM John Kelly of the RIF, has contributed to *Malta Remembered* as published by the George Cross Island Association. After recording that on 5 June full details of air raid precautions had been widely circulated and details given of the various siren notes to be used, she also comments that she and her family had been busy getting their shelters ready as the news from Italy was bad. Her entry for 11 June reads:

'War has really reached us at last and this morning at 6.55am we had our first air raid. What a thrill it gave to hear the Siren for the first time and to know that the enemy were at hand. I got so excited I was rooted to the floor for the moment. We went down to the shelter and the guns went off in earnest and the noise was terrific. I went into Valletta in the afternoon and had the odd experience of being the only person in the Strada Reale. Most of the shops were shut and I found it difficult to get food. From the bus I saw what damage had been done in the raid at Msida, several houses had collapsed, other damage was done to the Portes des Bombes. Fatal casualties amounted to eight, many more people are now off to the country. During the course of the day we had seven more alarms.'

Mrs Marjoribanks-Egerton's family would spend that night in the air raid shelter, but were so plagued by mosquitoes that they decided they couldn't possibly go through such discomfort again, so instead they would only go into the shelter if things really hotted up. Buying food was a problem as many of the shops were still shut; she comments that the Government had broadcast a warning that they would take over the shops if the owners did not open them soon. She also says: 'The civil population have borne their first raids well and if they continue to meet all others in the same way, then we shall have nothing to worry about.' More from her diary later. [6]

Above. Valletta was bombed as well as Hal Far on that first raid. Here smoke rises from enemy bombing in a subsequent raid, but on the initial one, 16 small 110kg bombs were dropped and damage was negligible. *IWM — GM 75*

Opposite top: First blood to the Fighter Flight would come when Flying Officer Woods shot up a Macchi MC200 Saetta ('Arrow'), severely damaging it. George Burges would shoot down an Italian bomber a few days later. Here civilians watch with interest as an RAF salvage squad strips a Macchi 202 fighter shot down by Flying Officer Beurling. *Bruce Robertson*

Opposite left: Pilots of Sea Gladiators receive a briefing. The first RAF defenders of Malta were flying just three of these obsolescent biplanes, which took on the might of the Italian Air Force. *IWM — A 8220*

Notes

1. *Malta Remembered* Issue No 1 of 1994.
2. Shores *et al: Malta: The Hurricane Years 1940–41.*
3. Ibid
4. Just one of the Gladiators, N5520, remains in Malta now. This aircraft was rescued in 1943, by Fitter Corporal William Brown and refurbished in 1961 by No 103 Maintenance Unit. Bearing the name 'Faith', it is currently on show in the War Museum. However, the aircraft is due to go to the new Aviation Museum that has been recently completed at Ta Qali, where it will be fully restored, using wings donated by the RAF and parts found in England and Finland. The restoration is possible thanks to sponsorship from the Bank of Valletta and should take two years to complete.
5. Philip Vella: *Malta: Blitzed but not Beaten.*
6. *Malta Remembered,* Issue No 3 of 1997.

Chapter 6

Operation *'Herkules'*

*'Without the occupation of Malta, the North African theatre is
in no way secured.'*
Field Marshal Kesselring

When asked which was the more important objective between
Malta and Crete, in order to ensure Axis success in the Eastern
Mediterranean, the operations officers of the OKW, had this to say,
according to one of the staff officers, General Walter Warlimont:

*'All officers of the section, whether Army, Navy or Air Force,
voted unanimously for the capture of Malta, since this seemed to
be the only way to secure the sea route to North Africa.'*

Keitel and his deputy General Jodl accepted the recommendation,
but when General der Flieger Kurt Student,[1] the commander of XI
Fliegerkorps, was asked for his opinion, he said that he favoured the
attack on Crete. Student was able to win over Hitler, who had
already almost convinced himself that Malta was too strongly garrisoned and would never yield to an airborne assault; Crete on the
other hand seemed an ideal target for the paratroopers. Göring, who
saw either plan as a way of rehabilitating the *Luftwaffe's* reputation
after its failure to win the Battle of Britain, did not really mind
which plan was used, provided paratroopers were employed, so he
supported Student fully. Events would prove that, although Student's paratroopers were able to capture Crete, the butcher's bill
would be so large as to put the Führer off considering any further
major airborne operations.

Planning the Attack Against Malta
Nevertheless, Kesselring continued with his planning, as he wrote
later in his memoirs:

*'Plans had to be translated into action. I did not consider the
African Theatre of Operations secure as long as Malta was in
British hands. For this reason I asked the Italian Supreme
Command and the Armed Forces High Command for permission
to complete my preparations and mount the Malta attack.*

*'My request was approved in the course of the previously
mentioned lively conference.[2] Thereupon and after a conference
with the Italian Supreme Command, we started work on the
attack plan. We began to assemble the necessary troops and
materiel. Forces were apportioned in such strength that failure of
the mission was impossible. We planned to use two airborne
divisions, one of which was to be the Italian Folgore Division,
trained by General Ramcke,[3] a very efficient paratroop
commander, in an extremely short period of time and with
excellent results. The division could be considered as elite.
Exercises, part of which I observed, showed that this division had
the real paratrooper spirit. The many difficulties were overcome
with noteworthy energy.'*

Kesselring also earmarked two or three Italian assault divisions,
picked from among the best Italian Army divisions, that would be
specially trained for Operation *'Herkules'* ('Hercules'), as the attack

on Malta was to be called. Units of the Italian battle fleet were also
to be employed in the attack on the island and in escorting the
assault boats that would carry the seaborne element of the operation. Large ships of the Italian merchant navy were to be used for
transporting the army units, whilst far greater numbers of air force
formations were to be provided for this operation than had been
employed in the initial aerial offensive against Malta.

After much detailed deliberation an outline plan was drawn up.
This involved an initial airborne assault by the German paratroopers on the high ground in the south of the island — to take place
on or about 15 August 1942 — which was to be preceded by heavy
bombing of the main airfields; this would then be followed by a
major amphibious landing, with heavy air support and yet more
paratroop landings. There would also be a diversionary seaborne
attack in the north of the island. However, during the final conference the Commanding Admiral of the Italian Naval High Command expressed his gravest concern with the plan, saying that in his
opinion the attack could only be mounted safely after all the guns
on the island had been silenced. Kesselring discussed the pros and
cons, citing examples, and tried his best to dispel Italian doubts.
However, afterwards he gloomily remarked: 'I wonder if the Italian
Navy was ever with us body and soul.'

Troops Available
With General Student in overall command, the force would
comprise both German and Italian troops, viz:

German 7th Fallschirmjäger Division under the command of
Generalmajor Bernhard Ramcke. (The division was still known
under its 'cover' name of 7th Flieger Division). The division basically comprised three paratroop regiments each of three battalions.
Support included an anti-tank battalion, an artillery battalion, an
MG battalion, an AA MG battalion, an engineer battalion, a signal
battalion, plus normal medical, supply and support troops.

The paratroopers would have in support a single tank company,
to be known as 66th Special Purpose Panzer Company. This company was thus the only German Army unit in the invasion force and
it was to be assembled at the Panzer Lehr Regiment's base at Wuns-
dorf, near Berlin, under the leadership of Knight's Cross winner
Hans Bethke. According to OKW instructions it was to comprise a
somewhat odd mixture of tanks: 12 up-armoured Panzer IV medium tanks; five heavily armoured but tiny Panzer I Ausf. F infantry
assault tanks; five also heavily armoured small Panzer II Ausf. J
reconnaissance tanks; all available (at least 10) captured Russian
StupzKw II(r), the assault version of the KV1 heavy tank armed
with a 152mm howitzer, and, as the photograph on page 63 shows,
fitted with a German cupola for the commander. This company was
clearly tailor-made for the job in hand, because of the anticipated
strong anti-tank defences on the island. Therefore the tanks were
chosen for their firepower and armoured protection, rather than for
their mobility and reliability.

Because of the air currents experienced over the Mediterranean, it
was decided not to load the transport gliders to their full capacity.
Therefore, no tanks would be able to be carried in the Me323 transport gliders even with their 24-ton capacity — the smallest panzers

Left:
Most influential of all Fallschirmjäger was General der Flieger Kurt Student, who convinced Hitler to use his paratroopers to capture Crete instead of assaulting Malta. The casualties they suffered taking Crete would heavily influence the Führer's decision as to whether or not to invade Malta.
IWM — HU 32007

Right:
Hitler had both
confidence and pride
in his paratroopers,
especially after their
success in Belgium
and Holland — he is
seen here decorating
some of them.
However, he was
greatly affected by
their heavy casualties
on Crete and was thus
against them being
used on Malta.
Author's Collection

Below:
The skies over Malta
would therefore not be
darkened by
paratroopers as seen
here being dropped
over Crete.
B. L. Davis

Above: Following up the paratroopers were to be the Gebirgsjäger (Mountain Troops) as had also been the case in Crete. Here men of 5 Gebirgs Division wait beside their Ju52s before take-off for Crete. *IWM — HU 55009*

Above: Largest of the German tanks to be employed in 'Herkules' were to be captured Russian heavy Stupz Kw II(r) tanks, fitted, as the photograph shows, with German-style cupolas. *Helmut Ritgen*

(the Panzer IF) weighing 21 tons. This meant that the tanks could be transported only in naval ferries (seagoing landing craft each carrying two tanks), or the Army's Siebel barges.[4] The intention was to land the 66th Special Purpose Panzer Company north of Kalafrana, in the Bay of Marsaxlokk, under cover of fire from a number of 88mm guns, mounted on more Siebel ferries. The armour would support the group in expanding their beach-head to the west.

Infantry support As with the Cretan operation, the paratroopers would be supported, if necessary, by a mountain (Gebirgs) division. These tough, highly trained infantrymen proved their abilities in Crete, so no doubt would have done equally well had they been used in Malta. The mountain division basically comprised two regiments each of three battalions, an artillery regiment, anti-tank, reconnaissance, pioneer and signals battalions, plus supporting units.

Aircraft The following aircraft and gliders were to be allocated to the mission: 500 x Ju52 and 12 x Me323 transport aircraft; 300 x DFS230 gliders and 200 new Gotha (Go) 242 gliders; 216 x fighter aircraft as escort; and 200 other mixed aircraft.

The old, reliable three-engined Junkers Ju52, known affectionately as '*Tante Ju*' (Auntie Ju), was ideal for parachuting and had begun life as a civilian airliner, under the clever subterfuge employed by the Germans to get around the Versailles Treaty that did not permit Germany to build warplanes. It could carry 13 paratroopers, or 18 air-transported troops or 10,000 pounds of freight out to a maximum range of 700 miles. When used as a glider tug it could pull two DFS230 gliders.

The newer six-engined Messerschmitt 323 was considerably larger, having been developed from the Me321 glider, with a wingspan of over 180ft (almost twice that of the Ju52) and a much larger carrying capacity. Similarly, the Go242 glider which carried a crew of two and up to 21 fully equipped troops, was a considerable improvement on the old DFS230 with its 8-troop capacity.

Italian

Matching the two German divisions were to be equivalent Italian formations — one paratroop, the *Folgore* Airborne Division; one infantry, the *La Spezia* Infantry Division — chosen from the three under training for such operations.

Aircraft The *Regia Aeronautica* would supply some 222 fighters plus 470 mixed bombers, torpedo-bombers and other assault aircraft.

Naval vessels Five battleships, four heavy cruisers, 21 destroyers and 14 submarines, plus motor torpedo boats and minesweepers, were to be allocated to protect the merchant vessels, landing craft, floating ferries and others.

In total, some 30,000 men were to be made available for the airborne assault, plus a further 70,000 to follow by sea. This was a far larger number than was actually allocated to Operation '*Merkur*' ('Mercury'), the operation to capture Crete. Although the airborne force was similar, the amphibious follow-up force had been nowhere near as large, and much of it had been destroyed by the Royal Navy before it could reach Crete.

Below: Air support would have come from both German and Italian bombers, like these Junkers 88 dive-bombers, preparing to bomb Malta.
Bundesarchiv — 80/90/13

Above: The other dive-bomber to make its appearance was the Junkers 87 — the dreaded Stuka which had supported the German Blitzkrieg throughout the early part of the war and regularly bombed Malta and the convoys bringing in supplies. *IWM — MH 5591*

Operation 'Herkules' — Plan

Phase 1: The Airborne Assault

The first wave of paratroopers of the 7th Flieger Division would leave Sicily just before first light and approach Malta from the west. At about 20 miles south of the island (at a point to be marked by a U-boat), each aircraft and its towed glider would turn to port, so that they approached the island from a southerly direction, in line abreast, aiming for the area of Qrendi to form a bridgehead between the small bays of Torri Zurrieq (between Wied iz-Zurrieq and Blue Grotto) and Ghar Lapsi. Qrendi airfield and any anti aircraft positions in the area would be captured and held, awaiting the arrival of further troops in Phase 2. The Phase 1 force would comprise most of the division less those elements needed for the airborne element of Phase 2.

Phase 2

Seaborne assault and airborne follow-up. At H+6 hours part of the *La Spezia* Division plus the German tank company would land from the sea in the Phase 1 bridgehead, whilst the *Folgore* Division, strengthened by part of the 7th Flieger Division, would drop in certain areas to the north-west of the bridgehead and capture Mdina and Rabat.

Phase 3

Attack eastwards. The seaborne troops would next capture Hal Far and Safi airfields, then the harbours of Marsaxlokk and Birzebbuga. Meanwhile the airborne troops would form a defensive line from Ghar Bitija (south of Dingli) up to Ll Qattara (northwest of Ta Qali) and then down to Kirkop. These airborne troops were to prevent the British using Luqa and Ta Qali airfields. If necessary, the force reserve, the German mountain division, was to be landed on the airfield captured during Phase 1.

Phase 4

The remainder of *La Spezia* Division would land at the harbours captured in Phase 3 and when this was finished, Valletta would be attacked. Supported by elements of the tank company, the Italians would then advance from the south and take the Senglea peninsula from the southeast. Airborne forces would simultaneously advance from the west and take Sliema. The two forces would then join up at the bottom of the Valletta peninsula, cut the city off and capture it. This would stop all further resistance and the island would then be completely under Axis control.

It was a good plan which clearly had a fair chance of success, but of course would never be put into action.

Radar Jamming

Tied in with their increased bombing raids and other preparations for 'Herkules', the Germans also installed some powerful new jamming devices on Sicily, to render British radar on Malta useless. This would deprive the Malta air defence of its early warning system, so it was vital to do something to counteract it. Eventually, the Air Ministry received a despairing signal from Malta, saying that they were now being very badly jammed and could British Scientific Intelligence provide any assistance. There was a simple response:

'I knew that the Germans judged the success of their jamming by listening to our radar transmissions to see whether, for example, they ceased to scan, as they might well do if they could not be used. I therefore signalled Malta to go on scanning as though everything was normal and not to give any kind of a clue that

they were in difficulty. After a few days the Germans switched their jammers off.' [5]

Ultra Knows All

And of course, Ultra had revealed Hitler's plans to capture Malta almost as soon as they were first mooted, so anti-invasion plans were also soon well advanced on the islands. They were given definite impetus after the fall of Crete in June 1941, but fortunately never had to be tested because of Hitler's wrong decision to permit only 'mental preparation' for 'Herkules' to be conducted, even after Tobruk had fallen in June 1942. How much he was influenced by the horrific casualties that had resulted from the assault on Crete is not clear. Certainly Kesselring remained puzzled about it, as he wrote after the war:

'To this day I do not understand why the two Armed Forces Operation Staffs in Rome and East Prussia failed to initiate decisive action with respect to Malta for such a long period of time. Hitler was inclined to consider the idea only after a very temperamental discussion. I should not like to state with certainty today whether or not he approved this operation completely. As an army man he undoubtedly imagined the attack was going to be more difficult than it actually would have turned out to be. One need merely compare the situation subsequent to the aerial assault on Malta, after which the island could have been taken with minimum losses. Perhaps Hitler thought that his approval for these operations would in future force him to agree to requests for transfers of troops and materiel at a time when the other theatres of war on which his thoughts were mainly concentrated would present their own demands which he could not ignore then.' [6]

Kesselring then goes on to comment, as already mentioned, that the Italians were obviously trying to avoid taking any risks whatsoever. He goes so far as to say that he did not think that the Italian Supreme Command had confidence in its troops being able to accomplish a mission of that kind. Is it any wonder that Kesselring added his remarks about the Italian Navy?

Alone on Malta

According to Cajus Becker's *Luftwaffe War Diaries* matters reached a head in early June, when Student was ordered to report at Hitler's East Prussian HQ at Rastenburg. The Führer listened to Student's report, asked some questions and even agreed that it might be possible to win a bridgehead on Malta.

'"But what then?" he asked impatiently. "I guarantee what will happen. The Gibraltar squadron will leave port at once, and the British fleet will come steaming from Alexandria. Then you will see what the Italians do. At the first radio reports they will go running back to their Sicilian harbours — warships, transports and all. And you and your paratroops will be left sitting on the island alone!"

'A dumbfounded Student started to protest but his Führer cut him short, saying: "I forbid you to return to Italy! You will stay in Berlin." And that was an end to it, all the months of planning and preparation had been wasted. What put the final nail in the Operation "Herkules" coffin was Rommel's capture of Tobruk and the subsequent approval given by Hitler for the "Desert Fox" to go on to strike for the Suez Canal and the glittering prizes of Cairo and Alexandria. Hitler was just as brusque with Kesselring when he criticised Rommel's plans as being madness while the Desert Air Force airfields were still intact. Kesselring was told to:

Above: Defending against the enemy armour would be tanks like this Vickers Light Mark VIC, armed with two machine guns, a 15mm and a coaxially mounted 7.92mm Besa. Note its distinctive 'stone-wall' camouflage.
IWM — GM 474

Right: Infantry, seen here firing their 3in mortars. A popular weapon, despite its relatively short range (2,750 yards) it was used in all theatres and by all Commonwealth forces, and no doubt would have played an important part in the defence of Malta, had 'Herkules' ever been put into operation.
IWM — GM 489

Isolate and Starve into Submission

'During the period 20 March until 28 April 1942, the naval and air bases of Malta were put completely out of action . . . In the course of 5,807 sorties by bombers, 5,667 by fighters and 345 by reconnaissance aircraft, 6,557,231 kilograms of bombs were dropped.' So read an Order of the Day published by II Fliegerkorps, based upon what could be judged from the air — and as is natural, the reconnaissance pilots saw only what they were able to see and there was no fifth column or spy network on Malta to confirm or deny such claims. Now as '*Herkules*' would never be put into action, the *Luftwaffe* was committed to continue bombing. Thereafter, even Kesselring considered Malta 'sorted'.

Would '*Herkules*' Have Worked?

So ended the proposed Axis invasion of Malta. It is difficult to say whether or not Operation '*Herkules*' would ever have worked successfully. Certainly the similar carefully planned assault on Crete worked, although it was an exceedingly close-run thing. Therefore, one is bound to say that the Axis would have had a similar chance of success had they invaded Malta. Fortunately it was the enemy who decided against taking the risk, both Axis dictators coming to the conclusion that Malta could be bottled up by air and by sea until it was forced to surrender. 'At Malta,' Hitler commented during one of his supper parties on 17 January 1942, when he was extolling the superior quality of *Luftwaffe* aircraft, 'our tactics consist in attacking without respite, so that the English are compelled to keep on firing without interruption.'8 According to Winston Churchill in Volume IV of his epic *History of the Second World War*, Mussolini was so 'elated at the prospect of conquering Egypt, he postponed the assault on Malta till the beginning of September', whilst Hitler was so confident Rommel would take Egypt that, 'without reference to either the Italians or to his own naval command, he postponed the attack on Malta until the conquest of Egypt was complete'. What both of them never fully appreciated was the strength of the indomitable spirit of the George Cross islanders — civilian and military alike — who were determined not to give in no matter what happened. In addition the Axis lacked answers to questions that could have been answered only by agents' reports and of course they had none on Malta.

Hitler's incorrect decision to cancel the Malta landing, along with the German failure to reach political agreement with Vichy France and Spain, surrendered the initiative in the Mediterranean to the Allies. They would capitalise on this with their highly successful offensives in North Africa that would eventually drive the enemy out, whilst Hitler would scatter the bulk of Germany's strength in energy-sapping gains in the vast steppes of Russia where massive advances rarely produced anything of real consequence, other than giving the Germans even more territory to administer. How different it all might have been if Malta had been taken and the Axis had become masters of the Suez Canal. Instead Malta remained a major thorn in the Axis side, preventing more and more supplies and reinforcements getting through to the North African theatre of war.

Notes

1. General der Flieger Kurt Student had been a pilot during the Great War, winning the Knight's Cross of the House Order of Hohenzollern for his bravery, then transferring back to the infantry postwar. In 1938 he became commander of the parachute and glider arm, was wounded in Holland in 1940, then was the author and overall commander of the paratroop assault on Crete in May 1941.
2. This was a meeting with Adolf Hitler in February 1942, during which Kesselring had 'forcibly presented' his requests. He quoted Hitler's response as follows: 'He took my arm and purred amiably: "Take it easy Marshal Kesselring, I'll do it." But of course he didn't.'
3. Hermann Bernhard Ramcke was a tough, uncompromising paratrooper, who won a Knight's Cross in Crete as commander of the 1st Parachute Assault Regiment. He would go on to reach the rank of General der Fallschirmtruppe and become the 20th recipient of the Diamonds to the Knight's Cross (having already been awarded his Oakleaves and Swords) as commander of Fortress Brest in September 1944.
4. The ferries were first produced at Antwerp as a joint Army-*Luftwaffe* project, but later built by the *Luftwaffe* and named after *Luftwaffe* engineer Major Siebel, who had run a special command in the *Luftwaffe* to test barges for the intended invasion of England — Operation 'Sealion'.
5. Quoted from R. V. Jones: *Most Secret War*. After the war Jones spent several days talking to General Martini, Director General of *Luftwaffe* Signals, when he was a POW. Martini asked him why his jammers had not paralysed Malta's radar and he 'laughed ruefully' when Jones told him of the simple stratagem he had employed and how it had worked so perfectly.
6. Quoted from General Kesselring's treatise on the Mediterranean War, contained in *WWII German Military Studies* Volume 14.
7. Cajus Becker: *The Luftwaffe Diaries*.
8. H. R. Trevor-Roper: *Hitler's Table Talk 1941–44*.

Chapter 7
Land Defences

BEACHPOST J.2.

'Concrete block and Malta stone, a lonesome dwelling we call home,
Down upon the rocky shore, six bunk beds and a cold stone floor.
Slits to poke machine guns through, and a primus stove to cook the stew
Whose turn next, let's have a look? "OH NOT HIM, let's stew the cook."
"STAND TO" drill it's fading light, preparing for another night,
Patrolling 2 hours on 4 off, along the goat track, and fell off,
Sliding, rolling down the cliff, climbing back all sore and stiff,
Get a grip be on your mark, now find your helmet in the dark.
Night binoculars to your eyes, sweep the sea and then the skies,
Alert for sneaking mine-laying Hun, with hard rock sticking in your bum,
"What was that?" you hear a noise, rifle bayonet quickly poise,
Approaching gently lump in throat, you nearly stabbed the bloody goat.
Moonlight shimmering on the sea, cold and lonely want a pee,
You'd like a smoke, but not that much, for if it's seen "your feet won't touch"
At last its 4am you've done, back to the post the next one's on,
Try to wake him, can you hell, he's snoring and his tootsies smell.
Tired of trying to gently wake, you grab him with a hefty shake,
Thinking it's a night attack, he jumps up, gives his nut a crack.
Then with his anguished cry of pain, wakes the whole lot up again.
And in darkness hearing groans, "INVASION'S Come" no time for yawns.
Pandemonium quickly spreads, as they tumble from their beds
And with enquiring rude retorts, grab their guns before their shorts,
So in remorse you light the light, confronted by a ghastly sight,
Knobbly knees and just a vest, they cross their legs to hide the rest.
With tousled hair and staring eyes, they turn to you and in surprise
Just like a herd of cows all moo, "WHAT THE BLOODY ELL'S TA DO?"
Explanations, blame on him, threats to clip him on the chin,
And once he's dressed and through the hole, back into bed you swiftly crawl.
In sweet contentment close your eyes, then suddenly across the skies,
Before you've time to curl your toes, the flaming wailing winnie goes,
With everyone competitive style, inventing curses rare and vile,
You're quickly wishing you'd go deaf or that you'd joined the RAF.
So to your posts look lively lads, we'll beat the Germans like our Dads
Two on the searchlight, three on guns, I'll brew them up, we've got some buns
And when tomorrow morning dawns, we may just justify our yawns,
Harassed, tired and weary too, but loyal comrades on J.2.'

R. Bleasdale, Malta, 1940-1

When the war began, R. H. Walter MM, was a member of the 24th Fortress Company, Royal Engineers, stationed in Lintorn Barracks, Floriana. In June 1940 he would volunteer with others to dig out an unexploded bomb at Sliema, which had been dropped during the first air raid on Malta. It would be the first of over 50 bombs which he and the other members of No 25 Bomb Disposal Section would deal with, that is to say, dig out, defuse and render safe. These bombs would range from enemy anti-personnel mines, both Thermos and Butterfly types, through 250-pounders, 500-pounders, 1,000-pounders and even two 2,000-pounders. He graphically recalled his initial experiences dealing with this first bomb in *Malta Remembered*:

'He [Major "Leggy" Jacobs the OC of 24th Fortress Company] briefed us on the operation by telling us that the unexploded bomb was located in Rudolf Street, Sliema. It did not appear to be a large bomb by the size of the hole in the roadway, and the civilian police had already evacuated the area. After we had collected the necessary tools and equipment, and a 30cwt lorry, we were to report to Sliema Police Station where we would be met by a Capt Jones and a Lt Eastman, both of the Royal Army Ordnance Corps who would be the officers in charge of the whole operation. This was because at the time we had no RE officers qualified in bomb disposal work. After our briefing Maj Jacobs thanked us for volunteering and wished us luck.

'Outside, Sgt King instructed me to go to the cookhouse and collect our rations which had already been prepared and meet him at the guardroom at 0945. In the meantime he would take the other two sappers to get the lorry and tools from the QM Stores. These included: pickaxes, shovels, crowbars, sandbags, planks, shoring posts, motorised water-pumps, ropes, lashings, a toolbox containing a wide selection of spanners, screwdrivers, pliers, hammers, 7lb and 14lb sledgehammers, field telephones and reels of cable, rubber gloves and rubber boots. The tools and equipment checked, I was picked up at the guardroom at 1000 and we moved off to Sliema, arriving at the police station at 1030.

'We were eagerly awaited and met by Police Sgt Orr who told us that Capt Jones and Lt Eastman had not yet arrived, but that he had supervised the evacuation of all the residents within a 400-yard area around the bomb and the area had been cordoned off and officers posted at various points. In fact everything had been done in order that we could start work as soon as possible. At 1045 Lt Eastman arrived and introduced himself to us. I was surprised that he was such a young man, but found that he was a pleasant and jovial person to work with. After introductions he said: "We will drive round to Rudolf Street and leave the lorry 100 yards from where the bomb is and walk to the location and have a look at the job." We boarded the lorry, drove round to Rudolf Street, with Police Sgt Orr and left it some 100 yards away. We all then walked down Rudolf Street, which was about 300 yards long, to where the bomb was located and found a hole in the road, three feet out from the south side pavement. The hole was about a foot in diameter, quite neat around the edges. You could see down into the hole for about 18 inches and then it was

Right:
Bomb disposal. Some of the bombs dropped did not explode so had to be rendered safe by the incredibly brave members of the EOD (Explosive Ordnance Disposal) squads. *NWMA Malta — 6842*

Opposite:
The larger bombs needed more men and more lifting equipment, but that did not make the job any safer or easier. *NWMA Malta — 1804*

Below:
Initially, as the first reminiscences show, men of the Royal Engineers formed volunteer EOD squads. Here is one such team with some of its 'trophies'. *NWMA Malta — 6740*

broken sandstone. We all thought there was a smell of explosives but none of us was sure about this.

'Lt Eastman suggested that we first marked the centre of the hole with a marker post. He felt it was a 250lb or 500lb bomb. He then instructed us exactly how we were to excavate — open up a hole five feet square, digging with sandbag covered spades, removing as much rubble as possible with gloved hands. Only two men could work in the hole until we got down to a depth of about three feet, then only one man would work in the hole but he would keep in touch with the rest of the team by field telephone; on finding any trace of the bomb, Lt Eastman was to be informed and we were to await further instructions from him.'

Having brought the lorry a little nearer the bombsite, they unloaded the tools they needed and began work. Sergeant Orr told them that the local bar-keeper had left a crate of 24 bottles of beer for them, which was promptly brought down to them. It was very hot, so the beer was most welcome and a second case was delivered during the afternoon. They had started digging at about 11.30, stripped to the waist, finding that once they had broken through the road surface and the first six inches of hardcore below it, then the ground below was easier to get out. By now they had removed the sandbags from their shovels and were able to get out the compacted sandstone with crowbars and shovels — working all the time with great care and removing much of the rubble by hand.

'During this first hour of digging Sgt King was replaced by our own Cpl Brewer, a burly likeable man whom we all knew very well. We never did find out why Sgt King was replaced. Lt Eastman left the site at 12.30 with strict instructions that should we find any trace of the bomb we were to stop working and await his return. He pointed out that the first part of the bomb to be exposed would be the fin section which in all probability would have been torn away from the actual bomb which would be found some distance deeper than the fin section. He also told us not to go any deeper than three feet and we were to break for lunch at 1pm and named a café some distance away which had offered to supply us with a hot meal and beer, but we were to leave a policeman keeping an eye on the excavation until we returned.

'By 1pm we had reached a depth of about eighteen inches and called a halt for lunch. Cpl Brewer called in the stand-by police constable to keep guard of the hole until we returned. We found the café some 400 yards away and sat down to a hot meal of sausages and chips, with peas and followed by apple pie and custard, with as much beer as we wanted, all provided free. It appeared that several of the local inhabitants had been round and made a collection of money to provide us with the meal and the beer. Lt Eastman wasn't with us for the meal. He had not yet returned. However, I did notice that during the meal and for that matter for the whole time we were digging, we had all been very quiet, none of the constant chatter normally noticeable when sappers are at work. I expect this was solely due to the job we were doing. I was tensed up to the point of being frightened and I did not relish the job at all. I suspected that the rest of the lads felt the same, but it was something none of us would admit.

'At 2pm we all returned to the site, after thanking the café proprietor and local inhabitants for their generosity. Off came our khaki shirts and we continued digging. By this time the sun was at its highest and it was extremely hot. We were perspiring freely, probably because of the beer. By 3pm we were down to a depth of 3 feet and had found nothing. We stopped work as ordered, sat down on the pavement for a beer and a cigarette, and during this

welcome break Lt Eastman returned. He was well pleased with our progress but surprised that we had reached a depth of three feet. Under his guidance we pressed on with the digging, except from now on only one man worked down in the hole for spells of just fifteen minutes each man, the remainder were some 50 yards away. Lt Eastman stayed at the hole and kept in touch with Cpl Brewer by field telephone, reporting to him exactly what we were doing and our progress. During my spell I found that the bomb had severed a sewer pipe and that raw sewage was seeping into the hole. It didn't smell very nice and the earth was wet. However, on exposing the sewer pipe, we plugged it with sandbags on each side of the hole which stopped the flow of sewage into the hole. We then cleaned out the hole and got rid of the evil smelling sewage and back to reasonable sandstone rubble, and we found that we were then able to make better progress, however, a lot of our pre-planning had gone by the board and we were behind schedule.

'By 4pm we had reached a depth of 4 feet 6 inches and exposed the fins of the bomb. Work stopped and Lt Eastman went into the hole by himself and completely uncovered the fins of the bomb and lifted them out of the hole. He called all the squad to see the fins and explained to us all that it was in fact a 250lb bomb. The fins had been damaged somewhat on entry into the ground but none the less they were all in one piece.

'From then on we carried on digging with much more care, as before with only one man in the hole, the remainder 50 yards away, Lt Eastman at the top of the hole with the field telephone reporting our progress to Cpl Brewer. At a depth of 5ft it was found that the bomb had altered its course slightly, but not so much as to cause us concern. We carried on digging until the light began to fade and Lt Eastman decided that we should finish for the day. The time was then 9pm Whilst we were getting cleaned up, collecting our tools and finishing off the beer, Lt Eastman told us that we would locate the bomb the next day and it should be a straightforward job to defuse it and make it safe, provided it was not some new sort of bomb. Cpl Brewer brought our lorry and we loaded up, covered the hole with a tarpaulin and anchored it down, then placed hurricane lamps (red) around the hole. Whilst we were doing this Lt Eastman called in the local police, told them what we had done and informed Sgt Orr that the area was to remain out of bounds to the locals overnight and we would return the next day and start work at 9am'

The squad then drove back to barracks, had a meal in the cook-house, then went over to the canteen for a drink and to talk over the day's events. Walter did not stay long as he was very tired, so went to bed early. In the morning he was refreshed but still somewhat apprehensive; however, he felt a lot better once he had met up with the rest of the squad at breakfast.

'We set off for Sliema at 08.30 . . . met Lt Eastman at 9am and lost no time in making a start. We removed the tarpaulin and hurricane lamps. It was a beautiful sunny day and the sun was shining down on us over the rooftops. The routine was the same as the previous day . . . and by lunchtime we had reached a depth of six feet and were able to see the base end of the bomb and from it protruded the blades of a brass propeller about five inches across . . . Lt Eastman called all the squad to the hole and pointed out to us the base of the bomb and the propeller protruding from it. He then explained to us that the propeller we could see should have been extracted from the bomb as it came down from the aircraft as the extraction of the propeller would release the firing pin to strike the detonator on impact with the ground. This was fortunate as it indicated that with the propeller still in place it could not fire the detonator and so we could assume that the bomb was in fact safe, but that we should take no chances. Somewhat relieved, we continued to expose the bomb and in fact soon found that it had split open and was in five separate pieces.'

They then stopped for lunch, left a constable guarding the hole, and once again ate at the same café, their meal being paid for by the locals.

'After lunch I was to spend the first fifteen minutes in the hole with Lt Eastman and we managed to remove the five pieces of the bomb and the explosive content. We placed the bomb on top of the hole and reconstructed it to make sure we had the whole bomb. When Lt Eastman was quite satisfied we called the rest of the squad to examine it for future reference. The explosive in the bomb was TNT which had obviously been poured into the bomb in a liquid form and had set into a solid mass. It was in fact an Italian 250lb bomb. The first unexploded bomb to land on Malta during the war and to be dug out successfully.

'For the remainder of the afternoon we cleared up the site, left the hole open so that repairs could be carried out to the damaged sewer pipe and loaded up our tools and equipment, together with the pieces of the bomb and the explosive. We left the lorry at the police station as we had been invited down to "Tony's Bar" on the seafront for a few drinks which the local inhabitants had treated us to in appreciation of our work. We all enjoyed the drinks in "Tony's Bar" and we were surprised by the attention the people of Sliema showed us. They clapped and shouted their thanks and they were so joyful that the bomb had been removed with no mishaps. They gathered outside "Tony's Bar" just to see and thank the sappers for their work. We for our part were very pleased and relieved and at 7pm we said goodbye to Lt Eastman who was returning to his barracks and thanked him for his guidance over the past two days.

'On arrival at Floriana Barracks we parked the lorry in the MT yards, went into barracks, had a bath and a change of clothing and then a hot meal at the cookhouse. I was feeling very tired and had an early night. The following morning Cpl Brewer

Above: More mundane was mounting sentry on important locations. This was in Kingsway, Valletta, near St Francis Church. Note the Maltese policeman and the sign saying that they are still open for business. *NWMA Malta — 6885*

contacted us and told us to be at the MT Yard at 10am On arrival we were met by Maj Jacobs, our OC, and our sergeant-major, who were there to see the bomb. This was shown to them, but we told them that the tail end of the bomb still contained the detonator and fusing device which were removed by Lt Eastman later in the day. Major Jacobs thanked us for our work on the project and told us that our Bomb Disposal Squad was to be enlarged to 12 men and was to become No 25 Bomb Disposal Section. Later that day Lt Eastman instructed us how to destroy the detonator of the bomb with a small explosive charge.'

The first unexploded bombed removed safely, the first Bomb Disposal Section was formed and was soon working under extreme pressure in the ensuing months. The following is an extract from the *Times of Malta*:

'To: The Editor, *Times of Malta*

Sir,

I, on behalf of the people living in the area of St Charles Street and Rudolf Street should like to thank through the medium of your paper, the Officers and men, also Police Sergeant Orr, for the excellent work carried out without thought for their own safety in not only removing the unexploded bomb from the said area, but also for the excellent morale instilled into the inhabitants under such trying conditions.

'I should like to thank the Officers and men of the Royal Engineers concerned for the work done under trying circumstances. I cannot express myself in words, but on behalf of the inhabitants of this area, once again thank them from the bottom of my heart.

'P. G. Mayo
'The Chief Engineer wishes to add his congratulations to the above report.'

Mr Walter added a postscript to his blow-by-blow account, in which he explained in some detail all the types of bombs the section had to deal with over the next 18 months, closing with the words:

'During my time on Bomb Disposal we lost five men — one officer and four sappers. The officer and two sappers were killed when they tried to recover an Italian conical shaped sea mine, and the other two sappers in dealing with anti-personnel mines. I have since considered myself very lucky as a Bomb Disposal man's life expectancy was three to six months.' [2]

So Many Heroes
The *Sapper* magazine also featured a short article about dealing with this first unexploded bomb (UXB) in which another member of the volunteer squad (ex-WO2 W. D. Scott) goes into some detail about the broken sewer pipe! He also explains that Lieutenant Eastman was awarded the George Cross in recognition of his bomb disposal work in Malta, and would later reach the rank of Brigadier. Captain Jones would be similarly decorated, both their awards being gazetted on 28 December 1940. Corporal Brewer received the MBE and Scott was twice mentioned in despatches — they certainly were an extremely brave band of men. Together with similar units from the RN and RAF, they defused or blew up some 2,500 tons of the 17,000 tons of bombs dropped by the enemy over Malta, rightly receiving the highest awards for their bravery which included the George Medal (GM) to Major Reginald Parker (27 May 1941), to Lieutenant Blackwell

(6 November 1942), to Lieutenant Cyril Rowlands, RNVR (2 September 1941) and Bar (7 November 1942) — the list is a long one.

And their work was not just restricted to bomb disposal. For example, Lieutenant Edward Woolley GM, was in charge of dismantling and making safe an Italian MTM explosive boat captured after the attack on Grand Harbour on 26 July 1941 (see later). With the voluntary assistance of Chief Petty Officer Leslie Hanlon, RN, he completed this extremely dangerous operation, thus enabling the islanders to learn all about such weapons and to work out plans to deal with them. His bravery earned him a Bar to his GM and a BEM for CPO Hanlon, who would later also be awarded the GM for other dangerous work. Acting Lieutenant-Commander William Hiscock, RN, was awarded the DSC for defusing sea mines and would later receive the posthumous award of the George Cross, whilst his successor, CPO Bargy received the DSM and later the George Medal.

Dealing with the Casualties
Of course the majority of the bombs did explode, causing widespread damage and many casualties to civilians and military alike. Soon hospitals were not only stretched to capacity but some were also extensively damaged, despite the fact that they were all clearly marked with the Red Cross. In addition to casualties caused by the bombing, others resulted from outbreaks of typhoid, caused, for example, by sewage contaminating the Ta Qali reservoir when bombing cracked the pipes, and polio brought on by malnutrition[3] and the generally very difficult and debilitating conditions under which everyone had to live. Dr Vivian Wyatt of Leeds carried out a study of polio cases overseas in World War 2 and of the use of iron lungs in their treatment. He kindly allowed me to see some of his research material, from which the following quotes are taken:

'I was indeed in Malta between November 1942 and April 1943 and I remember the polio epidemic well. I was second in command at Ta Qali at the time and all our men were in billets off the station, because it was too dangerous to live on and, anyway, all our buildings had been destroyed by bombing. The men lived in requisitioned houses in the local towns and villages. They had to be bussed to and from work. The housing situation was acute, so they were generally overcrowded. Also we were all undernourished at that time. And to add to that there was not only a water shortage but also of fuel to heat it. I never got quite used to washing six days out of seven with cold water and eagerly looked forward to one bath a week with only a few inches of hot water.

'In consequence we had little resistance to normally not very serious illnesses. We had a number of cases of polio on the station; somehow the figure eight sticks in my mind, but I may be wrong. One of my duties was to inspect a proportion of the men's billets daily and frankly I loathed it, as I had a great fear of getting the disease. We insisted on the highest possible standards of cleanliness and keeping the sleeping quarters aired, but there was nothing we could do about overcrowding.'

In his treatise Dr Wyatt states that during the actual siege from 1940 to late 1942 Malta had only one case of polio diagnosed. However, some children who fell sick on 15 and 21 November 1942 were found to have polio, though this was not initially recognised; the first of many service cases was diagnosed on 27 November:

'The end of the first fateful week found us with eight patients with severe respiratory involvement and one iron lung. It was soon discovered that an unorthodox type of artificial respiration (ie: a rhythmical pressure and release, applied centrally with the palm of the hand on either side of the sternum) was of some help

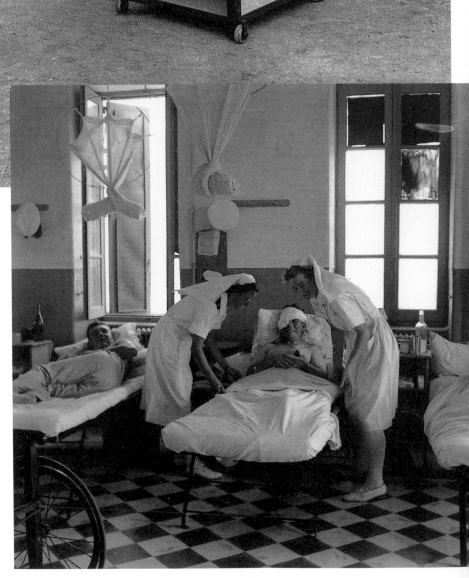

Above: An iron lung ready for use. As the text explains, polio was rife in Malta for a while and there were some 483 victims in total.
IWM — GM 3706

Right: Ministering angels. This lucky wounded serviceman has not one but two QAIMNS nursing sisters to get his bed made neatly — no doubt for Matron's morning inspection!
IWM — GM 3532

. . . and an SOS for volunteers to work in fifteen minute relays was immediately issued. The response was great. All male orderlies not on duty at that time (together with members of the Malta Auxiliary Corps) flocked to the ward and were soon dressed in gowns and masks, ready for action. When day staff finished duty they, too, hurried along to reinforce the volunteers.'

The iron lung was itself the brainchild of the then Chief Ordnance Mechanical Engineer (OME) Lieutenant-Colonel (later Major-General, KBE, CB) Leslie Tyler, who had an invaluable aptitude for improvisation and made the life-saving machine out of all manner of spare parts, including inner tubes and vehicle bonnet clips. The men on call had to operate a hand pump if the power supply failed. Tyler was also the leading light in keeping the precious anti-aircraft guns properly maintained and repaired despite the continual, chronic shortage of spares. For his contribution to the defence of Malta he was honoured with the OBE.

An article in the *British Medical Journal* in June 1945 gives more idea of numbers involved in the polio epidemic, stating that there were 483 victims in total, 426 of them civilians and of these almost all were children under the age of five, with a substantial number being under one year. Fortunately the death rate among civilians was low — only 3.5 per cent being directly attributable to the disease. However, it was much higher among the 57 service cases where one fifth died.

And Even Tanks

As we have seen, the Germans had intended to include tanks in their seaborne follow-up force. Whether or not they knew that there were British tanks on the island is not clear but, despite the fact that there was a shortage of 'good tank country' on Malta, as we shall see, a mixture of infantry, cruiser and light tanks, totalling 14 in all eventually served on the island. They arrived in two batches, the first in 1940, the second not until the spring of 1942.

Bill Green of Bristol served with the first batch, which was part of the 1st Army Tank Brigade and comprised three officers and 64 NCOs and men from the 4th, 8th and 44th Royal Tank Regiments (RTR), under the command of Captain (A/Major) R. E. H. Drury, RTR. Their journey to Malta began at Liverpool, where they were loaded on board the *Louis Pasteur*, a converted French liner, which took them as far as Gibraltar. Then they were loaded onto HMS *Greyhound* which took them to Malta, as Bill Green recalls:

'So into Grand Harbour, as yet virtually untouched by war, and soon marching through Floriana, Hamrun and on to Birkiekara to our first billets, an ex ice cream factory. No 1 Independent Tank Troop, RTR, had started in style. Actually it turned out to be one of our better "homes", but at that time we were blissfully unaware, and contented ourselves by looking at the local "talent", and weighing up where the local bars were. Our tanks were unloaded later and soon our "fighting strength" was assembled — four Matilda Mark II and two Light Mark VI. The former were named "Greyhound", "Griffin", "Gallant" and "Faulknor" after our destroyer escort.'

Bill couldn't remember the names of the two Light Mk VI; however, I have since learned that they were called *'Fortune'* and *'Fury'*.

'The tanks were soon tucked away, specially prepared hangars had been provided, and so they were out of sight of the daily reconnaissance flights of the Regia Aeronautica. Soon the tanks were to be repainted with a local "stone-wall" pattern which proved very effective camouflage indeed. During the next few weeks

the flag was shown round the local villages and main towns, very effective for morale as the Maltese had never set eyes on a tank before, and must have felt rather assured at the sight, but why they felt it necessary to cross themselves rather mystified us!'

The tank crews were then issued with bicycles, so that they could get around the island and discover, as Bill puts it, 'every bump and pothole, but better still every village bar'. The tanks did not often get an airing as fuel was in short supply, so instead the crews were given other jobs. They used either to drive their own unit's trucks or commandeered others to move the contents of ships' holds away to dumps in the country, or worked at navvying, creating blast shelters.

Early in 1942 6 RTR was ordered to reinforce the Malta Troop, so A Squadron, equipped with a mixture of elderly A9 and A13 cruisers sailed from Alexandria. Unfortunately, their convoy was heavily attacked and only eight tanks, plus 85 all ranks, reached Malta on 19 January. Later that spring, A/Major S. D. G. Longworth took over command. The enlarged Independent Troop was now to add a new skill to its current skills of sangar erecting, mining and 'trucking' as Bill Green recalls:

'Large parties joined their infantry mates and moved down to the airfields, mostly to become builders, not with the usual building bricks, but with huge slabs of local stone from the bombed buildings, which without the use of any lifting gear were to form "pens" — three sided shelters in which fighter planes were given a certain amount of protection from strafing 109s who usually came over 10 minutes or so after the Spitfires had landed from their flights off carriers and could be destroyed before they could be refuelled. Other pens were constructed of petrol tins filled with small rubble, also some of sandbags. They were so sited that no two open ends ever faced the same way, thus committing any hostile attacker to one target only. These pens were the saving of the fighter squadrons and from then on the majority of newcomers were so protected that they could be airborne again and joining in the defence of the island very quickly indeed. We even helped the RAF armourers with the ammo belts for the 20mm cannons and some worked on the petrol bowsers . . . This was definitely not the sort of work usually given to a tank soldier and the wide open spaces of the aerodromes made one feel a trifle naked, especially when subjected to low level fighter bombers. Needless to say we went to ground rather rapidly at the start, and tried to make ourselves as small as possible. My own experience of this was feeling rather embarrassed after having scrambled into the lee of a rather low wall, hearing a couple of North Country lads five or so yards away, blazing away with mag after mag of Bren, and discussing the best parts of a Bf109 to aim at! I went back to our half finished pen and continued with the next layer a rather chastened man.

'It was in April 1942 that the invasion "bluelight" was going the rounds, originating from the RAF lads, it gave us to believe that the PRU [Photo Reconnaissance Unit] Spitfires had spotted gliders on Catania airfield and that the runway there was being extended, as were two smaller fields. The PRU ace was Wing Commander A. Warburton, DSO, DFC, who even at the lowest points of Malta's fortunes, went out day after day as the "eyes of the island"; it takes a certain type of courage to undertake so many flights armed only with cameras and he was of that ilk. Naturally this was to be followed by another rumour of invasion barges, so it was a very anxious garrison that awaited what could have become another Crete. If everything had been normal, a parachute invasion from the German viewpoint would have been nothing short of suicidal, but already the AA crews were having

to ration their ammunition, and food had been cut to both the civilians and the services and was destined to get worse. However, the island went about its normal routine and prayed for the next convoy. As history now tells us, a golden opportunity by the German High Command went begging and the cancellation of the invasion spelt the end of Axis forces in North Africa.'

Bill Green goes on to tell of the miracle 'Pedestal' convoy and of the renewed German bombing as they tried to stop Allied aircraft from striking at Rommel. He then explains how the tankmen added a new skill to their repertoire:

'It seemed that among the first casualties suffered at Luqa was the entire pool of cranes and tractors, usually employed to tow crashed aircraft after belly flopping on runways, so with great excitement, I was included with two Matilda tank crews to join the RAF crash crew party. Our brief was to keep the runway open and if there was anything blocking it, it was: "tow ropes out and haul whatever happened to be there, off onto the grass verges". Here it was then cannibalised of its good parts, and the rest towed to the dump, which by now was reaching epic proportions. The RAF crash crew were a very professional bunch of "oddballs" and lived in a cave at the end of the runway, very short of discipline and quite eccentric on dress regulations. We got on very well with them and as the crashed "kites" usually contained rations of some sort or another, these were considered as "perks" and we therefore ate very well indeed. We bunked in the cave with them and were very busy indeed for the next 10 days that followed, each tow being just a bit different from the last. However, the number of enemy bombers getting through dwindled, not surprising really as the AA defences covering the harbour, docks and airfields were devastating and by the 20th it was virtually all over, the Luftwaffe had been thrashed.

'For me that was the turning point, a convoy got through practically untouched in November, and we tankies were trucking once again. Then a larger one in December made it. It was especially rewarding to our eyes to see that a good proportion was food, not only for us, but for the ordinary people of Malta, who had surprised us all by their outstanding resolution and courage despite their losses and the privations they had suffered. The tide had turned.' [4]

Attack on Grand Harbour

In the early dawn of 26 July 1941 the Italian 10th Motor Torpedo Boat Flotilla (X-MAS) launched a daring attack on Grand Harbour, Valletta, with the aim of wrecking dockyard installations and sinking any British ships that happened to be in port. The torpedo boats of this elite unit provided protection for eight small explosive craft, known as *Maiale* (Swine). The *Maiale* was a two-man human torpedo also called an SLC (*Siluro a Lenta Corsa*, literally a 'slow-running torpedo') 6.7m long, and with an electric motor giving it a top speed of 4.5 knots. It was armed with a detachable 200kg explosive charge which the two operators would endeavour to suspend under the target's hull, thus increasing the explosive effect. The two operators wore rubber suits and breathed pure oxygen and sat astride the craft — highly dangerous.

The Italians had initially decided that the best time to make the attack would be during the moonless nights between the end of May and the beginning of June 1941. Accordingly, they carried out two reconnaissances on the nights 25/26 and 27/28 May, and as a result were very encouraged by the fact that their torpedo boats were able to get within five miles of the coast of Malta without any reaction from the coastal defences. However, the powers that be would

not give permission for the attack at that time, so X-MAS was ordered to wait until the next new moon at the end of the month. This they did, but then had to abandon the operation almost immediately, as sea conditions were too rough and one of the torpedo boats got swamped in the choppy waves. They tried again the next night with the same results, so once more had to return to their base at Augusta in Sicily. After these two failures they were somewhat despondent but, nevertheless, determined to try again, so the operation was rescheduled for the night of 25/26 July. The day before, a convoy (Operation 'Substance') had arrived in Malta, so there were even more tempting targets in Grand Harbour.

The Defences

Before going into further details about the attack, a word on the local defences is appropriate. The entrance to Grand Harbour, between the two arms of the breakwater, was blocked by a boom and there was a second boom a little further down the harbour stretching from the tip of the Ricasoli breakwater to Fort St Elmo. At the St Elmo end there was a two-metre gap to allow access for small boats. There was also a steel bridge at the St Elmo end of the large breakwater arm; this was permanently blocked by a heavy steel anti-torpedo net stretching down from the bridge spans to the sea bottom. Covering the entrance was Fort St Elmo, which had six twin 6-pounder quick-firing guns[5], manned by 3rd Coastal Battery, RMA, and Fort Ricasoli which had three similar guns manned by 1st Coastal Battery, RMA. In addition to the guns, there were many searchlights and heavy machine-gun positions on the rocks below Ricasoli, which were manned by 1 Cheshires. A careful plan had been worked out so that each of the nine 6-pounder mounts had its own zone of fire and was responsible for attacking targets in its zone and only fired on targets in neighbouring zones if there were none in its own special area of responsibility. Although it was the intention to fit a fire control director to the guns, this had not been done when the X-MAS attack took place, so they were still independently controlled. They could fire at a cyclic rate of 120 rounds per minute and used special anti-flash ammunition to assist the gunlayers and to prevent them being blinded at night.

There were only some 600 yards separating the two gun batteries, which meant that any attacker would have to brave continuous, point-blank, enfilade gunfire, so, without complete surprise, any assault would be suicidal, especially with the additional direct fire from the heavy machine guns. Add to this the problems of getting through heavy seas in small boats and one can readily imagine how fraught with danger the whole assault idea really was, but the men of X-MAS were determined to continue and probably did not appreciate exactly what firepower they were up against. To lessen some of these risks it was decided to employ a mother ship to carry the lighter craft to within striking distance of Malta and to use a *Maiale* to blow a hole through the netting at the St Elmo end of the breakwater. This explosion was timed for 4.30am and it was hoped it would create a large enough hole to allow the torpedo boats to race into the harbour and attack the shipping. Another *Maiale* would also attack the submarines that were moored in Marsamxett Creek.

In addition to the seaborne operation, there would be extensive air activity. At 1.45 and 2.30am there would be small raids on Valletta — these were to help the naval element to fix on their targets — then at 4.30 there would be a heavy raid as a diversion, the resulting AA fire helping to drown the engine noises of the approaching boats. Then, finally, at 5.30am fighter patrols would take off from Sicily to protect the returning convoy.

The Italians set off from Augusta at 6.15pm on the evening of 25 July. The convoy comprised the sloop *Diana*, two torpedo boats (MAS 451 and 452), nine explosive boats, one small two-man boat

Left: Soldiers help to construct an aircraft pen out of stone blocks salvaged from bombed buildings. As will be seen in other photographs, pens were also constructed out of sand-filled petrol cans.
IWM — GM 987

Below: Soldiers lend a hand to move this Spitfire back into its protective pen after a sortie.
IWM — GM 2614

(to be used for navigation, command and control) and a carrier boat (Type MTL) carrying the two *Maiale*. *Diana* towed the MTL and had shipped on board the nine explosive boats. The weather was perfect and Commander Vittorio Moccagatta, who was in charge of the assault force, used *MAS 452* as his flagship. All went well on the first leg of the journey, until the force was some 20 nautical miles northeast of Valletta. Here *Diana* stopped, unshipped the explosive boats, then about an hour later withdrew northwards to wait for the assault force to return after the operation.

The two torpedo boats then began to escort the rest towards Malta. As *MAS 451* pressed on, the tow rope between it and the carrier boat fouled its propeller and the two boats collided. This caused damage to one of the human torpedoes, while efforts to free *MAS 451's* propeller proved unavailing, so after about an hour it was decided that this craft should return to Sicily, whilst the rest of the convoy carried on to its objective, with *MAS 452* now towing the carrier boat. Speed was of the essence as time had been wasted trying to untangle the two craft and night was slipping away. They set off again at a faster speed, then half an hour later had a stroke of good luck for a change: *MAS 451* rejoined them, its crew having managed to free the propeller. Shortly after 2.00am they reached a point some five nautical miles northeast of Valletta, then stopped to regroup. The two MAS stayed there, whilst the others began the last leg of their journey to the St Elmo bridge. Unbeknown to the attackers, their movements further out at sea had already been detected by radar on Malta, so they had been monitored for some hours — radar was something about which the Italian attackers knew very little, so they were completely unaware that they had been spotted. In addition, of course, Ultra knew all. A special liaison unit to distribute Ultra reports had recently been established on Malta and it was this unit which had initially alerted the garrison to the danger of a surprise seaborne attack.

After a while things quietened down and, as there seemed to be no further activity at sea, the Malta gun crews were stood down. However, they were not allowed to disperse, but rather were ordered to sleep in the gun and searchlight positions, with their guns fully loaded and aimed at the Grand Harbour entrance, whilst the searchlights were switched off but held at 30 seconds readiness. Thus, although the defenders were ready and waiting, they had temporarily lost touch with the Italians and did not know that they were quite as close as they actually were, despite all the problems which had occurred and slowed them up.

Just after 3am the Italians approached their final rendezvous point, only 1,000 yards off the St Elmo headland. More precious time was then used up launching the two human torpedoes, finding there were problems steering one of them and trying to correct its trim, because it had been damaged in the midnight collision. There was now hardly time for them to reach the St Elmo bridge on schedule, let alone detach the explosives to blow a hole in the net. Without hesitation, the pilot of the designated two-man torpedo (Tesco Tesei) decided that if he did not reach the net in time, he would explode the bomb without detaching it, even if this cost him his life. The other two-man torpedo pilot (Costa) made the same decision as he approached Marsamxett Creek.

Meanwhile the rest of the attackers waited some 1,000 yards offshore, listening for the explosion of Tesei's torpedo that would, they assumed, tell them that the way into Grand Harbour was clear. When the explosion had not occurred by 4.30, one of the small explosive boats was sent in to blow the net. Whilst endeavouring to carry out these operations, both this boat and the earlier *Maiale* exploded on the surface. Tesei was killed and the force of the explosion brought down one of the large bridge girders — effectively blocking the opening far better than the net had done.

Although the defenders had been taken unawares by the Italian assault, they quickly recovered. When the explosion rent the stillness they began engaging the enemy craft — although it was still extremely difficult to see their targets properly in the pre-dawn twilight, before the searchlights were able to be switched on. The explosion had been heard by the crews on the rest of the attacking boats who imagined that the way into the harbour was now clear. As they approached, they were suddenly illuminated by the searchlights and heavily engaged by the 6-pounders and the machine guns. As one historian put it:

'Searchlights from Forts St Elmo and Ricasoli were illuminating a wide expanse of the open sea and caught in that web of light was a tiny object moving fast trying to avoid the red tracer shells that were darting at it from the belching guns in the forts. The boat exploded and the searchlights and guns found another one with the same result.' [6]

Five MT boats and eight other small craft were soon completely destroyed. The remaining MT boats and all other craft still afloat then tried to make a run for it back to Sicily. They were pursued by Hurricanes from Malta. The pre-arranged Italian air cover now arrived and in the subsequent air battle, one Hurricane and two MC 200s were shot down. The Italian vessels were all were sunk, with the exception of the sloop *Diana* and *MAS 452*, which was badly damaged, and Commander Moccagatta and his crew all killed. *MAS 452* became a 'prize of war' when the pilot of the Hurricane which had been shot down, swam over to the drifting vessel, climbed aboard and discovered it was crewed by eight dead Italian sailors. Six hours later, a Fairey Swordfish floatplane arrived, took the small craft in tow and brought it triumphantly into Valletta.

Despite all their undoubted courage, the attack had been a complete fiasco almost from start to finish for the Italians and a complete triumph for Malta's defences.

The *Times of Malta* paid tribute to these defences which together had managed to throw back this very first organised seaborne attack on Malta. In its editorial of 28 July 1941 the newspaper commented:

'The suicidal bravery of the enemy was only equalled by the accurate fire of our gunners . . . Malta was first to receive systematic raiding from the air on Italy's entry into the war; today she is again the first British territory to repel enemy attack from the sea. The daring of the enemy crews last Saturday morning was reminiscent of the Luftwaffe pilots when they made
their spectacular attacks on the Illustrious *in the Grand Harbour. Both air and sea attacks on the Malta Harbours have failed. The enemy have now been made aware that the coastal defences of Malta are not a whit less powerful than Malta's air barrage, while the Royal Air Force and Navy work in complete harmony with the land defences.'*

Notes

1. Published in *Malta Remembered* Issue No 5.
2. Published in *Malta Remembered* Issue No 2.
3. It is interesting to note that during the siege Malta's food shortage was such that British troops had to be ordered to stop playing games and instead to have 'sleeping parades' in order to conserve their energy. This was not dissimilar to the situation which the German garrison of the Channel Islands experienced in 1944–5 during their 'Hunger Winter'.
4. Extracted from *Tank*, the Journal of the Royal Tank Regiment.
5. The British twin 6-pounder coast gun came into service in 1934 and would remain in use until 1956. Its weight in action was 22,132lb and it fired a 6.25lb shell, and had a maximum range of 5,150yd.
6. Quoted in Greene and Massignani: *The Naval War in the Mediterranean 1940–43.*

Left: Stores were taken from the dangerous docks area as quickly as possible, to safer, more secluded storage areas in the surrounding countryside. Here they are sheltered under some 'prickly pears'.
IWM — GM 1128

Right: One regiment in particular, namely the Cheshires, worked so closely with the docks that in February 1943 this large facsimile of their cap badge was unveiled on the harbour wall, by Mrs MacKenzie, wife of the Admiral Superintendent of the Dockyard, (holding bouquet).
IWM — GM 2944

Chapter 8
Air Defences

Ordeal From the Air

As we have seen in an earlier chapter, the bombardment of Malta from the air had begun on 11 June 1940, when the Italians launched their first air raid. The innumerable epic air battles that the handful of indefatigable pilots fought have earned their place in the history of air warfare. In total the AA guns accounted for 236 enemy aircraft and the fighters 893, so despite their small numbers, the air defences did not just survive but seriously damaged the Axis air fleets into the bargain. The situation had become much more serious in early 1941, Then the *Luftwaffe* (Fliegerkorps X) came to Sicily. Despite a methodical attempt by the *Luftwaffe* to destroy the island's airfields, nine hectic days in January 1941, for example, saw the destruction or damage of nearly 200 Axis aircraft in the Mediterranean area. In addition, bombers on their way to bases in Egypt visited the new German air base at Catania and destroyed 35 aircraft on the ground.

Malta's aircraft not only successfully protected the island but also presented a constant threat to Rommel's supply lifeline between Europe and North Africa. Indeed, Malta's ability continually to cut off his supplies had to be eliminated and the 'limestone aircraft carrier' as one historian calls it, put out of action. This nettle was now grasped by Kesselring, aircraft being hastily transferred from the Russian Front. Until then no more than 70 enemy aircraft had been operating against Malta; now the number tripled and the weight of bombs dropped went up by 10 times. This figure was then doubled during early 1942 and quadrupled in March, whilst in April 1942 a staggering 6,000 tons of bombs fell on the island. As Philip Guedalla says in his *Middle East 1940–1942, A Study in Air Power*:

'Malta entered a new order of chivalry. Hostile aircraft were perpetually overhead; bombing shifted from the airfields to the docks and painted churches and little alleys of Valletta, where angry citizens scrawled: "Bomb Rome" on broken walls. On the battered airfields soldiers working in twelve-hour shifts were building the new runways and dispersal pens; for the Services were never in a closer partnership. Overhead the fighters wheeled in uninterrupted combat; and as they mounted in the sky to meet the endless stream of German aircraft, they saw the dim Sicilian shore and the distant shape of Etna and the smoking, flashing island at their feet. Their own strength was running low, with 129 Spitfires and Hurricanes out of the race. But the rationed AA guns expended their daily 15 rounds with formidable skill, destroying 122 aircraft in the month. The fight in April cost the Luftwaffe 379 aircraft lost or damaged; and though it was known that they must get more fighters, AA ammunition and flour in the next few weeks in order to survive, Malta had contrived to live through April 1942.'

Those Who Fought the Battle

Here then, are some reminiscences from five people who were intimately involved in those battles — a Fleet Air Arm air gunner, an RAF fighter pilot, a Royal Artillery heavy anti-aircraft gunner, a section officer of an AA searchlight unit, Royal Engineers, and finally an RAF ops room floor supervisor. First then, the air gunner:

'I arrived at Hal Far, Malta on 10th January 1941, to join 830 Fleet Air Arm Swordfish Squadron,' wrote Nat Gold in the fifth edition of *Malta Remembered* published in 2000. He was taking up his duties as a Telegraphist Air Gunner (TAG) and was somewhat surprised to discover that the squadron was the 'front line defence of the island'. They carried out torpedo attacks on enemy ships, dive-bombed targets in Sicily and North Africa and also laid mines. The squadron sank some 110,000 tons of enemy shipping and damaged a further 130,000 tons during the seven months May–November 1941 — not bad for obsolescent prewar aircraft, known affectionately as 'Stringbags', which had no blind flying gear or torpedo sights. Nat Gold recalls:

'After I had been on the island for six months orders were given that operational tours for all FAA and RAF air crews would be nine months on the island. When I reached the magical nine it was further reduced to six months. I therefore assumed I would be on immediate draft but no such luck, due to lack of experienced crews I had to soldier on for 12 months.

'My last two months were very hectic, I never had a proper night's sleep, only cat naps, for example, after flying for several hours during the night, landing around 7am, being debriefed, a hurried wash and shave, a quick breakfast, then turn to at 8am to service our aircraft and finally be stood down at noon. Nuisance raids prevented us from getting on with our work during the morning and again in the afternoon more nuisance raids prevented sleep. Then a similar procedure the following night and day, and so it went on. Our accommodation was basic, we had RAF three sectional beds with hard biscuit mattresses. We were under RAF victualling — three meals as day against the Navy's four. For lunch, I did not think it possible to disguise McConnachies tinned stew in so many ways! Another horrible meal was very, very fat tinned sausages. Our last meal of the day was around 4–4.30pm, a typical meal would consist of lettuce, tomato, a spoonful of tinned salmon, a triangle of cream cheese, bread and margarine, sometimes a wedge of melon and sometimes a slice of fruit cake. We were also given a bar of plain chocolate wrapped in a plain white wrapper. Eating this kept us going for many, many hours. The naval ratings complained about the number of meals and finally the "powers that be" relented and at 6.30pm we had soup and bread. The RAF boys also enjoyed this small extra. Often we topped up our eating with a fried egg sandwich in the NAAFI . . .

'Many air raid alerts did not materialise, so we were instructed only to take shelter after the firing of a large smoke flare. Often this happened when the first screaming bomb was on its way down. The screaming part put a lot of fear into one especially when close by. Our squadron retaliated by clipping four screamers on each bomb fin. This gave us a lot of satisfaction when we went on a bombing raid. Sometimes we threw overboard empty beer bottles with a heavy stone tied to the neck. This screamed on its way down, ending up with broken glass.

'Jerry was very methodical, he had a set bombing routine and kept repeating it. For example, on large bombing raids we either went out into the surrounding fields or down past the old monastery on the edge of the drome to the edge of the cliffs where there were small caves to shelter in and a sheer drop of 250 feet down to very deep water.

'On Wednesday 5th March 1941 the sirens sounded and the word went around that a plot of 100 plus were coming in. As Luqa had been bombed last we knew it must be Hal Far's turn. Being air crew we had no action station, in the past it had been suggested that we took our Lewis or Vickers machine gun with a pan of 100 rounds of ammunition, into the fields, prop it on a wall and hope for the best. It was very heavy to carry and very cumbersome. The gun fired at a rate of 600 rounds per minute and made it impossible to get into position to fire upwards holding it steady, so we soon put a stop to that.

'When this particular plot approached we evacuated into the surrounding fields to take cover in an old redundant goat shelter before the first bombs came screaming down. The noise seemed to go on for ever, one Stuka bomber either hung up for a while and then broke free or the crew had spotted us, the scream of bombs sounded right over the shelter. We were lying flat on the floor almost digging into it, and finally the bombs exploded about 10 yards away. Because of the rock of the island and little soil, it created a greater blast effect. The explosions nearly burst our eardrums, rocking the shelter and blowing in the dust and grit, getting into our eyes and making us cough. The blast lifted me on top of an RAF leading aircraftsman who was lying next to me — he screamed thinking I had been hit. And I have no recollection of being lifted. When the bombing ceased we plucked up courage to venture outside only to scramble back again when a Bf109 came in very low up the valley firing his guns, the bullets hitting the walls and ricocheting off the roof. With our hearts racing, it was a little while before we ventured outside again. When we did, we went over to an Army machine gun post, where they had just received a message to say another 100 plus plot was on its way. Back we went into our goat shelter and waited for the nightmare to start again. Fortunately this time we did not have such a close encounter. The Stuka crews often threw hand grenades.

'When finally it seemed to be all over again, we checked with the Army post to ascertain if any more plots were on the way, there weren't so we made our way back to the drome . . . hurriedly past an unexploded bomb. We heard that eighteen enemy aircraft had been shot down . . .

'It used to amaze me watching the Hurricane fighters taking off — probably 10 at a time, they scrambled and took off in a very tight bunch. How the pilots in the rear aircraft could see one another through the dust they threw up I shall never know.

Below: First in line in the island's air defence were the radar stations, then the ground observers in their visual observation posts. At this RAF observer post the two RAF officers are joined by an RN observer, as they look for approaching enemy aircraft. *IWM — GM 1022*

Above: Information on enemy sightings was passed back to the operations rooms at War Headquarters, Lascaris. This one is the coastal defence room, with its plotters at work, but the air operations room was very similar (see photograph on page 152).
IWM — GM 2310

'The Swordfish of 830 Squadron flew at night. When ready for take-off, we taxied to the beginning of the single dim flare path lights — these were flashed on for a while then switched off, because Jerry often waited overhead to drop anti-personnel bombs. The pilot had to memorise the flare path position, then let the Swordfish roll into the darkness inevitably struggling to take off, as we could only take off down drome regardless of which way the wind blew. We might be carrying a crew of two, a full overload petrol tank in the Observer's cockpit and either bombs, torpedoes or magnetic mines. The weight was considerable, but with the odd exception we just managed to clear the stone wall at the end of the drome and make our rendezvous around Fifla Rock and then form into a tight "Vee" formation to set off on our operation. Some operations entailed over six hours flying in the old "Stringbags" and we often landed in the dark, trusting to luck that there were no bomb craters . . .

'830 Squadron occasionally became involved in picking up British spies — "Bowler Hat Boys" as we affectionately called them, from North Africa. Unfortunately we lost one aircraft on one of these operations by getting stuck in the mud; the crews were interned in Tunisia. A Heinkel He115 on floats was kept at Kalafrana and often took a "Bowler Hat Boy" to Sicily. They also had other means of transport. These British spies were marvellous,

it wasn't uncommon during briefing of a forthcoming operation that we learnt they had sent information through stating the names of the ships involved, what they were carrying, where they were sailing from, the time of sailing, where they were destined for and what their escort would be. With this information an RAF Wellington would be despatched to shadow the convoy, then we would follow later to deliver our attack . . . At one stage we were desperately short of torpedoes and the AA gunners were short of shells. Our Maltese armourers found some First World War torpedoes down at Grand Harbour which were adapted and used with fatal results — on hitting the water they went round in circles. We were very vulnerable but, fortunately, Jerry did not know about this.

'I finally left Malta on 25th January 1942 on the HMS Glengyle a little bomb-happy but overjoyed to be going home. We were escorted to Alexandria by the remains of the eastern Mediterranean Fleet, taking two and a half days of misery under constant attacks. To get to Malta I had travelled around the Cape and returned home the same way.'

Now, a fighter pilot recalls his first days:

'Well, anyhow, we flew out to Malta. We stopped in Gibraltar for a night and then went down the Mediterranean through the night — masses of electric storms. I remember bouncing about, low down of course, under the radar cover. And we landed in Kalafrana Bay just as dawn was breaking. As we got out of the Sunderland, onto the jetty, the air raid siren started to wail, which was par for the course in Malta; they were at it all the time. And suddenly one heard the throb of Rolls-Royce engines, Merlin engines, and they sounded very rough I may say. And here were five clapped out Hurricane IIs in an old fashioned vic formation — which we had given up in the Battle of Britain — just beginning to clamber up to gain height. And then about, oh I suppose, nothing more than about a minute or a couple of minutes later, high up, and you could just see it as the dawn was breaking on the haze, a lovely spring morning, February, there were these, about probably a Staffel [1] I suppose of 109s flying in that beautiful wide open, line abreast formation that they used to fly their Schwarms in.'

That is how the late Wing Commander P. B. 'Laddie' Lucas CBE, DSO, DFC remembered his arrival in Malta as a flight lieutenant, during a taped interview he made for the Imperial War Museum (Accession No 10763/10 dated 1989). The interview continues:

'It was a great experience actually, to fly those old Hurricanes before the Spitfires arrived. I was flying with Stan [Turner],[2] and it made one realise what those Hurricane pilots had been enduring against the Messerschmitt 109F. I mean, in France, the Spitfire V and the Messerschmitt 109F were very evenly matched and on the whole, as many no doubt will have told you, I think that those of us who were flying Spitfire Vs, thought that we'd probably got the edge on a 109. It was then the 190[3] appeared and that was absolute murder.

'Anyway, here, these Hurricane IIs were getting all clapped out. And they had been cannibalised, you know, in order to keep just a handful going. They were flying against these 109Fs and my godfathers, what those fellows must have done for a period of about five or six months I just really hate to think, because we had a fortnight of it . . . And I can always remember him [Stan Turner] because I learned more I should think in that fortnight or three weeks than I learnt from anyone else in the RAF. Stan was a Canadian in the RAF. He'd got a short service commission . . . And he said to me: "These are terrible old aeroplanes, these things, but anyhow, we've got to do the best we can." I was getting on well with him then. And he spent his time flying these blooming aeroplanes with the throttle right through the gate so that, I mean, it was a hell of a job to keep up, because he was trying to fly the aeroplane so fast, trying to get more and more speed out of them. And this was a man who was exhausted really . . . And Stan realised that with these masses of aircraft the Germans had in Sicily, and they were building up at the time . . . the only chance of real survival was that we should get the maximum advantage out of the pilots that we'd got there. Well, there's no way that you're going to do it with the old vic formations. The secret of flying in Malta had to be two aircraft in line abreast, each chap dependent on the other and so on.

'And he had changed that in 249 Squadron in about a week, to begin with. And then of course when the Spitfires started to come in, then things began to change a little. Although the Germans still had this enormous ascendancy of aircraft in Sicily. I mean, they had to begin with between 400 and 500 fighters plus in Sicily. Everything, bombers, fighters and so on. And what they were doing, they were sending the bombers in with a hell of a lot of fighters, maybe a dozen or so bombers in with a hell of a lot of fighters — maybe 80. And the idea was of course, to get the Spitfires up, so that they could shoot them down, and this was all a sort of prelude to the invasion.'

'Laddie' Lucas gives a graphic impression of the air battles that took place:

'And Woody [Group Captain A. B. Woodhall — "the best controller of fighter aircraft in the RAF in World War 2"] used to see these plots building up over Sicily, over the airfields in Sicily, with the bombers gaining height, and then the fighters would take off. And he would ring up, certainly when I was a squadron commander, he'd ring up our dispersal, our bombed-out dispersal, I think we had about three chairs with about two legs on each you know, bombed in structure there and we just had an operations telephone. He would ring up and say: "Look, there's a plot building up now, it's beginning to move from south from Italy, from Sicily." Well, that was 60 miles away. And he'd say: "I'll give you the order to scramble in probably about five minutes, then I'll vector you, get you up high, high up so you've got plenty of height with the sun behind, south of the island. Climb up really fast, and then I'll vector you on to these aircraft and then you ought to be able to see them."

'And that is precisely the way he played it. We'd get off, we'd scramble and we'd get up, plenty of height, climb well south of the island. That is to say, if the raid was coming in in the morning. These German raids used to come in like a railway timetable. They used to come in at breakfast, lunch and dinner, just before dinner, sort of high tea time. And just occasionally they'd put in four but normally it was three. And so, if it was a morning raid, old Woody'd get us up very high, 25, 26, 27,000 feet, south of the island. And then he'd start to bring us in and he would say: "Now the big job's with a lot of little jobs about and it's about 80 plus, approaching St Paul's Bay now. Suggest you come in now and come in fast." And then you would see them down there in the sunlight, marvellous visibility, you know, that Mediterranean thing, when there wasn't a haze of a mistral. Then we'd come in and we'd do the interception.

'Now because we'd been got into this excellent position with plenty of height — it didn't always happen of course, I mean this was the utopian concept, but it very often did happen because his controlling was so good — we'd get all the advantage of height and sun. And so we'd come in really fast and get in amongst them etcetera, etcetera, and eventually have a bit of a skirmish and then go down and land. The problem of course was that they had so many fighters and we had so few that they'd send these fighter sweeps in afterwards, after the main raid, to catch our fellows landing when they hadn't got any petrol.'

Describing another action, he tells of a similar build up when they:

'. . . followed the normal procedure, got the height and he (Woody) said: "There are three big jobs", in point of fact they were Savoia-Marchetti 79s, Italians, surrounded by about, oh, 80 or 90 Messerschmitts, doing high cover and close escort. And we were well above them, old Woodie had got us up well above the height of the incoming raid. And the last instruction he said was: "They're now approaching St Paul's Bay, St Paul's Island, soon be crossing St Paul's Bay and the coast. Suggest you come in now and fast."

'Well, I could see these three Italian bombers and I could see the stuff all around us and we had eight against, as I say, I think eighty to a hundred plus. I think he said: "There are 80 plus". And so I said to them, "My section will take the bomber to port," — they were flying in a vic of three, very tight, "and yellow section, take the middle one." The two aircraft on the other side took the outside one on the starboard.

'And we went straight through these and you know it worked, just one of those things. I remember getting right close into the thing and giving them a squirt and hitting it all over the

Left: Ground crews worked around the clock to service, maintain and bomb up the aircraft. Here RAF and naval ratings load a torpedo into a Bristol Beaufort torpedo bomber, which was a derivation of the Blenheim bomber.
IWM — GM 1024

Below: Naval ratings again assist RAF ground crews to prepare this tropicalised Spitfire Mk V for combat inside its protective pen, built from old petrol cans filled with sand. Two fill up the aircraft with fuel, whilst a sailor feeds in a belt of ammunition. *Bruce Robertson*

Above: A line of Spitfires belonging to No 229 Squadron at the Qrendi strip. Work had begun here in 1940 and its two tarmac runways were completed in 1942. *NWMA Malta — 6459*

blooming place. Then my number two got it and then anyhow, the long and short of it was we got all three. And they went down in flames, absolutely right on top of the island. And when we got down I said: 'Don't mix it now with these 109s, because we're outnumbered to such an extent. We've got the bombers and now we'll clear off.' And we went down to land and they never followed us down. And so it was a real sort of Wembley job, you know, a hundred thousand people cheering the chap shooting the goal.'

The Importance of Radar

'Laddie' Lucas goes on to comment on the radar, saying how good it was in Malta and that the Germans/Italians in Sicily had nothing to compare. He quotes one of the Italian fighter pilots of the period (who postwar was to become head of the Italian Air Force) as saying: 'Of course your great advantage was that you had the radar and we didn't in Sicily, and this made it very difficult.'

Anti-Aircraft Defences

Next the Ack-Ack gunner remembers the night the Germans came. The late Henry Clark was a member of 4th Heavy AA Battery, Royal Artillery, stationed on Malta and in a series of letters home to his sister Florrie, he tells of his recollections of nights of action, beginning with the night that the *Luftwaffe* began its first bombing campaign. His gun position was on a small hill, only some 200 feet high, on the south coast at Benghajsa, some mile or so from Hal Far airfield, which wasn't far from both Luqa and Safi airfields. They were thus only a few hundred yards away from the sea, near both a

submarine and a seaplane base. Also at the foot of their hill was a radio transmitting station which was the main communications link between the UK and the Middle and Far East. So they were, as he put it, 'bound to be in the middle of any trouble that the Germans were likely to cause'. In his first letter home to his sister he wrote:

'The night the Germans first came was a beautiful moonlight night, such as you only get in these parts of the world. Until that night we had been used to having two or three Italians over who gave us little trouble and who dropped their bombs almost anywhere — more often than not in the sea! The Italians were no likers of the barrage that we put up whenever they held their course for a few seconds and they also knew it was fatal to be illuminated by the searchlights as nine times out of 10 the fighters or the guns would get them. At about 10 o'clock on March 4th [1942], the GOR [Gun Operations Room] was asking all gun positions for an immediate identification of the aircraft being used, as already there had been about half a dozen aircraft over and there were still more on the way. It was about half an hour after this that a plane was illuminated to the south of our position well out to sea. The searchlights were usually more capable of getting their targets but it was always more difficult for them to operate when the moon was so bright. However, we immediately recognised the plane as a Junkers Ju88, the dive-bomber which the Germans had put so much faith in. As soon as we knew what we were up against we all gave up hope of getting back to bed again that night, so we settled down to our duties, determined not to let it get us down.

'Barrage after barrage went up! String after string of bombs came down! Have you ever heard a bomb coming down? It is the most horrible thing in the world. Sometimes it shrieks like a

Above: A flight of Fairey Albacores flying over the distinctive Maltese countryside. Designed as the replacement for the old Swordfish, the Albacore had many improvements, but in the end merely complemented the older aircraft rather than replacing it. *NWMA Malta — 6688*

train tearing along through the night, sometimes just a terrific rush of wind, which sends a shiver running up and down your spine every time you hear it. It always seems to me that it takes hours to come down and the suspense is almost unbearable. And then the crash and you feel the ground, solid rock though it is, trembling under your feet. But that is not all! After this comes the shrapnel, both from the bombs and from the shells which have been fired from the guns and blown themselves to pieces, to be almost as deadly to us as to the enemy should they hit us in a vulnerable spot. I have seen many casualties from this of which I will tell you later. To get back to this first night of the German raids. It was about 5 o'clock in the morning before we were given: "Stand Easy". We had definitely shot one raider down, but only the Germans know how many failed to return or how many managed to crawl back seriously damaged. Since that night the Germans have often admitted the loss of more planes over here than we have claimed. We crawled into bed just after 5 o'clock and Reveille was ordered for 10 o'clock. Since that night we have had few nights which we have been able to sleep right through. I don't think I shall ever be able to catch up on all that sleep I have lost. I have changed from one of the best sleepers in the world to a bad case of insomnia. There are even times nowadays which I get a chance to sleep but cannot do so because of the thought that we are going to be turned out at any moment.

'As the raids gradually increased during the hours of daylight it was realised that the men would have to have some means of getting at least a few hours' sleep each night, so the GOR organised a 'Rest Roster' in which all the gun positions were divided into three groups (known as "A", "B" and "C"). The system worked so that all the gun positions in 'A' group were out of action between 8 and 12. Those in 'B' group between 12 and 4 and those in 'C' between 4 and 8. Each night the periods were changed around so that we had a different period each night. Later on when the raids turned into all-day affairs as well as all night, each group was given an extra hour's rest during the day so that we could have at least one meal 'in peace' . . . Try to imagine a typical raid. The telephonist begins by plotting the raid soon after it leaves its base. If it is a clear day they give us our first information something like this: "Raid Six, Twelve plus," (this probably means 3, 4 or 5 bombers escorted by fighters), "Bearing 40 degrees, range 25 miles". The TI (Target Indicator) then begins to search that bearing: "Bearing 60 degrees, range 20 miles, Second class GL (ground location) height 16,000 feet," reports the telephonist. And so it goes on until the TI reports: "On Target! Six Ju88s escorted by fighters." Angles and bearing are immediately poured forth by the GPO Ack (Assistant to the Gun Position Officer) until both the Height-Finder and Predictor report: "On Target". When this has been achieved, the Predictor is switched on and the guns immediately "Blackout" or in other words go to the bearings and elevations which are being electrically transmitted to them. The Height-Finder gives us height, which is immediately set into the Predictor and as soon as the target comes in range firing commences.

'During this time the target has been travelling S or SW, but now, assuming his objective is the airfields, as had been the case nine raids out of ten, he changes course and heads straight towards us, owing to the fact that we are between the coast and the airfields. *Now try to put yourself in the position that I have found myself in so many times, that is keeping the Predictor which controls the guns on target. Six planes each carrying 2,000lb worth of bombs are gradually approaching, the guns are firing making your hands jerk just when it is vital to be steady as is humanly possible. Then, just before they are overhead they release their bombs. As you know they have to release their bombs before they reach the target owing to the fact that a bomb does not drop straight down, I watch the bombs leave the plane, perhaps one large and 3 or 4 medium ones, I have even seen 12 released in a whole chain from one plane. I get that scared that I feel like running miles, anywhere to get away from it all. However, the guns have got to be kept on target. Don't think that I am professing to be brave or a hero — far from it. There is only one thing that keeps me at my post and that is faith in the knowledge that prayers are answered . . . there is something more than just mere luck attached to it all.*

'But to get back to the raid and as I have said the bombs are on their way down. Soon after they leave the planes they pass out of sight but after what seems like hours, although it is only a matter of seconds, you can hear them whistling or rather shrieking through the air and all the while thinking: "Has he released them too soon?" Then comes the climax, the bombs burst with a terrific crash, one after another. The guns are blazing away with a deafening roar, the engines of the planes are screaming at their highest pitch as they come out of their dives, the light Ack-Ack opens up with a sharp staccato tone as the bombers come within range for them. In a few seconds it is all over. A deadly silence falls, save for the drone of the bombers as they recede. Perhaps one has been shot down, perhaps others will

crash on the way back, any that get back untouched will be very fortunate indeed. And what of the damage? Most of the bombs drop in open fields, and some don't explode. Occasionally a fire is started on the airfields and there is usually damage to civilian property and to the civilians themselves, but taking an all-round view, for all his efforts, the Hun hasn't achieved as much as he might have done bombing this island.'

In his next letter to his sister, Henry tells her all about another raid which was escorted in force by large numbers of German Bf109 fighters. The Bf109 was superior in performance to the Hurricane, but not the Spitfire which had just begun to arrive in small numbers. He wrote:

'The most vivid and horrible memory of all took place on March 7th [1942]. It was a Saturday and throughout the day we had raid after raid over, sometimes three, sometimes six bombers escorted by large formations of Bf109s. During the afternoon we had been immensely cheered by the arrival of a number of Spitfires. We went fairly mad with joy, the general reaction being: "It won't be long before they show the Messerschmitts where to get off!" However, we knew it would be a day or two before they would be ready for action, so we had to be as patient as possible. It was a glorious day and as each raid came over we engaged them with more determination than ever.

'Dusk was beginning to fall when what turned out to be the last raid of the day appeared on the plotting board. Given as 6 plus, it was soon identified as three Ju88s escorted by fighters. At the time I was doing the duties of No 3 on the Predictor [No 3 being one of the two layers]. The target was coming in on a course which had been very popular with German pilots and I soon decided that their objective was Hal Far which was south of our position. I was glad for this as I knew that it meant that the bombs would not be released over us as was the case for Luqa.

Below: Curtis Kittyhawks of No 3 RAAF Squadron based at Ta Qali. The Mk 1A version was in RAF service in large numbers and was also supplied to Commonwealth air forces. *NWMA Malta — 2065*

Above: Towing a petrol bowser with a somewhat antiquated-looking tractor, RAF ground crew drive past a crashed Wellington bomber at Luqa airfield. Note also the camouflaged staff car in the rear. *NWMA Malta — 1836*

'"Lay on the right hand plane" ordered the GPO and then: 'It's changed its position and is now centre plane.' I carried out this order and could see it was obviously the leading plane of the three. As I followed it changed position once again. At this time we were firing and as I learnt later, the bursts were well amongst them. Suddenly I saw the plane we were following cross the course of the other two and it was then that I realised I had stopped traversing the Predictor, meaning that the plane was coming straight towards us. A few seconds passed, we were still firing and then I saw a stream of bombs, between 12 and 15 of them, leave the plane. It was a sight that would make anyone dive for cover, but I have seen hundreds of them and for the time being thought little of it, other that they were going to be very close. Next came what we all dread to hear: "Target above angle." It was then that I was glad that we were unable to keep on to a target directly overhead. The Predictor had to be turned completely round and the target picked up and engaged while receding. It was while we were turning the Predictor and the guns round that I heard the bombs coming. Very few did, the noise created by the gun, etc, is pretty deafening. I dropped flat on the ground and during those horrible seconds which seemed like years, I prayed to God to keep me safe once again, as I had done so often during the past few months.

'Once again my prayers were not left unanswered. The first thing I knew, after landing on the ground was that another fellow had been knocked down by the blast. Then, when I realised the nearest bombs had exploded, I started to get up, but the GPO who had stood throughout it all was shouting to everyone to keep under cover. I realised then that something was wrong and so I moved nearer the sandbags. I dragged myself through pools of blood on the ground. "No 4 Gun has been hit," said the GPO. Horrified I looked up to where he was standing. The sight I saw I will never forget. It was far more dramatic than any film producer could ever imagine. The GPO, only a young fellow, was standing in between two sandbag walls which came up to his waist. His steel helmet was gone, but he was still holding his binoculars. I could hear the shrapnel whizzing through the air. The atmosphere was thick with dust, smoke and fumes. A more impressive scene just couldn't be realised. The noise died down.

'Half dazed I stood up and looked at No 4 gun which by the way was the nearest gun to the Command Post [CP]. There was a fire in the gun pit and stumbling from it came one of my mates who until quite recently had been on the CP. He came over, rolling up his shirtsleeve to show an ugly looking piece of shrapnel in his arm. "I'm all right," he said, "but there's some dead 'uns over there." Death! How horrible it is when you come up against it for the first time. I just couldn't believe it. For a few moments I was like a helpless fool. Fellows around me and in the CP itself had been hit. One of them looked at me with such an appealing look in his eyes. "Help me! Save me!" he seemed to be saying. Others went to his aid. Suddenly my senses seemed to come back to me. Fellows around me who had been hit were being taken care of so I dashed across to the gun. I grabbed two cans of water

Above: An Italian Macchi 200 fighter overflying Hal Far airfield. This was the first airfield to be built on Malta and was opened in 1923. Its stony surface was initially liable to waterlogging, but by 1940 four runways were available. *NWMA Malta — 4917*

and hurried into the gun pit scared though I was that the ammunition in there was liable to go off. But the sight I saw on entering the gun pit made me forget everything. It was the most ghastly sight that human eyes could ever see. I won't try to describe it. I've tried to forget it but I know it cut too vividly on my mind ever to be forgotten.

'By now they were calling for stretcher bearers to remove casualties from the gun park to where the HQ buildings were, ready for the ambulances to take them away. Having got them there I obtained some tea and gave cigarettes to those who wanted them. The faces of those who had been in the gun pit were terrible. A lot of ammunition had gone off and burnt them so they looked like men with iron masks on. That any came out alive of what must have been a blazing inferno is nothing short of a miracle. An MO [Medical Officer] arrived on a cycle and told us that the road by which the ambulances were coming had been hit and unless it was repaired they wouldn't be able to get through. The word went round and soon we were on the spot with shovels and spades working like demons to repair the damage. It was almost dark when we had finished. The ambulances, four of them, had by then arrived. I shuddered as I passed by, and knowing their mission it was enough to make anyone feel ill.

'We made our way back to the gun park. The bodies of those who were past our help were being placed on a Matador [lorry] which had brought the Colonel from RHQ. We all gathered around the CP where a hot drink was provided and as we stood there the "All Clear" was sounded in the villages and towns. It was the most tragic and eerie all clear I have ever listened to.'

Peter Kent had arrived in Malta in January 1938, being posted there as a section officer in 16th Fortress Company, RE (AA Searchlight). The role of his unit was to man all the anti-aircraft searchlights in Malta. Each section had six searchlights stationed at mobile sites scattered throughout the island. At first each station had a 90cm searchlight and a very old-fashioned type of sound locator. Detachments lived in barracks and only manned the sites for 'night runs' and for the ever-increasing number of political 'flaps'. Thus he was with the unit from the very beginning and remained with it as more and more sophisticated equipment was issued (eg 120cm searchlights and Mark VIII Sound Locators) and detachments eventually moved into stone buildings. As the war progressed it became clear that more troops would be needed and, in November 1940, the 4th Searchlight Regiment, RA, was established, comprising a Gunner searchlight battery, Royal Malta Artillery, and 16th Fortress Company, Royal Engineers. Although largely a Gunner unit, it was commanded by the ex-OC of 16 Company now promoted to lieutenant-colonel and at the same time Kent was promoted to major to command 16th Fortress Company. Morale in the unit was very high, even when, in December 1940, a new CRA (Commander,

Royal Artillery) arrived on the island and demanded that 16 Company should wear Gunner badges. This ruling was strongly opposed and eventually the CRA gave way and they remained Sappers.

In January 1941, when HMS *Illustrious* came into harbour, the first German raids began with 100-plus aircraft instead of the 'gentlemanly' five to ten Italian planes flying in formation at some 17,000 feet. As the most experienced sub-unit, 16th Fortress Company defended the southern sector of the island, which contained the harbour, dockyard and the two main aerodromes. In March 1941 a parachute mine landed on Company HQ, killing seven men and wounding many others. The technical store caught fire and most of the spare equipment was destroyed. During the summer the frequency of raids slackened off somewhat and an opportunity was taken to switch detachments around to relieve monotony. The searchlight emplacements were also given local defences — nine rifles and a Lewis machine gun! Raids increased in intensity again in the winter of 1941 and the searchlight stations suffered some direct casualties, whilst rations became very short. Peter Kent relinquished his command in March 1942, having seen them through the worst period of the siege.

The Lady Plotters of Malta

Henry Clark has told about action at a gunsite and mentioned briefly how the enemy aircraft were detected, then shadowed all the way to their targets, so that up-to-the-minute information could be passed to the aerodromes and the gunsites. Douglas Geer, RAF, who was a radar operator by trade, but had been seconded to Lascaris Fighter Ops because he had previous training and experience at Biggin Hill Fighter Ops. He became a Floor Supervisor and helped train the female civilian employees who had volunteered to become plotters in the ops room. He recalled:

'I think that there were up to 60 ladies taken on by the RAF as civilian employees at Lascaris. They were divided into four crews or watches, to man the Ops Room telephone lines around the clock. The plots originated from information picked up by radar stations at Dingli, Tas Silq and Madliena. These were passed through to the RAF Filter Room at Lascaris. Here the tracks were analysed instantly and given appropriate labels: "H" for Hostile, "X" for Unidentified and "F" for Friendly, and plotted on the grid reference on the Filter Room plotting table. The Filter Officer was aware of all friendly aircraft movements, such as aircraft in transit, passing through to Middle East, via Malta or vice versa; delivery fighter aircraft flown off carriers to Malta from Gibraltar, plus any action by Malta-based bombers, torpedo bombers or our photographic reconnaissance planes. All these plots had to be dealt with. It was essential that information received from radar was interpreted accurately and as speedily as possible to give the Duty Controller as much notice as possible, particularly with an enemy air raid building up and approaching the island.

'As soon as the tracks were labelled by the Filter Room they were read off their plotting table and passed by phone to the girl plotter in Fighter Ops (wearing a telephone headset) by quoting the grid reference on the map. Here a message would be passed, for example: "Hostile Raid No 15 in M for Mike, Four Six Two Eight, 25 plus aircraft at 15,000 ft South West." The girl plotter would then place a coloured pointed counter on the Ops Room table map on the appropriate grid reference. The plotters pushed the plots out to the centre of the table when necessary by using long wooden rods to enable them to reach the required grid reference. A small wooden block was always moved along with the latest plot at the head of each track, giving details: Raid Number, Number

of Aircraft and height if known. Any up-to-date changes to these details were altered on the blocks as the tracks moved along. Before placing the plot on the grid reference on the table, the plotter would glance at the Ops Room clock to ascertain which coloured counter should be used, as all Sector Ops clocks have three separate colours painted on the dials, ie: from nought to five minutes past the hour the colour was red; from 5 to 10 minutes past was yellow; and 10 to 15 minutes past, blue. The corresponding counter colours would be used. The same colour sequence was used on the clock face for the next 45 minutes to complete the hour. This would indicate to the Duty Controller the time that the plot had been put on the table. As the tracks built up the counters at the tail end were removed. The plotting table was situated in the well of the Ops Room and covered an area approximately 12ft by 12ft. The map painted on the surface included most of Sicily to the north, showing enemy airfields as far as Gerbini and to the east the islands of Linosa and Pantelleria. Our radar stations were often able to detect enemy aircraft when they were airborne from the Sicilian dromes. The Duty Controller sat in the centre of the dais, situated above the plotting table. This gave him a clear view of all tracks being plotted. At the same dais, seated at telephone sets were the Deputy Controller, Guns and Searchlight Liaison officers. Up to fourteen girls were designated to each crew — A, B, C and D Watches. At times, three girls would be plotting at the table at the same time, all connected to the one line from the Filter Room. Usually two girls [worked] on the east side of the table and one on the west side.

'The Ops Room also contained a DF Room situated under the dais. The Direction Finder Room was linked by phones to three spaced out Direction Finder Stations situated on the island. These listening stations picked up bearings from transmissions when our airborne pilots spoke on their radio telephones and these bearings were passed to three girls on separate lines in the DF Room. The three stations each had a string running from their respective position on the circular DF table. Also painted around the edge of the table were three sets of degrees, one for each station. On receiving a bearing from their stations the girls would each place the furthermost end of their string on the bearings received on the appropriate degree. The position of the aircraft was secured by reading the grid reference where the strings crossed on the DF Table map. This would be read off the table by a teller to a plotter who would mark the plots by chalk on the large blackboard (also marked up with the grid reference) situated on the right-hand side of the main table. All these DF bearings were recorded in a log book also giving the exact time.

'If a fighter pilot was shot up and in difficulty and about to bale out, and he was able to do so, at the last second he would switch to a special RT frequency and call out: "MAYDAY!... MAYDAY!... MAYDAY!" Each Direction Finder Station would then get a bearing on his voice And these would be passed through to the DF Room at Lascaris. The separate girl plotters would place the bearings on the table and a grid reference would then be worked out of his last known position. An Air/Sea rescue search would then be co-ordinated by the Duty Controller and a high speed launch would be despatched from Kalafrana and directed to the last plotted grid reference to hopefully pick up the pilot from the sea. For this purpose also, the bearings from the DF Stations and the resulting grid reference were recorded in a log book.

'The purpose of my job as Floor Supervisor was to ensure the smooth running of the watch and system at all times and that information received was dealt with as speedily and accurately as possible and that it was plotted in the correct square. Had for

instance a track been incorrectly plotted in the grid square 'M' for Mike instead of 'N' for Nan, the track would have been sixty miles out and this would have endangered intercepting pilots in the air. I was able to listen in on the main plotting line to monitor the pilots from Filter Room to Fighter Control, at any time if considered necessary, by means of a separate phone which I was able to plug into the line. Lascaris was the final "nerve centre" of the RAF defence on the Island during the siege which lasted from June 1940 until April 1943.

'In addition to the shortage of food and other siege conditions the lady plotters experienced very severe conditions and in the early days, some had to walk miles, often through air raids, day and night, in order to arrive at Lascaris for their duty watch. It was only their individual loyalty, allegiance and resolute staying power that enabled Lascaris Fighter Control to operate through those dark and dangerous days. On 4 June 1943, six civilian girls who helped hold the front line during the siege were each awarded the British Empire Medal. These included three of our own plotting girls from Lascaris Fighter Ops: Irene Cameron, Mrs M. Fletcher and Christina Ratcliffe. I regret to say that one of our 18-year-old girl plotters was killed on the 1st March 1942.'[4]

Douglas Geer goes on to comment about the 'great injustice perpetrated' when surviving Lascaris plotters were excluded from the Malta George Cross Fiftieth Anniversary Commemorative Medal issue in 1992, due to the fact that they were civilian employees and not in uniform during the siege. I would certainly entirely agree with him that these brave ladies fully deserved their medals. What a shame it is that so often heroes are treated so shabbily due to stupid red tape — the mandarins of Whitehall have a lot to answer for.

On the Other Side of the Hill

So much then for a brief look at those who were defending the island. However, as well as covering the small selection of the members of the services and the civilians who were together responsible for the air defence of the island, it is also relevant in this chapter to look in some detail at the planning of the German aerial offensives against Malta which are set out very clearly in 'Smiling Albert's' postwar treatise. Whilst he wrote this, as already mentioned, without having access to any reference material or adequate maps, he still presents a clear and comprehensive enough picture, to make it well worth including here, especially with regard to his conclusions because of course they give the *raison d'être* of the defenders. In it Kesselring wrote:

'*The Aerial Offensive against Malta, 2 April to 10 May 1942.*
Although the long-lasting preparations proved a strain on the nerves considering the precarious situation in Africa, they paid off when the attack itself was started. Prior to the attack I was able to establish the following facts:
(1) The minimum force of bombers, fighter planes and sea rescue planes was standing by. It had been trained for its mission in an exemplary manner.
(2) Fuel, ammunition and spare parts were on hand in sufficient quantities. The supply system was well established. It could be relied upon to fill expected requirements.
(3) The command organisation of II Fliegerkorps, in charge of operations, was well co-ordinated and the liaison system was of top-notch quality.
(4) Ground elements were sufficiently flexible and adequately protected by anti-aircraft artillery.
'During the command conference I satisfied myself that the basic idea behind the offensive had permeated the entire

command and that orders were clearly understood. While inspecting the formations I was able to ascertain their confidence in the success of their mission. I noted that they were raring to go. Under these conditions the attack was bound to lead to the expected victory, accompanied by moderate losses on our side.
'The basic idea of the order issued by Second Air Force was the following:
(1) Enemy fighter aviation to be neutralised in a surprise raid or its effectiveness to be reduced to a point where it will no longer constitute a threat to subsequent bombing missions. British fighter planes to be engaged in the air. The three aerodromes on Malta to be strafed and otherwise attacked with heavy bombs and light fragmentation bombs, at the same time and within short intervals, in order to destroy or damage planes on the ground and render runways useless at least temporarily. Anti-aircraft (AA) artillery to be neutralised.
(2) Subsequent attacks by bombardment wings were to accomplish the following:
  (a) Inflict further damage on airfields, interfere with their repair and bomb them until rendered completely unusable.
  (b) Render useless dispersal revetments and shelters on airfields.
  (c) Destroy harbour facilities and ships, as far as possible city areas to be spared.
  (d) German daytime raids, combined with fighter protection, were to be flown without interruption and in accordance with main effort attacks; in this manner British fighters were to be kept away from the formation making the bombing run; German fighters were to pursue British interceptors until these were annihilated.
  (e) Make periodic night time nuisance raids by individual planes in order to interfere with clearing and repair work; the few British ships expected to arrive at Malta were to be destroyed by dive-bombing attacks and 'contamination' of harbour entrance by mines dropped from the air.
'The execution of this plan required extraordinary efforts on the part of all formations. The mission was accomplished successfully and entailed moderate losses. The following factors made the assault on Malta more difficult:
(a) There were natural installations, such as dispersal revetments for planes, depots, shelters, etc, blasted out of the rock along the edges of the airfields and in the harbour area. Against these shelters the one-ton bombs at our disposal had no effect. An attempt at blasting the entrances with bombs dropped by fighter-bombers was unsuccessful. Enemy aerodromes were also subjected to area bombing in the course of which light bombs equipped with contact fuses were dropped. These raids were, perhaps, the most successful of all.
(b) The strong concentration of British AA artillery and its reinforcement by shipboard AA guns for the protection of the harbour formed a curtain of fire which took great courage to penetrate and which, of course, resulted in a loss of planes.
(c) The weakness of dive-bombing attacks lies in the "roll-over to the dive run" and in the "release point" at the end of the dive, because the speed of flight is decreased and the formation disperses. We were able to cut down on losses resulting from these weaknesses of dive-bombing manoeuvres by arranging for close-escort fighter formations to dive with

the dive-bombers and by providing a bottom cover squadron committed in the altitude of the release point. This squadron was also responsible for shielding bombers until they had reformed back into flights and squadrons.

(d) The British fighter formations deserve praise and admiration for the gallantry, their manoeuvrability in dog-fighting and especially, for their dive-bombing tactics which they had practised to perfection. The British would dive from maximum altitudes through compact German attack formations. The British unloading organisation likewise deserves praise. Tankers and cargo vessels were unloaded in an almost incredibly short period of time.

'In this field worthy opponents met.

'In the planning and execution of the attack, HQ II Fliegerkorps, Messina, turned in an extraordinary performance which was matched by the morale and devotion to duty of II Fliegerkorps' flying formations. The aerial assault on Malta had to be interrupted whenever it became necessary to divert formations to attack enemy convoys, the destruction of which were a prerequisite for the continued success of the Malta operation. In bitter fighting we succeeded in sinking these enemy convoys, with the exception of a few ships.

'The main German attack commenced on 2 April 1942. On 10 May 1942, I was in a position to consider the mission as having been accomplished. German command of the sea and air in the sector of the Mediterranean containing our supply lines had been secured with the neutralisation of Malta. The supply system was now sufficiently well established to fill all requirements. Special honours to the Luftwaffe for keeping the action limited to purely military objectives. The British appreciated this. It would have been easy to seize Malta after the bombing offensive. In not capturing the island the Axis command made a mistake which bore bitter fruit later on. Primarily, however, the Axis aerial offensive against Malta had removed all threats to our supply routes. Our Army, Navy and Air situation seemed stabilised . . . In view of the aerial victory over Malta, the Armed Forces High Command (OKW) believed itself justified in contemplating the transfer of most aerial formations from the Mediterranean area, especially since those formations were needed in the East. At that time I could well understand that the air force as a decisive arm of the Armed Forces was urgently needed elsewhere. I still say, however, that we should not have been satisfied with the destruction of enemy installations merely in order to get by for any length of time with the minimum of aerial formations. Of course, there remained in the Mediterranean a number of planes sufficient to observe and patrol Malta, attack enemy convoys and protect Axis convoys. The number was, however, not large enough to prevent the enemy for any length of time from restoring Malta to the status of an effective base and replenishing its supply stores. The Mediterranean was too large and Malta too well protected by its underground installations to enable minor Axis forces to keep the island neutralised for any length of time. A strong reinforced Malta was bound to constitute precisely the same threat to the African supply lines as during the

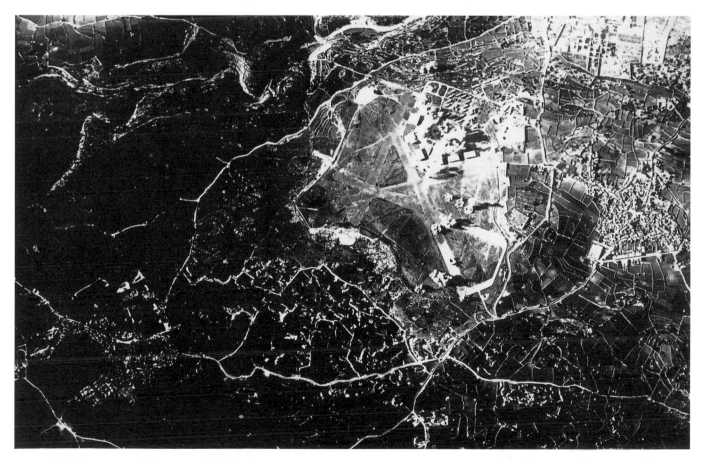

Above: Bombs bursting on Luqa airfield, which became the principal RAF station on Malta, after having been used prewar as Malta's civilian airport. The three main tarmac runways were commenced in October 1939 and completed in April 1940. Facilities included taxi-tracks, dispersal areas and aircraft pens. *NWMA Malta — 15668*

summer and autumn of 1941. This caused me at an early date to win over the Italian Supreme Command to the idea of seizing Malta. I also renewed my efforts with the OKW in this respect. I was successful in obtaining OKW approval in February 1942. It was possible to commence with the preparations in March. Axis aviation had command of the air until July. The assault on Malta was planned for the beginning of July. Our domination of the Mediterranean weakened gradually as a result of three factors. The British increased their sea and air activity against Axis convoys; they were able to reinforce Malta because we abandoned our attack; our aviation thus bore a heavier load.'

A German Victory?

It is interesting to see how mistaken 'Smiling Albert' was about the success or failure of the aerial offensive he had waged against Malta between 2 April and 10 May 1942. Clearly he continued to be mistaken even after the end of the war, as this report shows — or was it perhaps that he did not want to have to admit, even at that late stage, that he had failed to achieve his primary mission? When one remembers that this mission was 'to secure and protect Axis supply in the Mediterranean', a mission that he considered to be (to quote his own words) 'of paramount importance', and also that the way he proposed to do this was (again in his own words) by 'putting enemy naval and air installations on the island of Malta out of action', then why did he think that he had succeeded when everyone on Malta knew otherwise?

A Second Bite at the Cherry

Kesselring goes on to complain how Hitler had been personally responsible for shelving the plan to invade Malta — as already explained in Chapter 6 — and then, somewhat later in his account of the war in the Mediterranean, talks about attacking Malta again under the heading 'New Measures for the Improvement and Security of Supply: The Second Air Offensive against Malta' in which, after explaining that warfare against the supply fleets of both sides continued unabated, he says:

'The defences of the island of Malta were again restored completely. This fact manifested itself most clearly in the increasing enemy interference in Axis convoy traffic. We could not secure our free movement in the Mediterranean by fighting a purely defensive battle . . . I just could not bear seeing us strangled to death slowly. Once again, backed up by the Italian Supreme Command, I urged Hitler and Göring to approve a purely aerial offensive against Malta. I was aware of the obstacles. Malta was fully able to defend itself. Its fighter forces had been increased considerably. The Allied practice of transferring fighter planes from Gibraltar by air became more frequent. There were no effective measures that we could possibly have taken. Although we were able to detect approaching enemy planes on our radar, our fighter planes arrived too late to intercept the enemy planes that were being transferred. Every pilot knows how difficult it is to put fighter planes into a given area on short notice. Furthermore, we were outnumbered and our formations were engaged in escort duty. Finally, the British had learned their lesson from the first battle of Malta. They had expanded their base and had achieved the highest possible degree of bomb protection.

'On the German side, the C-in-C of the Luftwaffe did everything that could be done at the time. It was impossible to accede to all demands. Our fighter wings were tried in combat with the British. The bomber formations were flown by experienced men, who, as a result of years of action, knew how to handle planes not only over land but also over water. We planned to use Ju88s for daytime sorties chiefly. The slower high-altitude bombers were employed mainly at night. We could not count on Italian bombers and fighters. These were obsolescent. Their crews lacked proper training in night flying. The air offensive was again under the direction of the seasoned II Fliegerkorps. The attack did not result in the desired success although tactical requirements had been met and although the human element involved did its part. I was forced to discontinue it in the beginning of October 1942 on account of excessive losses and particularly in view of the Allied invasion which was to be expected then. I should like to cite the following reasons:

(1) There was no surprise element. Bombing raids against air bases spent their force. Our pilots had to engage enemy fighter planes in the air and attack them on the ground where they were protected by bombproof dispersal revetments. This made things more difficult for us and diminished the effect of our attacks.

(2) Escorting German bombers became an extremely difficult mission. German radar was for the first time neutralised by tin foil dropped from the air.

(3) British defensive tactics had improved. Their activities had been extended in time and space. The British simply had more planes.

(a) Diving manoeuvres by individual fighter planes from maximum altitude (10,000m and higher) through German formations was still successful. The employment of German fighter formations in stagger formations did not faze enemy fighter pilots who persisted in making their individual dive runs.

(b) The stagger formations of enemy fighters took into consideration the weak spots of German dive-bomber formations, shortly before the latter rolled over into the dive and after the pull-out until the formations had reformed. Countermeasures were of course, in the nature of defensive moves and could not counteract the effect of the attack.

(c) Ground control was made more difficult, since our radar was eliminated by enemy tactics described in point 2.

(d) Damaged planes needed special protection which was furnished by escort formations. Detailing planes for missions of that type diminished the combat strength of fighter formations.'

Notes

1. The *Staffel* (plural *Staffeln*) had a nominal strength of nine aircraft and was the smallest flying unit in general use in the *Luftwaffe*. The commander bore the title Staffelkapitän and was usually an Oberleutnant or a Hauptmann. The *Schwarm* was the standard four-aircraft tactical formation used by German fighters; when copied by the RAF it became known as the 'finger-four'.
2. Squadron Leader (later Wing Commander) Stan Turner is described in *Malta: The Spitfire Year 1942* as being a 'tough, no-nonsense character — nicknamed "Bull"'. He was a Canadian who had fought both in France and in the Battle of Britain and was now commanding 249 Squadron in Malta.'
3. This was the Focke-Wulf 190 which, when introduced, was significantly superior to the best contemporary RAF fighter, the Spitfire Mark V.
4. From *Malta Remembered*, quoted, Issue 4.

Above: A Hurricane burns on Ta Qali airfield. It had been used prewar by civil airlines, its main customer being Italian Ala Littoria. It was subjected to heavy bombing during the war. Mdina and Mtarfa can be seen in the background. *NWMA Malta — 370*

Above : Malta-bound on Operation 'Calendar'. These tropicalised Spitfires are being loaded onto the aircraft carrier USS *Wasp*, destined for delivery to Malta, April 1942. 46 arrived safely. *NWMA Malta — 7064*

Chapter 9

Sea Defences

Malta Shows its Teeth

Although initially the Royal Navy had but few surface vessels or underwater craft stationed at Malta, as we have seen that situation changed considerably. I will be dealing with the vital business of convoy protection and especially with the all-important 'Pedestal' convoy in other chapters, but here I want to give just a few examples of the diverse gamut of tasks which the Royal Navy (and even in one case the Royal Air Force) undertook in this aspect of the defence of Malta.

The Malta Striking Force

Orders for setting up the first such formation were issued on 8 April 1941 and the initial composition was to be four of the most modern British destroyers then operating in the Mediterranean: *Jervis* and *Janus* — both 1,690 tons (armed with 6 x 4.7in guns and 10 x torpedo tubes) plus two Tribal Class: *Nubian* and *Mohawk* — both 1,870 tons (8 x 4.7in guns and 4 x torpedo tubes), making up 14th Destroyer Flotilla under Captain P. J. Mack, who also commanded *Jervis*. They were at sea when the order was signed. All

made it safely to Malta by daylight on the 11th, and began operations almost immediately.

As well as actively protecting convoys and running the gauntlet to bring in much-needed supplies, the Royal Navy continued to operate aggressively from Malta. For example, during the summer and autumn of 1941 ships from the Malta Striking Force — 14th Destroyer Flotilla, Force K and Force B — attacked enemy convoys en route from Italy to North Africa. They were of course helped by Ultra's advanced warnings of enemy convoys, which then had to be disguised, for example, by being attributed to aerial reconnaissance, so that the enemy would not guess that their codes had been broken. A typical example occurred in mid-November 1941, when, in response to urgent requests from the DAK for AFVs, fuel and ammunition, a convoy of five merchant-

Below: HMS *Kandahar*, a destroyer of the Malta Striking Force dropping depth charges during a convoy protection operation. She and HMS *Neptune* would hit mines off Tripoli on 19 December 1941. *Kandahar's* after magazine exploded, causing severe damage; both vessels eventually sank. *Author's Collection*

men and two tankers was despatched to North Africa, heavily protected by escort vessels. Force K (comprising the cruisers *Aurora* and *Penelope*, plus the destroyers *Lance* and *Lively*), set out from Malta, intercepted the convoy and sank all the enemy cargo vessels and tankers. They also sank one of the escorting destroyers and damaged a further three, one of which was finished off by a submarine attack. The victorious quartet returned to Valletta during the afternoon of 9 November, without a single casualty. Philip Vella, in *Malta: Blitzed but not Beaten*, quotes the Italian Foreign Minister, Count Ciano, as saying:

'An engagement occurred, the results of which are inexplicable. All, I mean, all, our ships were sunk and one or maybe two or three destroyers. The British returned to base having slaughtered us. Naturally, today our various headquarters are pushing out their usual inevitable and imaginary sinking of a British cruiser by a torpedo plane; nobody believes it.'

The Submarine Flotilla Plays its Part

The 10th Submarine Flotilla (also called the 'Malta Force Submarines') comprised both RN and Allied subs, operating from the shore establishment, HMS *Talbot*, at Lazzaretto Creek. They inflicted considerable losses on Axis shipping, the 15 submarines racking up a grand total of just under 400,000 tons of enemy shipping sunk during the period 1 January 1941 to 1 May 1942. Top scorer was HMS *Upholder*, which sank 128,353 tons including two destroyers, three submarines, three transports, 10 supply ships, two tankers and a trawler. Sadly, *Upholder* was lost on her 25th patrol — which would have been her last one before returning to England.

Francis Gordon Selby was a British coxswain who served aboard various submarines in the Mediterranean, including *Upholder*, *P39* and *Olympus*, all being based on Malta. He recorded his memories of the period on a tape for the Sound Archive of the Imperial War Museum (Acc 16738). He explained how he had joined the RN in 1935, received his initial training at HMS *St Vincent* at Gosport, served on the battleship *Ramillies* (he considered it too big and impersonal and he says that he never found his way around the massive vessel), then the cruiser *Galatea* off Spain during the Spanish Civil War. He subsequently volunteered to join submarines in September 1938, so he was well established in his new trade when war was declared. After some patrols around the UK, including one lying submerged just off the French coast during the withdrawal of the BEF from Dunkirk, he sailed from Portsmouth on 10 December 1940, bound for the Mediterranean as a crew member on *Upholder*, serving under Lieutenant-Commander David Wanklyn DSO, who in May 1941 would become the first submarine VC of the war. Selby describes his skipper as being a 'quiet gentleman' who was always soft spoken, calm and thoughtful. He was also clearly a man who inspired confidence in others. His crew were all regular prewar sailors with just one exception — that tended to be the 'norm' on *Upholder* — when it moved from Gibraltar to Malta in early January 1941.

Life in *Upholder*, as in any submarine of the time, was arduous and stressful:

'During daylight the sub was submerged, surfacing well after dark to recharge batteries. The crew — most of whom did not see daylight for days or even weeks — were organised into three watches, two hours on and four off. Two hours was considered the maximum period that a man could hold his concentration.'

That is how historian John Laffin describes submarine life in his book *British VCs of World War 2* and he goes on to say this about Wanklyn:

'Upholder under Wanklyn made one patrol after another from Malta. Towards the end of his seventh patrol, Wanklyn had sunk five vessels — supply ships from 5,000 to 8,000 tons — and had probably sunk two others. His first victim, the 8,000-tonner, Wanklyn attacked at night on the surface to conserve torpedoes. Upholder was itself close pressed by Italian warships; in one short period after a successful torpedo attack the Italians dropped 26 depth charges.'

Selby was present throughout all these attacks, undramatically yet vividly recounting what happened to *Upholder* during these patrols. He explained: 'Everyone was naturally calm, especially the skipper, who was a quiet person by nature and set the pace for everyone else.' In the early weeks of 1941 they were constantly on patrol from Malta, being away for anything up to 14 days at a stretch, leaving Malta (he calls it their 'patrol billet') late in the evening and returning in the early mornings, after being dived all day and only on the surface at night to recharge batteries. Once their skipper had 'got his eye in' their patrols became more and more successful, with *Upholder* becoming one of the top-scoring subs in the Mediterranean. Wanklyn would soon be awarded the Victoria Cross, the citation reading:

'In May 1941 in the Mediterranean, south of Sicily, Lt Cdr M. D. Wanklyn, commander HM Submarine Upholder, *torpedoed a troopship which was with a strongly protected convoy. The troopship sank and* Upholder *endured a strong counter-attack in which 37 depth-charges were dropped. By the end of 1941, Lt Cdr Wanklyn had sunk nearly 140,000 tons of enemy shipping, including a destroyer, troopships, tankers, supply and store ships.'*

Selby's welcome to Malta had been somewhat traumatic. They had been tied up very close to the aircraft carrier *Illustrious*, and a few hours later she had been subjected to heavy dive-bombing by German Stukas. As their submarine was only some 50 yards away, they were almost too close for comfort. However, they were not hit. Their patrols took them off the coasts of North Africa and of Sicily and the southern part of Italy. He describes their attack on the convoy in which they sank the troopship *Conte Rossa* near the Strait of Messina, the convoy being protected by at least six Italian destroyers. They also destroyed an enemy transport that had been beached near Sfax, going alongside, putting a boarding party on board and setting off demolition charges. On other patrols, because of defective instruments, Wanklyn had to fire his torpedoes on the surface, making his judgements by eye, yet managing to hit his targets successfully. 'A very confident crew and a good captain,' is how Selby explains their continued success.

However, after a good deal of heart-searching because he was loath to leave *Upholder*, Selby was transferred, on promotion to coxswain, to *P39* in late February 1942. Not long afterwards, whilst at Malta, they were subjected to yet more heavy dive-bombing attacks, a near miss doing considerable damage to *P39*, which necessitated them going into the dockyard to replace their battery cells. Unfortunately, in late March, whilst in the dockyard under repair, they were bombed again and *P39* had her back broken. The crew were fortunately not on board at the time and without a sub of their own to man, were thereafter used as a relief crew for other submarines patrolling from Malta, so that their crews could get a break. They also unloaded stores at the dockyard and generally made themselves useful until they were put on board the submarine *Olympus* bound for the UK. Unfortunately, just some seven miles off Malta, they hit a mine and had to abandon ship. Although most of the 90-plus seamen made it to the surface, only a handful managed to reach shore. Selby had been in the petty officers' mess when

Right: HMS *Una* enters harbour. The small U Class submarines took a steady toll of enemy shipping. Note also the Maltese gondola-like *dghaisa* in the foreground.
IWM — A 14385

Below: Lazzaretto Creek by Manoel Island. This was the base for the 10th Submarine Flotilla (Malta Force Submarines) which operated from HMS *Talbot*.
IWM — A 6919

they hit the mine, had heard the enormous thump of the explosion, and the order to abandon ship, had reached the upper deck and swum off the rapidly sinking submarine. With no life-saving equipment and seven miles to swim, the sailors tried to stay together and to help each other; however, as Selby explains, only seven in his group made it. His late captain off the *P39* got to within a few hundred yards of the beach, but then disappeared and was drowned. There were some soldiers on the beach who helped to take them to hospital and then back to the submarine base. However, they did not stay there for long, being hustled aboard the cruiser HMS *Welshman*, which then steamed flat out all the way home, reaching Milford Haven in record time.

Such experiences clearly did not put Selby off submarines and he went on to serve in the Far East, then stayed in the submarine service postwar, until he left in 1951 and emigrated to Australia. Like his captain, he was clearly a modest and unassuming man, and tells his dramatic story with little emotion, although clearly he was considerably affected by it.[1]

Even Smaller — Midget Subs

Sailing from the Clyde on 26 November 1942 and destined for Malta was a very special party of 11 officers and 15 ratings, led by Commander G. M. Sladen. They would join the 10th Submarine Flotilla; however, their craft were tiny midget submarines (known also as 'chariots'). Three normal submarines (*Thunderbolt*, *Trooper* and *P311*) were detached from the flotilla to work with the chariots and fitted with external containers to take them to their target areas. This was a new method of transport and not exactly a submarine commander's dream:

> *'The Submarine Service normally expects, for the pains and risks it must endure, frequent opportunities for engaging the enemy. To become a ferry-boat for someone else who is probably going to be presented by you with the chance of a lifetime and to be told into the bargain that no potential targets below the rating of capital ships may be engaged until after the operation, can only be the sort of assignment that one wishes for one's colleague. Furthermore it entailed incurring the greatest of all submarine risks, that of proceeding close inshore into water too shallow for a successful evasive dive. It is to the great credit of the men concerned, therefore, that in no instance was their undoubted dislike of the work ever manifest in the presence of charioteers or X-craft personnel. Co-operation was always of the highest standard. It was bettered only by the hospitality.'[2]*

All chariot crews began night runs, in order to prepare for an operation that Sladen had been planning, the three 'carrying' submarines sailing from Malta on 28/29 December 1942 and by 9pm on 3 January 1943 two of them were in position a few miles to seaward of Palermo in north Sicily. Operation 'Principle' had begun. *P311* never returned from this mission, nor did it arrive at its rendezvous, so it must have been lost with all hands before getting to the target area. With the crew died 10 charioteers (three two-man teams and four 'dressers'). This left five teams in all (two on *Thunderbolt* and three on *Trooper*). Conditions worsened whilst they completed the arduous job of 'dressing' and getting their final briefings — the wind was now about Force 4 (a wind speed of 11—16 knots), coming directly off the shore; waves were breaking over the casing as the crews made their way cautiously for'ard from the gun-mounting and conning tower area to where the two machines were housed. They had to struggle hard to maintain their grip but eventually managed to scramble onto their machines. Thereafter neither Lieutenant Richard Greenland nor Leading Seaman Alec

Ferrier (one crew) saw the submarine *Thunderbolt* again or the other chariot crew (Petty Officer Miln and Able Seaman Simpson). However, when they headed around onto the compass bearing and made for the harbour, they were able to pick out a light which marked the entrance.

Keeping on the surface, they were badly affected by the heavy sea, although the waves eased slightly as they got closer inshore. The two of them communicated with each other, using Morse Code (tapping on each other's hands) and agreed to dive to correct the chariot's trim. Having done so they surfaced again and made their run in to the harbour, only to find their way blocked by a large, heavy anti-submarine (A/S) net. Eventually they managed to get through it unscathed, although thereafter it was apparent that it had had an adverse effect upon their compass readings. The sea was still very rough inside the harbour and next time they broke the surface they saw yet another line of buoys holding another A/S net. Fortunately they were able to pass under this one without further incident. Now they were inside Palermo harbour. Despite the darkness they were able to make out the outline of their target, the Italian cruiser *Ulpio Traiano*, just out of the fitting-out yards, the commissioning crew still aboard as they had not yet completed their trials. Soon they were alongside, had forced their chariot down under the cruiser and secured the warhead. Greenland then set the timer on the explosive charge for two hours. However, they were not finished. Each team had also taken four 5lb magnetic charges, which they proceeded to fix to three submarine chasers and a merchantman. Unfortunately, whilst withdrawing on the surface from between the second and third chaser, they fouled an anchor chain. This caused their screw to come out of the water and race violently, the noise causing someone on the chaser to look over the side, but fortunately he did not see them. They then headed seawards, but in the pitch black collided with a merchantman whilst going flat out. The noise seemed to be magnified in the dark, but again they were not seen or heard. However, the crash had completely ruined their compass and they realised that there was no chance of navigating to the agreed RV.

They were now near a naval dockyard, so Greenland drove the chariot alongside a small motor launch, and as he was now out of oxygen, climbed onto the launch whilst Ferrier took the chariot out into the middle of the small basin and sank it. He then swam back to join Greenland and they got rid of their breathing gear and diving suits by tying them to their lead soled diving boots and ditching the lot into the dark water.

'Dockyard steps gave way to quayside, whither two of the Royal Navy's more scruffy looking units made their way in search of somewhere comfortable to sit. They felt peckish. One of them produced some chocolate, and they munched quietly for a few minutes before deciding on which direction to move off. Perhaps the big bang would not be long.'[3]

The other team from HMS *Thunderbolt* (Miln and Simpson) launched perfectly happily despite the heavy weather. However, during the run-in they had a battery explosion and the machine dived rapidly. Miln tried desperately to free Simpson who was badly tangled up, but eventually, suffering from oxygen poisoning himself at a depth of some 95 feet, he had to surface and swim to safety. Simpson was presumed drowned, whilst Miln was taken prisoner.

Sub-Lieutenant Dove and Leading Seaman Freel were one of the teams to leave *Trooper*. They reached and attacked their target — the *Viminale*, an 8,500-ton troop transport. They then made the way ashore and were taken prisoner. Another of *Trooper's* chariots (Sub-Lieutenant Stevens and Leading Seaman Carter) could not find the harbour entrance, and after some five hours' searching, during which Carter's breathing apparatus developed a fault and he had to be left for some time on a convenient buoy, whilst Stevens

Top: Mark I chariots and containers mounted aft on a T Class submarine. *Author's Collection*

Left and above: Two stages of dressing a charioteer. He waits whilst the headpiece and apron are passed over his head, then his boots are secured and his belly-clamps fastened. *Author's Collection*

continued the hunt, sadly in vain. They decided to return to their submarine, but could see no sign of it. However, they were picked up safely by *P46* which had been sent in expressly to pick up stray chariot crews. The final chariot, manned by Lieutenant Cook and Able Seaman Worthy, was unfortunately destined for tragedy, Cook being drowned and Worthy having to swim ashore, where like five others of his colleagues he was taken prisoner.

Nevertheless, their achievements had been spectacular. Six of the vessels in Palermo harbour had been attacked, Greenland and Ferrier had been the most successful — sinking the cruiser *Ulpio Traiano* and damaging three submarine chasers and a merchantman, whilst Dove and Freel had badly damaged another merchantman (the *Viminale*). It had been worth it.

Mine Clearing off Malta

Sydney Nigel Bush applied to join the RNVR in 1938 and, after training in Devonport Barracks, joined the communications section on HMS *Witch* on convoy duties off Great Britain in the early part of the war. Some months later, after being selected for officer training at HMS *King Alfred*, Hove, he was commissioned and posted to *Motor Launch 134* which was part of the 3rd Minelaying Flotilla. After preparing for Mediterranean service in the Hamble and fitting long-distance fuel tanks, they sailed for Gibraltar, arriving there without incident. After some months operating from the Rock, the flotilla joined the Operation 'Harpoon' convoy bound for Malta in June 1942. They had a difficult journey, at one stage the motor launches having to be towed by an accompanying merchant ship, the *Orare*, in order to try to make better speed. However, progress was still painfully slow, because the tow ropes kept on parting. Eventually they had to be left on their own to make their best speed. The convoy was heavily attacked and some of the merchantmen sunk. Then as they approached Malta, one of the escort vessels, the Polish destroyer *Kujawiak*, which was acting as rearguard, struck a mine and began to sink. Realising that they must be in the middle of a minefield the convoy stopped, including the MLs who were near the rear and thus fairly close to the sinking destroyer. Lieutenant Bush, who was commanding *ML 134*, heard the despairing shouts of the Polish sailors begging to be rescued — it transpired that they were being badly stung by a swarm of jellyfish. Together

with the closest destroyer and another ML, Bush took his vessel into the mass of swimming sailors and the three boats together managed to rescue all of them. They then made slow but safe progress on to Malta. Their arrival at Valletta was a considerable shock to Bush, who had never been there before and was forcibly struck by the devastation caused by the continual bombing — he comments that there was hardly a ship left afloat or undamaged.

Once they had settled in and got their bearings the ML flotilla began its minesweeping duties in earnest, sweeping a mile-wide channel down the southern and eastern sides of the island, creating a safe lane for shipping some 100 miles in length, from which they took out some 400-plus mines. This was vital work as, until then, both surface ships and submarines had been continually sunk by mines, as other naval reminiscences confirm. Then, when the battered convoys arrived, the ML flotilla had to guide them into harbour along the swept channel. Bush vividly recalled the arrival of the 'Pedestal' convoy in August 1942 and the state of the battered tanker *Ohio*, kept afloat by two destroyers (see Chapter 12). He also tells of the difficult food situation on Malta, where their staple daily rations were half a tin of corned beef and half a loaf of bread. Nevertheless, they saved up part of their meagre rations so that they could hold a Christmas Party (on 25 December 1942) for the Maltese children who lived near their waterfront base. Later, in March 1943, his was one of the escort vessels for the monitor HMS *Aphis*, when it bombarded the Mareth Line. He eventually left Malta for Gibraltar by air in April 1943.

Success for the Motor Torpedo Boats

It was not until 1943 that the motor torpedo boats (MTBs) based on Malta had their first major successes. Four MTBs (*260, 264, 267* and *313*) left Malta on 19 January to patrol towards Tripoli under the command of Lieutenant Peter Evensen, of the 20th MTB Division. After some eight hours one of the boats developed engine trouble and had to return to base, but the other three continued towards the North African coast and reached Tripoli about half an hour later. As they approached the harbour they saw a hospital ship just leaving with all its lights on and its Red Cross signs illuminated. Unfortunately the departure of this ship prevented them slipping into the harbour unseen. However, after cruising along the coast for about an hour they came across three enemy tugs towing a submarine off a sandbank. They attacked with torpedoes and using their guns. The torpedoes missed but they scored numerous hits on the tugs, one of which was set on fire. All three tugs then abandoned the submarine and headed for the safety of Tripoli harbour with two of the MTBs giving chase. The MTBs followed them in as far as they could until they came under heavy fire from the shore batteries. Despite this they scored more hits on a burning tug, which then ran aground just south of the harbour entrance. Meanwhile the enemy submarine had been engaging the third MTB with cannon-fire as it came in on a depth charge attack. However, that had to be aborted as the submarine was still stuck on the sandbank, so that there was insufficient water to drop depth charges. Instead the MTB opted for a torpedo attack. Just as they were starting their run-in, they saw an enemy destroyer leaving harbour at top speed, so they sensibly withdrew some miles out to sea. When the excitement had died down, they crept back at slow speed for another attack on the submarine. One MTB engaged it from about 400 yards with torpedoes, scoring a hit just aft of the conning tower and then watching the target disappear under the water. The shore batteries then opened up again, so

Left: Motor torpedo boats. A gaggle of MTBs, MGBs (motor gun boats) and MLs (motor launches) are seen here berthed at Haywharf, Floriana, on VE or VJ Day. *NWMA Malta 7051-35*

they decided to withdraw under cover of smokescreens. They arrived back in Malta on the 20th and were delighted to hear a few days later, when Tripoli was captured, that the Italian submarine *Santorre Santorosa* had been found severely damaged and abandoned in the shallows about a mile from the harbour.[4]

Call-Out

Air-Sea Rescue was one of the many important wartime tasks carried out on Malta by RAF personnel involving, as it did, saving the lives of airmen who for one reason or another had baled out or been forced to ditch their aircraft in the Mediterranean. The activities of the Malta-based high speed launches have recently been documented in an enthralling new book, *Call-Out*, written by Frederick Galea, which deals with many of the attempted rescues, a staggering 270-plus of which were successful. Here is a typical successful rescue recorded in the book, which took place on 15 November 1941:

'*Three Wellingtons of the Overseas Air Delivery Unit (OADU) were attacked by five CR42s. One Wellington was shot down in flames, crashing at position Latitude 36 degrees 15 minutes North, Longitude 12 degrees 50 minutes East, nearly 90 miles west of Kalafrana and well beyond the enemy occupied island off Linosa. Crockett[5] wrote: "We left base (in HSL128) at 1645 hours and with a fresh wind from the east setting up a moderate sea, we made very good time until half way to position when our port engine started giving trouble — periodically backfiring and sending out great sheets of flame out of the open exhaust. As it started to get dark this was really awe inspiring — making me think that even if enemy boats were in the vicinity and saw or heard this exhibition, they would imagine we had 6in guns and clear off in fright.*

'"*In spite of the engine trouble we were approaching position shortly after dark, but by then the weather conditions were deteriorating and the Swordfish aircraft, which we had been told by wireless had located the Wellington crew in their rubber dinghy, must have lost it some time before. Now and again we could hear the Swordfish buzzing around somewhere overhead but could not see it.*"

'*Spotting a light on the starboard beam three miles away, Crockett made for it in complete darkness as they were in enemy waters, only to discover that this was HSL 129 from St Paul's Bay out on the same search! Crockett continued: "'Well let's get on with it. Nicolls, you had better start a square search round this point. I will go back to my original position about four miles west of here and start a square search there.'" "My launch had been on its square search for about five minutes when I saw the quick flicker of a white light about two miles away. Six men were huddled in a rubber dinghy — all RAF sergeants. Popper, Leonard and Welch were English, Barlow and Cameron were Canadian and Duncan was from New Zealand. Their Wellington aircraft had ditched successfully, so none of them had been injured on impact with the sea. Unfortunately their dinghy had inflated upside down but they managed to turn it right way up whilst standing on the fuselage of their sinking aircraft and they then stepped aboard with only their feet wet and watched their Wellington disappear slowly through the clear Mediterranean waters into the depths below.*

'"*With no real idea where they were when they ran out of fuel and having had to ditch, they were relieved when the Swordfish search plane spotted them in the middle of the afternoon. They had seen two messages float down to them from the observer of the Swordfish, giving them their position 90 miles from Malta and to say that a rescue launch should reach them by nightfall,*

but the rising wind carried the messages a little distance away and they had no means of moving the dinghy. Their paddles, as well as most of the dinghy's other rescue gear, had been lost when it inflated the wrong way up."

'*HSL 128 had accomplished her first pick-up, returning to Kalafrana at 0100hrs on the following day, having travelled a distance of 186 miles during this mission. HSL 129, with Nicolls being more discreet in his navigation, held off until daylight before attempting to get back to his base at St Paul's Bay.*'[6]

Somewhat less typical of the strange jobs undertaken by the rescue launches was an incident which had occurred on 28 March 1941, when a Sunderland flying boat had approached Malta, bound from Cairo carrying a load of VIPs, who included Anthony Eden (Foreign Secretary), General Sir John Dill (Chief of the General Staff), Robert Watson (Chief of Radar Development), Admiral Lyster (head of the Fleet Air Arm) and two Americans — one being an admiral who was Commander Submarines USN. They were en route back to the UK, but flying only by night for security reasons, so they had to stage in Malta, then Gibraltar. Flying Officer (later Group Captain) Edward Hardie, who was to become Deputy Director of RAF Marine Craft, recalled in an after-dinner speech during a visit to Malta in 1975:

'*We had one epic evening when we got a signal from HQ Mediterranean that there was a Sunderland on its way from Alexandria to Marsaxlokk and by the time we got this signal there was a storm blowing and when the swells worked up at Marsaxlokk they used to hurl huge boulders up the slipways right up to the hangar doors. We couldn't possibly have laid a flare path into the bay but the aircraft was past the point of no return and she had to come on.*

'*On board there was the Foreign Minister, Anthony Eden, and the Chief of the General Staff, Sir John Dill, so we were in quite a quandary about how we were going to get these august people down. After consultations I told the CO that I was prepared to take some of our launches out and put the searchlights on as far as possible into line and when the Sunderland approached we would ask the gunposts all to switch theirs on too and by the grace of God we got them down in one piece. They finished up nearly into Delimara Point.*'[7]

Below: Call-out! High Speed Launch 107 berthed alongside the pier at St Paul's Bay, with Sunderland House in the background. HSL 107 made 82 rescues during her service in Malta in the RAF Air-Sea Rescue Service. *NWMA Malta — 21046*

A Strange Air-Sea Rescue

Navigator Norman Harper of 39 Squadron had a fascinating tale to tell about the crew of a Beaufort of his squadron that was shot down off the coast of Greece on 28 July 1942. The crew comprised pilot — SAAF Lieutenant Ted Strever, navigator — Pilot Officer Dunsmore, RAF, and two New Zealanders, Sergeants Brown and Wilkinson. Harper writes:

'They were picked up by an Italian Cant 504 which was circling round their dinghy. They were taken aboard and received an excellent reception. The Cant then taxied into Kerkira harbour in Corfu. They were given dry clothes, taken to the Officers' Mess and well fed — a change from bully beef. They were asked not to run away — dinner was served at 2000hrs, with good food, wine and cigarettes — and then allocated officers' quarters. In the morning, following a photo call with their hosts, they were put aboard the same Cant flying boat and set course for Taranto, with two pilots, an engineer and a wireless operator plus a corporal guard. Wilkinson, awaiting an opportunity, smashed his fist on the engineer's jaw and seized the corporal's revolver which he handed to Ted. The 2nd pilot's gun was also wrestled from him. The corporal appeared in a poor way — very airsick and was propped up against an open port — very thoughtful!

'Ted took over the controls with the assistance of the 2nd pilot. When the toe of Italy came in sight, three Spitfires appeared. The Navigator, Bill Dunsmore took off his white vest and waved it outside. Ted ordered the pilot to land, and as they did so, the engines stopped — no fuel! The crew clambered out and waved to the Spits who flew off. The crew, of course, felt remorse after the way they had been treated. They were then all picked up by the Air-Sea Rescue. An interpreter explained their regrets, but the Italians took it well. They opened a bottle of wine from a suitcase — taken with them because the crew were to have gone on leave after reaching Taranto! . . . Ted and Bill Dunsmore were awarded the DFC, Brown and Wilkinson the DFM. Ted was badly burned in Ceylon in 1944. He died in 1977, aged 77.'

In the same section of the George Cross Association newsletter (No 39 of September 1999) is confirmation from First Coxswain Haffenden of HSL 107, who, on 29 July 1942, had been called to investigate a ditched aircraft one mile off the Madliena Tower:

'As we approached the plane, somebody was waving something white as he was standing on the wing. There were no Spitfires in the area and 107 towed the Cant to St Paul's Bay . . . Lieutenant Strever told me the Italians had treated them very well when they were shot down and they spent a couple of nights in Corfu. The Cant was flown away the following day and the story goes at the time that it was put on special duties.'

HMS *Welshman*

One of the most remarkable vessels to be based on Malta was a fast minelaying cruiser, the 2,650-ton 40-knot HMS *Welshman*, which brought all manner of scarce commodities to the island. Its cargo might consist of food (eg flour, powdered milk, canned meat or dehydrated foodstuffs), ammunition, aero-engines, glycol coolant, paravanes, even troop reinforcements, in fact anything that was needed urgently. The Germans continually tried to sink the ship, especially when it was in harbour; smokescreens were often employed to hide the ship whilst it was being unloaded.

Alun Tebbutt served aboard this remarkable vessel from 1941 until she was torpedoed off Tobruk by *U617* on 1 February 1943.

He wrote in the George Cross Island Association newsletter (No 46 of December 2001) about his experiences and commenting upon a previous article in the newsletter about his ship:

'HMS *Welshman* indeed bore a resemblance to a French cruiser. We were, in fact, because of the French capitulating and leaving France to go to all different places in the Med, flying the French ensign. I do not know if I should say this but the flag came down 50–60 miles from Malta and all hell was let loose. Both Jerry and Italian bombers did their best to stop the unloading, yes, quite true it was unloaded in about 8–9 hours and back to sea. Welshman could mass up around 45 knots flat out, and we needed it . . . After the next trip, carrying all sorts of needs for Malta, we then started to travel between Malta and Alexandria. It was on a trip back to Alex that we were torpedoed. Contrary to the statement of only lasting minutes, we kept her afloat for two and three quarter hours. Anyway 'Abandon Ship' was about 7.30pm . . . I personally, along with a hundred others, was not picked up until 9.30 the next morning, covered in oil etc, by HMS Beaver and HMS Tetcut, two Hunt Class destroyers and landed at Alexandria . . . One of the jobs we had was picking up 800 troops in Haifa and taking them to a rest camp in Cyprus — this took about a fortnight. They were Gurkhas and men of the 51st Highland Division.'

Another member of Captain W. R. D. Friedberger's crew of this 'jack-of-all-trades' minelaying cruiser, was Leading Seaman Jim Taylor who also wrote in the *Newsletter* (No 25 of April 1996):

'Beginning another trip, we loaded what to us was another strange cargo consisting of powdered milk, seed potatoes, seed tomatoes, ammunition, wooden crates (which I now know to have been aero-engines) and many other commodities for the successful prosecution of the war. Our first port of call was Gibraltar and, after passing through the Straits and entering the "Med", we guessed our destination was Malta . . . we were spotted by reconnaissance planes and several times during the day we were attacked by Ju88s and Stuka dive-bombers. Owing to our speed and the excellent seamanship of our Skipper, Captain Friedberger, the bombs missed their target. We finally arrived and entered the Grand Harbour, Malta, through the breakwater, during the early hours of the next morning to the tumultuous applause and cheering of the naval, military and civilian population high on the cliffs on our starboard side which elated us all. No sooner had we secured alongside the dock in Frenchman's Creek, we were invaded by the navy, army and the civilian population whose primary job was to off-load, with our help, the valuable cargo we had brought, and this enabled us to have a quick turn-around for our trip back to Gibraltar. Five or six times during the day this was interrupted with the usual aerial bombardment that the population of Malta endured daily. Many hours later, unloading completed, it was "Hands to Stations for leaving Harbour" and we were finally on our way back to Gibraltar, which was reached after surviving the usual air attacks. The "Powers that be" then suggested that, having done it once, it could and would be done again.

'On our next occasion in this theatre of war, the star attraction was that we donned cowls on our funnels, bolts of black canvas on our waistline, and from fo'c'sle to stern regaled "A", "B" and "Y" turrets with the French tricolour, intending to disguise the ship as a Vichy French Leopard Class destroyer. We, the crew, were ordered to keep out of sight! This seemed to have done the trick, as the Axis reconnaissance planes circled over us and from then onwards, we were left alone and reached our destination unscathed. However, next morning we were sighted in harbour and became a prime target for the Luftwaffe, who intended to put this ship out of action once and for all. Before this could happen, however, we brought in a new line of defence, in the shape of smoke canisters, which were lit as soon as the air raid warning sounded, thus obliterating the target they sought.

'It was some 41 years later, when I was on holiday in Malta for nostalgic reasons, we met four elderly gentlemen of whom I asked: "Could you point out Frenchman's Creek please?" and one answered: "Were you an ex-serviceman?" "Yes" I replied, "Navy". "What ship?" "Welshman". At which he stood and shook me by the hand and said: "Yes, I was one of the dockyard mateys that helped to unload you on your arrival. You did a great job, but it was marred by an episode. When the first air raid warning sounded and we repaired to our sandstone caves, unknown to us you lit your smoke canisters and when we switched on our fans, they sucked in the black smoke. We choked and spluttered and wondered what the bloody hell was going on!" To which I replied: "Which was the lesser of the two evils?" He smiled and said:

"Thanks again" and pointed out Frenchman's Creek which later in our holiday we manoeuvred towards on a different kind of cruiser, namely Captain Morgan's harbour cruises.'

Store-Carrying Submarines

In addition to HMS *Welshman* several submarines made regular trips to Malta, carrying all manner of vital items. These included *Rorqual, Osiris, Porpoise, Urge, Cachalot, Clyde* and *Talisman*. On the first run by the *Rorqual*, she carried two tons of medical stores, 62 tons of 100-octane petrol, 45 tons of cooking oil, together with passengers and mail. Until 1942 when the robust German 'Jerrican' was adopted, petrol was carried in very flimsy British-made cans that were easily damaged — this made refuelling aircraft dangerous as the flimsy cans had to be lifted onto the wings of aircraft and then emptied into the fuel tanks. You can see examples of these cans, filled with sand and used in the construction of aircraft pens, so they were of some use after all. During the second half of 1941 some 16 store-carrying trips were made by submarines and in the spring of 1942, when perhaps Malta's need was greatest, a further 20 such trips were made. In total this amounted to over 65,000 tons of vitally important items carried by submarines. What is even more remarkable is the fact that not a single submarine was lost during these dangerous missions.

Notes
1. IWM Sound Archive Recording No 16738.
2. C. E. T. Warren and James Benson: *Above us the Waves.*
3. Ibid.
4. IWM Sound Archive Recording No 13300.
5. George Ronald Crockett MBE, skipper of one of the High Speed Launches (HSL) wrote his memoirs 'An Airman is a Sailor', but died before they could be published. Galea quotes from them in *Call-Out.*
6. Frederick Galea: *Call-Out.*
7. Ibid.

Below:
HMS *Kingston* under repair in Malta. She was also part of the Malta Striking Force. IWM — A 9636)

Above: HMS *Welshman* enters harbour, 15 June 1942. This fast minelaying cruiser was one of the most remarkable ships of the Malta battles. Disguised to look like a French cruiser with clinker tops on her funnels, she carried a wide variety of cargoes to Malta, making full use of her 40-knot top speed. Alas, she was eventually torpedoed and sunk. *NWMA Malta — 1832*

Chapter 10
The Convoys Must Get Through

Anxious about Malta

Writing in his memoirs about the Mediterranean theatre in the early summer of 1942, Winston Churchill comments that, whilst he was content with the way the battle in the Western Desert was going (this was just before Rommel attacked the Gazala Line), he was still 'anxious about Malta'. He quotes the following communication of 2 June 1942:

> *'Prime Minister to General Auchinleck and Air Marshal Tedder*
> *"'There is no need for me to stress the vital importance of the safe arrival of our convoys at Malta, and I am sure you will both take all steps to enable air escorts, and particularly the Beaufighters, to be operated from landing grounds as far west as possible . . ."'*

The Prime Minister had every reason to be worried about Malta. What with the almost continuous air raids, the shortages of food, fuel, ammunition and weapons of war, combined with the threat of invasion, Malta's situation was getting more and more difficult. Even when Hitler finally decided against invasion, he was still determined to bomb and starve Malta into submission, so the convoys that were sent to keep the island's military and civilians supplied were vital and had to get through no matter what the cost might be in ships and lives. This was a time of great sacrifice for both the Royal Navy and the Merchant Navy as they battled against almost continuous attack. Outline details of the most important convoys are given in Appendix I to this chapter. Here are just a few examples of the actions that took place.

HMS *Foresight*

Chief Electrician Thomas MacPherson DSM, BEM, recorded some of his reminiscences of convoy work on board the F Class destroyer, HMS *Foresight*, in *Malta Remembered*:

> *'At the commencement of the war HMS Foresight was attached to the Home Fleet where we continued operations until February 1941, when we joined Force "H" at Gibraltar under command of Admiral Somerville. Our operations in the Mediterranean commenced on that date and were to feature Malta on many of our trips until we were eventually sunk on the Santa Marija ['Pedestal'] convoy in August 1942. We carried out most of our escort trips when the carriers were flying off Hurricanes and Spitfires to Malta and also supply convoys. One of the convoys ['Tiger'] — one of the most significant convoys to reach North Africa in 1941. Sent by Churchill in May, it was a 'fast convoy' and brought additional armour (nearly 400 tanks) and aircraft (50 Hurricanes) — stands out in my memory, besides "Pedestal", was the one when we were ordered to go to the assistance of the merchant ship* Empire Song. *The incident occurred during*

Above: Malta Convoys. Gun crews wearing anti-flash headgear as they man their 4.5in AA guns. Note also the wings of the Walrus biplane reconnaissance amphibian (nicknamed 'Shagbat') on the catapult on this cruiser. *H. Langford*

daylight hours when she had struck a mine and as we arrived we could hear ammunition or something exploding inside her. Officers and crew were immediately taken off her and HMS Foresight *then withdrew to a safe distance and waited. One must remember that the* Empire Song *was a large merchant ship loaded with ammunition and war material for Malta and to lose her would be quite a loss.*

'HMS Foresight *waited for a period of time until the noise of exploding ammunition had subsided and all seemed quiet.* Empire Song *officers decided to re-board their vessel and try to*

Above: A tired crew of a multiple pom-pom (nicknamed the 'Chicago Piano')
have a quick smoke between enemy air attacks. These 2-pounder AA guns
could be fitted in single-, four- and eight-barrel mountings. *IWM — A 11180*

sail her to Malta. HMS Foresight *approached the stricken vessel
and lowered her sea boat to take the officers back to their ship.
The sea was reasonably calm as the sea boat approached the
jumping ladder previously lowered over the side of the* Empire
Song *and just as the first officer was about to step onto the
ladder, the* Empire Song *gave one almighty roar and blew up,
taking all her cargo to the bottom of the Mediterranean. The
fortunate part of this episode was that HMS* Foresight *was so
close to the other vessel that most of the heavy deck cargo was
blown right over us, but we did sustain some damage. I believe a
Bren Gun Carrier bounced on top of our torpedo tubes and then
into the sea. At a later inspection we found that one of our
torpedoes was stuck in its tube due to a dent made by the Carrier.
Miraculously, as far as I can remember no lives were lost as, even
though the sea boat passengers were blown into the water with
the blast, none were lost. The only casualty as I know was one of
the sea boat's crew, an Able Seaman, who was supporting another
person in the water after the explosion. It was not until we
picked him up that we discovered our AB had lost a leg in the
explosion. He was awarded the Albert Medal.*

'*At the time of the explosion I was standing under the "X" gun
flare and it sounded like being under a corrugated roof in a
heavy rainstorm but instead of water it was ammunition etc
from the* Empire Song. *HMS* Foresight *rejoined the convoy and
instead of returning with Force "H" we were ordered to proceed*

*with the convoy to Malta and have the damage sustained during
the* Empire Song *episode, repaired. During the passage through
the Strait of Sicily on the last night before our arrival in Malta
we were attacked practically all night by "E" Boats and aircraft,
but arrived safely in Malta. With dockyard help and our own
staff we made good our damage. One thing I can remember was
all the ship's company, Duty Watch excepted, had to go ashore at
sunset and sleep in Corrinda Tunnel. I can remember slinging my
hammock in the tunnel and sleeping well all night. On the
completion of the repairs HMS* Foresight *was to run the gauntlet
on her own, with everyone at Action Stations all night. The luck
was with us, being on our own and able to proceed at full speed
we did not hear or see anything during the passage, at daylight
we were through and soon able to join "H" Force again. We were
then ordered back to the UK and with our sister ship HMS*
Forrester *carried out a convoy escort with HMS* Edinburgh *to
Murmansk in Russia which is another story . . . However,
eventually we joined a Gibraltar convoy en route for Malta.
This was the famous "Santa Marija — Pedestal".'*

SS *Empire Song*

On board the SS *Empire Song* at the time of these events was G. R.
Myers, then a lance corporal in the 8th Royal Tank Regiment, and
he too recorded his memories of that fateful voyage in the same volume of *Malta Remembered*:

'*We were in convoy outward bound to Alexandria, part of the
convoy was bound for Malta but not the* Empire Song *which
had on it the entire battle equipment of 8 RTR which had been*

loaded at Glasgow and was bound for North Africa. There were seven RTR NCOs and one officer aboard as escort for the vehicles. The ship was armed with a 4in gun mounted at the stern and on the port and starboard bridge wings were mounted two "Harvey Rocket Projectiles", the likes of which I have never seen before or since and would never ever like to fire one again! [Known as the '3-inch Harvey LS Projector' and made by Messrs G. A. Harvey of Greenwich, it was a very simple device for firing a single rocket from two guide rails. It had basic sights and was fixed electrically. It was trialled in 1940 and used both on land and at sea (mainly on Merchant Navy vessels).]

'I don't know what damage it did to enemy aircraft, but I do know what damage it caused where it was sited. The one and only time I fired it, it badly injured a merchant navy officer, bent the bridge wing guard rails and melted the pitch on the bridge decking! We also had four tanks lashed on deck and these were armed and were used against submarines and low flying aircraft, so the ship was not defenceless. She also had paravanes mounted and strung out for mine cutting.

'And so it happened, one hell of an explosion on the port side just off the bow. The seven of us RTR NCOs were asleep in the paint store in the bow at deck level. I was blown out through the open door and sent headlong on my stomach to finish up at the bottom of the steps leading to the bridge. Here I received a head wound of

Below: The ubiquitous Bofors LAA gun was also to be found on many types of ships including merchantmen. Here a crew stand easy between air attacks. IWM — A 11182

which I was unaware at the time. Then the second explosion came, this one was also on the port side. By now the SS Empire Song had taken a slight list to port, the first officer came from the bridge and partly removed one of the forward covers to discover the hold was on fire. As stated, we were loaded with tanks, lorries and ammunition, so we had a problem. The ship slowed down but was still making headway; however, the list was increasing. The two starboard lifeboats could not be launched because they were swinging inboard due to the list, one port side boat had been attempted to be launched and was hanging stern first in the water. This left one boat which was duly launched and quickly filled. The captain gave orders to abandon ship but called for volunteers to stay aboard, to try to keep the ship afloat and make for Malta. This action by the way was taking place off Pantelleria and the seven of us stayed aboard and took up fire drill duties.

'Two hours after the second explosion conditions were getting worse, smoke was pouring out from the hold ventilators and the pitch in the decking planks was starting to melt. The list had increased and the order "Abandon Ship" was given. The list was so great that we didn't have to jump, we just slipped into the sea, with our lifejackets on of course, and switched on our little red lights so that we could be located for pick-up. Our main objective was to swim as far away from the ship as possible; this we did and luckily for us we had done so before, in a huge explosion, the SS Empire Song blew apart and went down in flames and steam. Then we saw them, two grey shadowy hulks slowly circling where the Song had gone down and it wasn't long before they saw us and closed in. They were drifting in towards us and we could

Opposite top: Ammunition and repair parties snatch a few moments rest between actions, as the convoy steams on towards Malta with its precious cargoes.
IWM — A 11183

Opposite bottom: Engaging the enemy. A cruiser, part of the protection force of this Malta-bound convoy, fires its 4.5in AA guns. This was another photograph taken by Eddie Beater, who, after his ship was bombed and sunk, was picked out of the sea and taken to Alexandria, given new kit and then served on HMS *Peony*
H. Langford

Above: Going down. A merchantman sinking; some lifeboats can be seen, also seagoing tugs, so they must have been quite near to Malta when sunk.
H. Langford

Left: Launching a lifeboat to help pick up survivors, as destroyer H.97 races past. Eddie Beater finally served on the aircraft carrier HMS *Argus* and was in Freetown when the war ended.
H. Langford

now see the scramble nets being lowered over the side and shortly afterwards we were scrambling up to be grabbed by two matelots and flung onto the deck of HMS Foresight and the other ship HMS Fortune.

'We headed full steam for Malta followed by part of the Italian air force who were strafing and bombing us. We made it to Valletta but not without casualties to some of the naval crew members. And that is how I came to be stationed on the George Cross Island for a while.'

Operations 'Vigorous' and 'Harpoon'

Much has now been written postwar about the remarkable breaking of the German codes by the team at Bletchley Park's Hut 3, where men like John Prestwich, who died in early February 2003, were responsible for intercepting messages sent between Rommel and the OKW during the Desert War. Less well known is the fact that, in the autumn of 1941 while the USA was still neutral, the Italians had stolen a code book from the US Embassy in Rome, copied it and then returned it before anyone realised it was missing. The American representative in Cairo used the same code to keep Washington informed of developments there, so the Axis could work out in detail the Allied plans, not only for fighting the war in North Africa but also the convoys to Malta. This meant that when such convoys as *Vigorous* set sail from Alexandria, comprising 11 merchantmen, escorted by seven cruisers and 28 destroyers, the enemy knew exactly what was going on. The convoy was in danger not only from the *Luftwaffe* but also the Italian fleet. The answer would have been simpler had a single aircraft carrier been available but this was not the case, so the RAF had to endeavour to provide cover, despite all its other ongoing commitments. The basic plan therefore was for the convoy to defend itself against air attack, whilst the RAF took on the job of warding off the Italian fleet for which it would need a considerable number of aircraft — but in the end all it could muster was a small force of fewer than 40 planes (15–18 from Malta and 21 from Egypt). It had also been decided that the old target ship *Centurion* (brought out of retirement in Bombay and 'coaxed' to Suez) would pretend to be a major capital ship and be positioned in the centre of the convoy to draw enemy fire. A feint convoy would also sail some 36 hours earlier in an attempt to draw the Italian fleet out prematurely, whilst all available submarines would form a screen between the convoy and the enemy's expected line of attack. Finally, commando raids were planned on *Luftwaffe* aerodromes, whilst the merchantmen were loaded secretly at isolated ports in Egypt.

The feint convoy sailed from Alexandria on the evening of 11 June 1942. It contained four merchantmen, escorted by the cruiser HMS *Coventry* and eight destroyers. After an uneventful first night, they were about to reverse course and join the main convoy, when they were found by enemy dive-bombers. The largest of the merchantmen SS *City of Calcutta* was so nearly hit that its engines were badly affected and it had to drop out and proceed independently to Tobruk. Communications with convoy control in Alexandria were exceptionally difficult and those endeavouring to control events were constantly short of up-to-date information.

The main convoy contained seven merchantmen, seven cruisers and 18 destroyers, plus a number of smaller vessels. They left at noon on the 12th, but almost immediately some of the merchantmen were in trouble — first the SS *Elizabeth Bakke* could not keep up with the rest of the convoy and had to be escorted back to Alex; then the SS *Aagterkirk* had the same problem as did two of the corvettes — HMS *Erica* and HMS *Primula*. The *Luftwaffe* soon began its attacks, sinking the *Aagterkirk*. As if the convoy hadn't enough problems, the weather then turned against it, blustery winds blowing up a heavy sea which battered some of the accom-

panying motor launches so badly that one foundered and the rest had to return to Alexandria.

By the end of Day 2, the convoy had already lost six warships, albeit small ones, and three merchantmen. They were now approaching the Narrows and were under enemy air attack. During the morning of Day 3, they were helped immeasurably by two squadrons of Kittyhawks and Hurricanes, which had been switched from desert operations and were able to break up a number of attacks and to shoot down or damage some 12 enemy aircraft. However, by the afternoon, the convoy had moved further westwards, so the friendly aircraft could spend less and less time overhead; then finally they reached the limit of their endurance. As soon as they disappeared, the enemy began to increase their attacks and for the next three hours the convoy was subjected to wave after wave of dive-bomber attacks by up to 12 aircraft at a time. Remarkably only one merchantman was sunk (SS *Bhutan*) and most of her crew were picked up by escort vessels. However, more worrying was the exceptionally high expenditure of ammunition — the gun crews were also totally exhausted after over 12 hours of continuous action, whilst over 50 per cent of their ammunition had been expended in just one day. Even after last light there was little chance of rest, as the darkness merely replaced attack from the air by attack from the sea, the enemy E-boats then closing in.

Admiral Vian, who was commanding the convoy, had expected such an attack and had brought the convoy into a tightly packed mass of merchantmen, with a screen of escorts both ahead and on either side. This formation kept both the E-boats and enemy submarines away for most of the night. Then the worst possible news — an emergency signal gave notice that the Italian fleet was at sea and racing to intercept the convoy. Admiral Vian gave the order to turn back on the same track. One can imagine the chaos, as some 40-odd ships endeavoured to carry out this order in the pitch black, with E-boats all around. The cruiser HMS *Newcastle* was torpedoed in the bows, the destroyer *Hasty* amidships and became a total loss. In addition, the expenditure of both fuel oil and ammunition had now reached danger point. The convoy was by now back in the Narrows, between the North African coast and Crete, an area known as 'Bomb Alley', still waiting anxiously for news that the RAF had halted the Italian fleet, but no signal came.

The Italian fleet was sighted at 7pm on the evening of the 14th, by a reconnaissance plane which saw two battleships, four cruisers and eight destroyers leaving the Gulf of Taranto on a course of 160 degrees and at a speed of 20 knots. This was confirmed by another aircraft from Malta; however, there were fatal delays in informing those who were controlling the convoy from Alexandria and thus delay in ordering the RAF strike force to intercept. In addition the initial 'strike force' from Malta comprised just four Wellington bombers, each with two torpedoes — totally insufficient to deal with a modern enemy fleet of this size. Their attack was hampered by the enemy ships making smoke which hid them from view. Only one of the aircraft was thus able to drop its torpedoes, both of which missed. Next it was the turn of 12 Beauforts that left Malta in the dark and arrived over the Italian fleet at dawn. They attacked at once and the leading aircraft managed to hit one of the heavy cruisers (the *Trento*). Torpedo hits were also claimed on the two battleships but in fact neither was hit. Despite the slowing down of the *Trento*, the rest of the fleet continued inexorably southwards, intending to cut across the path of the convoy. Next came eight Liberators, who attacked and hit the *Littorio* on its A turret, but did little damage. A final attack was then made by a depleted squadron of Beauforts — they had been intercepted by some Messerschmitts en route and seven had been shot down. The other five bravely continued, but despite them dropping their torpedoes from close range no hits were scored, although claims were made that both a battleship and a cruiser had been damaged. Undoubtedly the reports received in Alexandria of the results on all these raids were very optimistic, so much so that it was decided that it would be better to brave the 'remnants' of the Italian fleet than to go through 'Bomb Alley' again. Therefore it was decided to turn the convoy around again and head for Malta.

Everyone at Alex now waited for good news, especially for the confirmed results of the RAF raids which, as noted, were initially wildly optimistic. Then at 8.30am news came that a reconnaissance aircraft had seen the two Italian battleships with the rest of their fleet — undamaged — and heading directly for the convoy which was now only some 150 miles away. Vian was ordered to turn the convoy around once more and head in an easterly direction. Next in this chapter of accidents came the reports from the last attack by the Beauforts from Malta, which claimed two hits on each battleship. More confusion as the controllers at Alex decided that these last claims were subsequent to the reconnaissance report and so the convoy was ordered yet again to change direction. Admiral Vian received this order at 1.45pm — the fourth change of direction he had received in a period of 12 hours. To make matters worse, it came to him in the middle of a heavy air attack in which the cruiser *Birmingham*, one of his key escort ships, had just been disabled. As Ian Cameron comments in *Red Duster, White Ensign*, his story of the Malta convoys: 'Like Nelson, he turned a blind eye to his C-in-C's signal and continued to withdraw to the east.' This undoubtedly took a lot of moral courage. Fortunately it was the correct decision to make, because had Vian obeyed the latest signal from Alex, turned and headed for Malta, then he would have run straight into the Italian fleet and his entire force could have been annihilated. Finally, after receiving a whole host of contradictory signals — one for example claiming 20-plus hits on the Italian fleet, whilst others said they were sailing undamaged towards the convoy, Admiral Harwood (now commanding the Mediterranean Fleet) in Alex, eventually sent Vian a signal to use his own discretion. This was an admission of defeat by Harwood and Tedder (C-in-C RAF Middle East), confirming that they had lost control of the situation and could do no more to influence events. Vian was thus left on his own. All he could do was to try to get back to Alex as speedily as possible, braving the almost continuous and accurate air attacks which had badly damaged at least three of his escort vessels and sank four more (one AA cruiser and three destroyers). Understandably, he was not happy when it was then suggested that he should give chase to the Italian fleet who had now decided to give up the pursuit and head back for Taranto. Checking his ammunition holdings reinforced his decision not to comply, as he had under 20 per cent left on most of his destroyers. At last light that evening Harwood gave the order: 'Return to Alexandria with your whole force.' Operation 'Vigorous' had failed, with the loss of one AA cruiser and three destroyers.

Operation 'Harpoon'

The Operation 'Harpoon' convoy the same month had been just as bad. It had left Gibraltar with seven merchantmen, escorted by a battleship, two aircraft carriers, three cruisers and eight destroyers. Five of the merchantmen were sunk, including the tanker the USS *Kentucky*, so only two merchantmen reached Malta. The escort's casualties were three cruisers damaged, and three destroyers, two corvettes and an MTB sunk. Thus, the two convoys between them had cost the Royal Navy and Merchant Navy a total of 11 ships damaged and a further 11 sunk. The RAF had been equally badly hit, having lost in total some 40 planes, whilst very little had managed to get through to embattled Malta.

But it was not a total failure. Undoubtedly, both 'Vigorous' and 'Harpoon' had been complete wash-outs, but several vitally important lessons had been learned which undoubtedly helped future inter-service planning. Ian Cameron comments:

'It is interesting to note that the vast inter-Service projects later set in motion in the Mediterranean were planned with meticulous attention to detail; while the system of remote control was never again used in a convoy to Malta. So, although Operation "Vigorous" was a failure — and a failure which came near to losing us Malta — at least its lessons were well learned and its mistakes were never repeated.' [1]

Air Cover from Malta

Once the convoys were in range of the fighter aircraft based on Malta, then the attacking enemy dive-bombers did not have it all their own way. The late 'Laddie' Lucas tells of one typical engagement in his book *Malta — The Thorn in Rommel's Side*:

'"OK fellers, I see them. Eighty-eights at two o'clock, flying south. Same level. About a dozen of them."

'The Ju88s were flying straight and level in quite tight boxes of some four aircraft in each. They hadn't seen us coming out of the darkening eastern sky. I gave the instructions. We would dive another 1,000 feet and, with all the speed we wanted, pull up underneath and attack from the quarter into astern position. Lint and Wattie would take the starboard box, and Jonesie and I the one to port. Then both pairs would have a go at the centre formation if we could. This would give the best chance of breaking up the attack. After that it would be each man for himself.

'Our assault came off to a T. The rear gunners never saw us as we attacked upwards from underneath, against the dark waters below. It wasn't until we had closed to 150 to 200 yards' range and the flashes from the four cannons in our Spitfire VCs and the strikes from them began to drive home that the German crews realised what was happening. Then there was mayhem, with the 88s breaking all over the place, not knowing how many Spitfires were attacking them. There might have been a couple of squadrons of us for all they knew.

'It was a splendid steal from which we extracted about as much as we could reasonably expect in the fading light. It was difficult to see the results, but Wattie and I reckoned we shared an 88 between us, Jonesie got another — a flamer — while Lint and I felt we had severely damaged an additional 88 apiece. But more important than the score, was the fact that the attack had been thrown into disarray. The Luftwaffe really had little idea what had hit them.'

Bringing in the Fighter Planes

Whilst strictly not convoy operations, the use of aircraft carriers to sail part of the way to Malta and then to fly reinforcing fighter aircraft on to the island was a continual and vital process, without which Malta could not have survived. As Appendix II to this chapter shows, this had begun in August 1940 and continued until October 1942, by which time over 700 aircraft had been flown in, the vast majority arriving safely, although a number sadly were lost en route. As the appendix shows, early on the morning of 2 August 1940 12 Hurricanes, each fitted with underwing long-range fuel tanks, were flown off the carrier HMS *Argus* from some 450 miles to the west of the island. They were accompanied by two Fleet Air Arm Skuas for navigational purposes. It was a long, exhausting flight and the numbers involved were not large; nevertheless these were the very first fighter aircraft reinforcements specifically designated for Malta and they all arrived safely.

Above: Light cruiser HMS *Penelope* given the nickname HMS 'Pepperpot' (later 'Porcupine') after being engaged for 12 days whilst in a dry dock in Malta and riddled with shrapnel from near misses. Eventually, with her holes plugged, she managed to sail to Gibraltar. *IWM — A 8602*

It was on 7 March 1942 that the first Spitfires were sent, from two aircraft carriers, *Eagle* and *Argus,* which between them they flew off 15 Spitfires which all arrived safely. George Beurling DSO, DFC, DFM and bar was one of the Spitfire pilots who made the same journey three months later in June 1942 and, as he later recalled:

'That night we were briefed by the wing commander, who told us we would take off in flights of eight and head east until we picked up the jut of the Tunisian coast. Then we would fly south by east for a while and swing east again across the last gap of water into Malta; about 745 miles in all, it turned out to be. Each Spit carried two cannon, loaded, but no machine guns, because room had to be found in the wings for kit. Radio silence would be maintained in flight for anything but "May Day". We could receive from the carriers and from Malta as we approached the island.'

The wing commander who was briefing them then gave some words of warning about keeping their eyes open for German aircraft, especially between Tunis and Pantelleria, where previous ferry flights had been ambushed. He also gave them some advice on the technique of carrier take-offs. Then it was off to bed with an early start the following morning.

By 6.00 the next morning they were all strapped in and ready to go. Beurling recalled:

'The Eagle was lying about fifty miles off the coast of Algeria, nose into wind and ready to turn in her tracks and run for Gib as soon as the Spitfires left her. The weather was cloudy but we were told to expect excellent visibility at Malta. By 6.05 the first eight were on their way, leaving the flight deck about two minutes apart. As each plane became airborne it climbed and

made left-hand circuits of the carrier until joined by its mates. At 2,000 feet they formed up over the ship, then legged for Malta, climbing hard. I went away with the third flight at 6.30. Malta came into view at 9.50 from 20,000 feet. My gang made Ta Qali, all right side up at 10.30. Right then the war began in earnest for Sergeant Beurling!' [2]

Unloading the Convoys

As explained in an earlier chapter, one of the important and unusual jobs carried out by some infantry battalions on Malta was the rapid unloading of merchant ships, a vital task that was made all the more difficult by the hazards of having to dodge enemy bombing and work with unstable cargoes in damaged ships' holds. However, their job was made easier by the fact that every merchant ship sailing in the Malta convoys invariably carried two masters, one to command and navigate, the other, who was known as the sea transport officer (STO), with responsibility for the military cargo, and able to deputise for the master should the need arise.

In National Newsletter No 35 of the George Cross Association 'Rags' Rickard tells about one of these STOs, a Captain Sam Jago of the SS *Brisbane Star,* who happened to come from his home town of Falmouth in Cornwall. He writes:

'To facilitate the speedy unloading of cargo, a detailed and clear cut plan had been worked out. Soldiers reported to the dockside where the ships were unloading and without previous experience

soon mastered the skills of keeping crates, boxes and sacks moving, to be loaded onto waiting lorries. Some were flimsy containers with hard biscuits, plain chocolate or fuel. Rigid containers later made coffins. Sometimes a sack of lentils would split during unloading and enough would be salvaged to produce a good lentil stew. But the effect on an empty stomach could be disastrous, more especially because the latrines on the campsites were at a distance!

'As soon as your truck was loaded you "put your foot down" to distance yourself from the vulnerable area of the dockyard. Bombing, as we all know was intense, so you did not hang around . . . Dispersal routes were colour marked and, dependent upon your load, you followed the appropriate signs:

eg Ammunition — Red Route
   Petrol (including paraffin, heating and cooking oil) —
   Yellow Route
   Food — Blue Route
   Miscellaneous Stores — Green Route
(Colour codings are possibly wrong as my memory is not at its best.)

'At the dockside, awaiting unloading, I mentioned to a seaman during conversation that I hailed from Falmouth in Cornwall. He said that I should go aboard and ask for Captain Sam Jago — the STO — as he also was a Falmouthian. This I did, to be received with open arms — he said that he understood we were a little short of necessities in Malta — was this an understatement?! "Come back this afternoon and I will have something ready for you." Later, returning on a motorcycle, I was given a liberal supply of soap, chocolate, Scotch whisky, together with many edible goodies. All safely stowed inside my battledress jacket, I resembled a "Michelin Man" advert. The next problem to be overcome was getting past the civilian Maltese Dockyard Police, but I am pleased to report that was successfully accomplished. Thank you Captain Sam Jago of the Brisbane Star!'

Notes
1. Ian Cameron: Red Duster, White Ensign.
2. George Beurling and Leslie Roberts: Malta Spitfire — The Diary of a Fighter Pilot.

Above: Running the gauntlet to Malta. Aircraft carriers were extremely valuable for convoy protection; however, they were very large targets for both enemy dive-bombers and submarines to attack. The Royal Navy lost both *Ark Royal* (torpedoed 13 November 1941) and *Eagle* (torpedoed 11 August 1942) to U-boat attacks. *IWM — A 11294*

Appendix I

Main Convoys Sent to Malta

Date	Codename	From	Result
August 1940	'Hats'	Alexandria	One merchant ship damaged, 40,000 tons of supplies delivered.
November 1940	'Collar'	Gibraltar	All arrived safely 29 November with 20,000 tons of supplies.
January 1941	'Excess'	Gibraltar	1 cruiser sunk; 1 carrier, 1 cruiser and 1 destroyer damaged, but all 14 merchant ships arrived safely on 10 January.
July 1941	'Substance'	Gibraltar	1 destroyer sunk; 1 cruiser, 1 destroyer and 2 merchant ships damaged, 11 arrived safely on 24 July with 65,000 tons of supplies.
September 1941	'Halberd'	Gibraltar	1 battleship damaged; 1 merchant ship sunk, 8 merchantmen arrived safely on 28 September with 85,000 tons of supplies.
March 1942	MW 10	Alexandria	3 destroyers, 1 submarine and 1 merchant ship sunk; 3 arrived with just 5,000 tons of supplies, but were sunk after arrival.
June 1942	'Harpoon'	Gibraltar	2 destroyers, 2 corvettes, an MTB, 4 merchant ships and one tanker sunk; 3 cruisers and 3 destroyers damaged; only 2 merchant ships arrived in Malta on 16 June with 25,000 tons of supplies.
June 1942	'Vigorous'	Alexandria	1 AA cruiser, 3 destroyers and 2 merchant ships sunk; 2 cruisers, 1 corvette and 2 merchant ships damaged. None arrived; convoy had to turn back.
August 1942	'Pedestal'	Gibraltar	1 carrier, 1 cruiser, 1 AA ship, 1 destroyer and 9 merchant ships sunk; 1 carrier, 2 cruisers and 3 merchant ships damaged; 5 merchant ships arrived safely on 12/13 August with 55,000 tons of supplies.
November 1942	'Stoneage'	Alexandria	1 cruiser damaged; 4 merchant ships arrived safely to relieve Malta on 20 November with 35,000 tons of supplies.
December 1942	'Portcullis'	Alexandria	All 5 merchant ships and their escorts arrived safely on 5 December.

NB: There were in addition a number of smaller convoys and solo supply runs by merchant ships. The actual total number of convoys was 24 plus 7 solos. There were also numerous runs by submarines and fast minelayers.

Source: *Malta: Blitzed but not Beaten* by Philip Vella.

Above: HMS *Ark Royal* sinking. This major loss was caused on 13 November 1941, when the carrier was torpedoed by *U81* and severely damaged. *Ark Royal* sank the following day; however, most of the ship's company were rescued. *IWM — A 6332*

Appendix II

Aircraft Flown to Malta from Aircraft Carriers 1940–2

During the siege the RN and RAF made heroic efforts to get aircraft, especially fighters, to Malta. Firstly, these were mainly Hawker Hurricanes in 1940-1, then Supermarine Spitfires in 1942. Space does not allow me to deal with this part of the story in the detail it so richly deserves but I would recommend to the reader who wants more information two brilliant and highly detailed books by Christopher Shores, Brian Cull and Nicola Malizia, published by Grub Street (details are listed in the Bibliography). This appendix gives just the bare facts. Please note:

a) Numbers shown — The numbers of aircraft shown as being transported by aircraft carrier to Gibraltar and then flown on to Malta are just those which Malta needed to fight its battles. These aircraft were invariably escorted either by Fleet Air Arm aircraft (eg Skuas or Fulmars), RAF bombers (eg Blenheims) or maritime patrol aircraft (Hudsons) which then eventually returned to Gibraltar and are not always specified as having actually landed at Malta. In other cases experienced pilots were transported to Gibraltar from Malta and then flew new aircraft back, at the same time acting as guides for the others.

b) Numbers lost — As can be seen, not all aircraft transported were then flown successfully to Malta. Some crashed on take-off from the carrier, others were lost en route for a variety of reasons and some crashed on landing at Malta. It is, therefore, difficult to tie down all the loose ends.

Operation	Date to Malta	Carrier	Number and Type of Aircraft (+ Guides Where Known)	Number Arrived
'Hurry'	2 August 1940	Argus	12 Hurricanes (+ 2 Skuas)	12
'White'	17 November	Argus	12 Hurricanes (+ 2 Skuas)	4
'Winch'	3 April 1941	Ark Royal	12 Hurricanes (+ 2 Skuas)	12
'Dunlop'	27 April	Ark Royal	24 Hurricanes (+ 3 Fulmars)	23
'Splice'	21 May	Ark Royal and Furious	48 Hurricanes (+ 5 Fulmars)	46
'Rocket'	6 June	Ark Royal and Furious	44 Hurricanes (+ 9 Blenheims)	43
'Tracer'	14 June	Ark Royal and Furious	48 Hurricanes (+ 4 Hudsons)	45
'Railway I'	27 June	Ark Royal	22 Hurricanes	21
'Railway II'	30 June	Ark Royal and Furious	42 Hurricanes (+ 6 Blenheims)	34
'Substance'	24 July	Ark Royal	7 Swordfish	7
'Status I'	9 September	Ark Royal	14 Hurricanes (+ 2 Blenheims)	14
'Status II'	13 September	Ark Royal and Furious	46 Hurricanes (+ 2 Blenheims)	45
'Callboy'	18 October	Ark Royal	11 Albacores, 2 Swordfish	12
'Perpetual'	12 November	Argus and Ark Royal	37 Hurricanes (+ 4 Blenheims)	34
'Exile'	7 March 1942	Eagle and Argus	15 Spitfires (+ 4 Blenheims)	15
'Picket I'	21 March	Eagle	9 Spitfires (no escort designated*)	9
'Picket II'	29 March	Eagle	7 Spitfires (no escort designated*)	7
'Calendar'	20 April	USS Wasp	47 Spitfires (no escort designated*)	46
'Bowery'	9 May	Wasp and Eagle	64 Spitfires (no escort designated*)	60
'LB'	19 May	Argus and Eagle	17 Spitfires (no escort designated*)	17
'Style'	3 June	Eagle	31 Spitfires (no escort designated*)	27
'Salient'	9 June	Eagle	32 Spitfires (no escort designated*)	32
'Pinpoint'	15 July	Eagle	32 Spitfires (no escort designated*)	31
'Insect'	21 July	Eagle	30 Spitfires (no escort designated*)	28
'Bellows'	11 August	Furious	38 Spitfires (no escort designated*)	37
'Baritone'	17 August	Furious	32 Spitfires (no escort designated*)	29
'Train'	29 October	Furious	32 Spitfires (no escort designated*)	29
Total	765 aircraft ferried	720 delivered		

Of the 46 aircraft which did not arrive, 12 returned with the carriers, but 34 were lost.

Source: *Malta: Blitzed but not Beaten*, by Philip Vella.

* Records do not always specify if there were escorts, especially for the Spitfire deliveries when experienced pilots from Malta appear to have been transported to Gibraltar to fly new aircraft back and act as guides.

Chapter 11

The Civilian Population

Through a Young Girl's Eyes

Mrs Daphne Barnes was the daughter of the late Major Edward Fowler, Royal Engineers, who was the Deputy CRE (Commander, Royal Engineers) on Malta. She was only nine years old when the siege began, living on the seafront near Sliema. When the first bombs began to fall the family moved inland to a safer area at Mtarfa. There were very few Army schools left standing so they had to use their Army quarters instead, as she later recalled in *Malta Remembered* No 2:

'My classroom consisted of three desks in a small bedroom, outside the bathroom. The other classes were similar. Every time the siren sounded we would troop down to the shelter which was dug deep in the rock. We used blackboards and chalk to pass the time by having spelling games with such words as: "awkward, necessary and queue" until we got them right, and it stood us in good stead for our future lives. Our family shelter was very good and held a family of seven including a baby born in the middle of an air raid in October 1940. The beds were hospital stretchers resting on pipes which were drilled into the rock walls. We brought bundles of bedding up every morning because it was so damp, then took them down again at night — we had to do this for two years. The shelter was 20 steps down deep into the rock and what was dug out was put on top and cemented over for extra protection. My father had put up a lot of fairy lights to keep the children happy. The shelter would have stood anything but a direct hit. Mtarfa was on a high hill and during the air raids we could look down to where the bombs were falling and see where the smoke was, which was mainly in the dock area, though the whole island received its share.

'As the war went on there was very little food in the shops, eggs cost half a crown each, bananas were only for children under five with a green ration book. It got so bad that the food was sent to a "Victory Kitchen", where it was cooked and we were rationed to one meal a day. I used to queue up to collect our seven portions in a saucepan. The menu consisted of soup with a few vegetables floating on top called: "Ministra". Another day we had an awful sweet called "Helwa", which was grey in colour — God alone knows what it was! Another day it was macaroni cooked in salt, no flavouring or anything with it. Our family had a bit more than the civilians as our father had army rations extra.'

Below: Policemen clear away debris in Kingsway, Valletta, opposite the Royal Opera House. *NWMA Malta — 6275*

Right:
The women of Malta sift through the rubble of their houses in Floriana, looking for items to salvage. *IWM — GM 904*

Left:
'Business as Usual!' Despite the bomb damage all around, this emergency shop in Floriana still displays goods for sale. *NWMA Malta — 2108*

Right:
'We are not amused!' Once this statue of Queen Victoria stood in a beautiful square beside the Royal Library, Valletta; now the buildings around it lie in ruins, but the link to the British Empire remains as strong as ever. *IWM — GM 554*

An Officer's Wife

We met Mrs Marjoribanks-Egerton, the wife of a major in the Royal Irish Fusiliers in an earlier chapter. She kept a detailed diary throughout the siege. She too had to spend nights down in a shelter, which she commented was 'a very damp place'. On 13 July 1940 her entry tells of the public interest that had been aroused by a 'miracle' at the Tal Figura Church on the Pawla Zabbar road near Tarxien:

'It seems that after the raid on the 11th, the statue of "Ecce Homo" [1] was found headless and the head was resting in an aperture made by a bomb splinter in the wall of the church. The head crowned with thorns was gazing out over the harbour as though taking it under Divine Protection. As may well be imagined this has been taken as a miracle by the devout and there has been a pilgrimage made.'

The raids continued, getting worse and worse as the days progressed. The entries for the three days 29 April to 1 May 1941 give a graphic impression of what it was like:

'April 29. Woken from a deep sleep at 1.30am by the alarm. Another Blitz staged. Not as severe as that at 8.55 yesterday but quite noisy enough. The usual flares and bombs thrown about. Alarms at 7.50am and 10.55am No action. Alarm at 6.45pm and a sharp raid took off. Bombs dropped in the Grand Harbour. One bomber broke in half and the crew baled out. Three of them fell near here and were picked up by troops from Madeliena Tower. Philip [her husband] was in for this raid and told me that one of our posts was hit last night at Naxxar, one killed and two seriously injured. He had to clear up and I could

see that he was shocked but of course wouldn't own to it. Alarm at 9pm and once more a Blitz. This is the biggest we have yet had and went on until 00.10am Two very large fires were burning in the High Street of Valletta which turned the sky a lurid red and wreaths of smoke all over the scene. It looked like some picture from the 'Inferno'. The fires burnt for about an hour before diminishing. Four land mines fell on Valletta and the explosion out here (seven miles away) was terrific. It was a most awe-inspiring sight and at times even the searchlights were hidden by the smoke from the fires. Valletta has certainly taken a good knock.

April 30. Alarm at 1.15am and another fierce attack was on us, flares, bombs kept the scene lively and the dull thuds of the latter were pretty regular. The raid lasted until 2.20am and Valletta was the main target. Alarms at 8am and 8.20am On the last raid only one plane was over and the barrage was lively. It was soon on its way out to sea after its peppering. Jean K rang to say that Valletta had caught a good dose last night. A number of shops on the Strada Reale were gutted — Muscats, two chemists, two drapers, part of the Law Courts. The Union Club and two cinemas were damaged. Amazing escape from harm was recorded from those who had been in the Club, most of the injuries were slight and were due to glass. Alarms at 11am and 11.45am, a good deal of noise in the last raid, about six bombers dropped stuff on Valletta and after a sharp spot of fire they passed out to go home. Alarm at 8.45pm and once more we were in the middle of a Blitz. Flares dropped in great numbers and lighted

Valletta which was again the target. One or two fell near here but soon went out. Clouds of smoke poured out close to the Palace and it seemed that it must be on fire. Bombs of a heavy type were used and also mines. To my mind these mines look most sinister, being suspended from green silk parachutes and they drift slowly as they come down and it is difficult to say exactly where they will land. When they do come down the whole area is blasted. I saw three of these things go down in Valletta and as usual the explosions rocked our house. At times the enemy planes swooped so low by our house that I could swear to feeling the rush of air as they passed. It may be remarked that during the whole raid the barrage was so intense and what with the whine of shells, the crash of bombs etc one hadn't time to be anything but thrilled. Alarms for the month were 88.

May 1. Alarm at 7.40 for an hour but no action. Heavy smoke still coming from Valletta after last night's raid. Jean rang up to say that they were safe though they had a direct hit on their shelter below Port Reale. The St James was hit and caught fire and the guests were in the cellar underneath but were all uninjured. From what she said Valletta must be in a pretty good mess. I went to Valletta later in the morning and found nearly all Strada Reale roped off and a number of shops blasted. Sliema had a good bit too and the corner of the street by the Post Office was down. A mine was caught up in a tree in Lady Bernard's garden and by the providence of heaven hadn't gone off. These mines are nine feet high and about four feet round. I went to see the tailor and he had an amazing story to tell of his escapes last night whilst on Home Guard duty. Alarm at 11.30am No action. Alarm at 4.55pm and fourteen bombs were dropped around a coastal vessel lying in the Grand Harbour. It was a near thing that it was not hit. The AA fire was brisk. After a Hurricane had buzzed about for a time the enemy made off. Alarms at 4pm, 7.35pm, and 8.25pm During my visit to Valletta this morning I went to the Great Britain and saw Jean, also met a Naval man who had just come from the Grand Harbour where a destroyer had been blown up by a mine with the loss of 100 lives. Only 34 survivors had managed to swim ashore, plastered with oil. I made a short tour of the wrecked part of Valletta and saw how the Cathedral of St John had suffered. The vast West Doors were torn off and all the glass from the windows was lying in the road. I hear that a valuable painting of the Crucifixion was shattered. The Bell Tower on the left side of the west door was peppered with shrapnel. Vandalism has come to Malta. Philip in for leave.'

A year later and things had not changed much, except that in this raid they were themselves the target.

'April 25. Alarm went soon after 6.30am and at 8.30am we got a raid on this camp and St George's. Took us all by surprise and we were not out of the house. The bombs screamed down and I got Phillippa under the stairs and then the door glass blew in on top of me and I was bruised. More bombs fell and the blast took my breath away. Philip and Roulston (our batman) were out in the garden at the time and they came in and we all went to the slit trenches somewhat shaken. When we got back to the house after the All Clear went we found it in an awful mess, glass and plaster everywhere. Incendiary bombs were dropped near us and set the grass alight, several didn't go off. A bomb fell about 30 yards from our trench. After breakfast I went into Valletta feeling very done in, got all the shopping done and came back with Mac in her car. Alarm at 12.45pm and another heavy attack was made on the Camp. We went into the trench and

went through a trying time, the bombs never seemed to stop coming down and the planes roared down to drop them, blast swept in and the whole place rocked. We were having our second round of bombing at close quarters and though alarmed we were not frightened. We looked out to see what was going on and found the whole area wrapped in a heavy cloud of dust. Philip arrived soon after having come down from Naxxar on hearing that this place had been attacked again. The house is in a dreadful mess but still standing. Alarms at 2.15pm and 3.15pm, but no action. Philip in soon after the alarm went at 5.45pm then we were in the heaviest attack of the day. We saw large plots approaching and awaited the worst in our trench and before long we got it good and hearty. Screaming of the bombs filled the air, roaring of the planes and the barrage, rocking the shelter. Showers of stones and debris swept over the trench nearly choking us. We gave up counting the bombs and just hoped for the best, the blast made me feel so sick. Phillippa was amazingly good and no tears. I lay over her at times to keep any blast off. Philip unperturbed and keeping us all in good heart. At one moment it all went dark and I thought the house had gone and was falling on us, but it was an immense dust cloud from over the end of the fields where two large bombs had fallen. We looked out when the worst had passed and found that the house was still there, a great relief. We climbed out leaving Phillippa in and saw that bombs of a large type had fallen by the mess, in front of the quarters up by the clock tower. We set off to the quarters thinking that people might be in trenches outside, one was blocked, the other badly damaged. We called and got no answer so I ran over to the main shelter and after enquiries found that they were all there and that no one was in the trenches. Back to Philip with the news and then he went off to see how all our families were. I went back to the house after the All Clear and found everything in the most awful mess again. Glass all over the place and inches of dust. Algy and Roland came along to see how we were. Damage to the two camps (St Andrew's and St George) was very great. The 39th Hospital was wrecked, most of the barrack blocks, Nos 2 and 3 Officers' Quarters shattered, the RC church wrecked, the Clock Tower clock gone, dining hall and half the NAAFI, all the MT Sheds and bomb craters everywhere. No doubt at all that this attack was very deliberate and carried out at low level. Over 300 bombs dropped. We went to bed completely exhausted.'

The following day, the intrepid Mrs Marjoribanks-Egerton and her husband made a tour to find out how all the families were, finding them in good form and amazingly cheerful despite many of them having lost everything. There were more raids that day and her entry closes with good news that, despite there having been over 7,000 people in both camps, the casualty figure had been only 18. Her diary continues right up until 10 August 1942, when the family left to go to Egypt, after four years and seven months. Even on that last day there was an alarm: 'a brisk action' is how she described it, with two Bf109s shot down. Despite all the hardships they had been through, she found it a sad moment and longed to stay. How could Hitler and his ilk have ever thought they could win when they were up against such formidable ladies?

The 'Voice of Malta'

Another intrepid lady was the Honourable Miss Mabel Strickland, daughter of Lord Strickland,[2] who had been Malta's prewar Prime Minister, and whom Mussolini's agents had attempted to assassinate in 1930. During the war she was the managing director of Malta Newspapers and editor of the Times of Malta. Born in Malta and

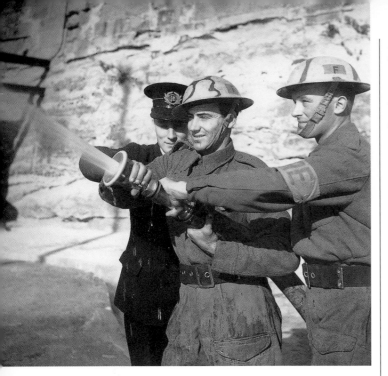

Above: Malta's fire defences. Superintendent T. B. Goodman of the London Fire Brigade, who was sent to Malta as an advisor, helps two soldier firemen with a spray nozzle. *IWM — GM 244*

resident throughout the siege, she gave an interview to BBC commentator Macdonald Hastings that was recorded for the IWM Sound Archive (Accession No 1173) in which she gives a blow-by-blow account of those tumultuous days. Hastings gave her the accolade of being 'a great Englishwoman' — and undoubtedly she was.

'In Malta,' she said when explaining how those who had been 'bombed out' of Valletta and the other towns, sought refuge with their relatives in the country, 'the family is always the unit and these grew to almost uncomfortable proportions — thirty or forty or more as they all crowded together. Eventually every town and village on the island had its bomb scars.' She then explained how over 13 miles of shelters had been cut out of the rock by hand and how most people slept in the shelters, but tried to carry on as normal during the day 'running like rabbits for their holes when the bombers appeared!'

The period from the end of 1941 through the spring of 1942 was, she considered, the worst one, what she called 'total war'. She explained that at that time all the farmland that adjoined the gun sites and aerodromes was soon carpeted with large craters and bombs were ploughing up the food supplies, 'not that Malta could hope to feed all its people anyway, for more than a few days, with some 2,200 people to the square mile'.

She talks in stirring terms of the AA artillery crews — British and Maltese — as all being heroes. In March/April they fired almost non-stop for 372 hours (the equivalent of 15 days' continuous firing). 'Soon ammunition began to get short and worry gripped the civilians, especially as the very brave fighter defence had been reduced to just seven planes. Whilst they flew in the skies above, the soldiers mended the craters, serviced the aircraft, unloaded the ships and all the rest, even though they were under continual air attack.'

She proudly goes on to say that, despite everything, she and her company went on publishing their newspapers seven days a week without a break, never missing an issue. As few civilian families had

radio sets, the newspapers provided the only link they had with the outside world. The papers were, in addition to the *Times of Malta*, *The Sunday Times of Malta* and *Il Berqa*. She also makes the point that tremendous credit should go to the newspaper boys who then had to make the deliveries — it would have been pointless printing the papers had they been unable to distribute them. And they were never short of news: 'We had the front line at the front door and on the front page!' is how she explains it. Surprisingly the printing machines were all above ground, being too big to move. However, they were grouped around a deep well-shaped shelter for staff protection.

Food conditions were especially grim and cruel in 1942. With 300,000-plus mouths to feed, the Governor, Lord Gort, soon made it clear that they were on what he called 'siege rations'. Miss Strickland said they were working towards what she called the 'target date', which was the name given to the day when the bread, the fuel, the ammunition and all the rest, would run out. With the convoys being unable to reach the island, Malta had to live on its own resources, but luckily by then it was coming up to the warm days of summer. Gort had made the farmers realise that this was the time to share and not to hoard. Everyone had to receive their fair share and if one person over-ate, then someone else went hungry. Wheat came straight from fields into the flour mill, whilst the rabbits, the poultry and seven out of every 10 Maltese goats had to be killed to feed the starving people. Even though Malta had once exported potatoes, now the time was foreseeable when they would not be able to plant the seed potatoes as these had to come from cooler lands. Thus she considered the early tomato crop to be a real godsend. August was also the month when the first vital convoy ('Pedestal') got through, but it was many months after that date — well into 1943 — before there was sufficient food for everyone.

A by-product of the lack of food was a lassitude that caused a dropping of standards, especially towards dirt and such related problems as scabies and other skin complaints, that were prevalent because of the continual filthy surroundings in the heavily bombed buildings. The newspaper offices, for example, were overrun with fleas.

It was similarly a battle of endurance for the troops who were all on half rations — with sleep parades being ordered to conserve energy. Severe penalties were imposed for stealing food — there was a two-year prison sentence for anyone caught stealing a small tin of corned beef. When the siege was lifted Miss Strickland said that Lord Gort quoted the words of General Monck about suffering: 'There is as much honour to be gained by suffering want patiently, as by fighting valiantly; and as great an achievement affected by the one as by the other.'

A Housewife Remembers

Another taped interview held by the IWM (Accession No 1165), this time anonymous, contains the reminiscences of a teacher who lived with her husband in Malta over a period of some four years, two and a half of which were during wartime, so she had vivid memories of Malta and its friendly people both in peace and war. She was very green when the air raids began and says that she couldn't at first tell the difference between guns firing and bombs landing. She and other women who worked in the dockyard area (she taught at the RN Dockyard School) thought, quite wrongly, that they were safe from harm when they sheltered in an old boathouse at the docks, but soon realised that they were only safe when under some 60 feet of solid rock! She recalled that, initially, many of the civil population left the coastal towns and sought refuge inland, so that the centres of the towns were deserted apart from swarms of hungry cats. However, once they all got used to the ineffectual Italian air raids, they mostly came home. However, this wasn't the case with the German bombing which was far more accurate and persistent:

'They kept up a steady time-table of raids at dawn, midday and dusk, plus extras, so work and meals had to be fitted around them. We used to have to get up at dawn and have an early breakfast before the bombing began — it was always easier to cope with it after having had something to eat!'

However, it was clear that when the frequency of raids was stepped up, people had to spend more and more time underground:

'The deep shelters were divided into family cubicles and during an air raid a family would sit in its cubicle whilst father chipped away at the rock, making a small alcove. Once this had been cut, then the family would move in and a small shrine [would be] put into a niche in the wall. Father would then go on chipping, whilst the family got on with their chores — mother peeling

vegetables or doing some mending. When a reasonably sized room had been hollowed out then beds and other items of furniture would be brought in. In some cases they became almost permanent dwellings, the size depending upon the nature of the rock and the numbers to be accommodated.'

The children, of course, found the raids very exciting and soon could recognise each of the different types of aircraft. However, the raid she remembers most vividly was one against a non-military evacuation camp that was attacked by some 50 dive-bombers. She and her husband were caught in the raid and 'lay face down in a small trench, our faces covered against being suffocated by the dust'. A little dog suddenly leapt in on top of them, then crawled to one end of the trench almost mad with fright. She remembers that his fur was standing stiffly on end. Some 150 bombs were dropped and they were very lucky to get out alive.

'Sunday, 10 May 1942, was a "Red Letter Day" for us and our spirits soared. The Spitfires had arrived and the Jerries didn't know! Crowds of Ju87s and 88s attacked in swarms of over 50 each, but the Spitfires met them head on. Despite the falling shrapnel, cheering crowds watched the air battles from the seafront, during which 36 enemy planes were shot down in under an hour. This was the last of their big raids.'

Below: Maltese policemen assisted with the control of traffic leaving the dock area, the improvised signing pointing out the routes to the various dumps in the country where supplies were hidden. *IWM — GM 1119*

She also mentions the scarcity of food and lack of fuel for cooking and heating. This led to the establishing of the Victory Kitchens used by all for obtaining one cooked meal a day, served either at noon or 5.00pm She recalled seeing 'the orderly queue of saucepans and pots which no one disputed', but also remembers receiving such minute portions as three small sausages and 15 peas between three of them, plus a tiny portion of bread. Eggs she recalls, when available, were 15 shillings a dozen and the news of anyone leaving Malta drew crowds of people, to see if they had anything to sell — foodstuffs or clothes perhaps, and shops dealt largely in second-hand clothes. She once bought a rabbit for 17 shillings and sixpence, but then had a guilty conscience because it was probably the shopkeeper's children's pet.

> *'Hot water was also in short supply. One could achieve warm water by putting a tin bath on the roof of the house and letting the sun get to work. However, for boiling water one had to search for wood from bombed houses, but even this became scarce and only the Victory Kitchens were allowed to use it in the end.*
>
> *'For lighting, we used a bootlace or a piece of string, in a potted meat jar containing a small amount of paraffin — just enough to see our way around the room.'*

As mentioned already, she taught at the RN Dockyard School and was amazed at her pupils' determination to get to school no matter what. One boy regularly took between one and one and a half hours to get there in the morning, but never missed a day. They had great difficulty in obtaining the necessary papers to take the Oxford School Certificate, but they managed it in the end and all the students passed.

When it eventually became time for them to go they found it very hard parting from all their Maltese friends and it was difficult to say goodbye. And when they reached Cairo, they told the waiter in the hotel that he didn't need to ask them what they wanted to eat — they would have 'everything on the menu' — and they did so for the next few days!

Notes

1. 'Ecce Homo' — 'Behold the Man' — the words of Pontius Pilate to the accusers of Jesus which denote a picture or sculpture of Christ crowned with thorns.
2. Baron Gerald Strickland KCMG (1861–1940) was born in Malta and succeeded as sixth Count della Catena in 1875. Formed Anglo-Maltese Party and was Prime Minister and Minister of Justice of Maltese coalition government (1927–30), then leader of elected members, Council of Government (1939–40). Unceasingly opposed Italian influence on Malta. Founder of the *Times of Malta* and other newspapers.

Below: After patiently waiting in the queue at a Victory Kitchen, this Maltese family received their daily soup ration. *IWM — GM 2866*

Top left: Patiently chipping away, a Maltese man digs out a shelter for his family from the solid rock that formed the foundation of his island home. *IWM — GM 178*

Left: Some of the civilian shelters were very large indeed, like this one where women and children sleep on wooden bunk beds made out of planking. *IWM — GM 191*

Above: At a Victory Kitchen. Christina Ratcliffe was one of the girls who worked in the Fighter Control Operations Room (and also in the chorus line — see the later photograph on page 124). On 6 October 1942 a War Office cameraman had the pleasant task of filming her during a 24-hour leave period. *IWM — GM 1657*

Above: Examples of paper currency issued by the Government of Malta during wartime. *RE Library*

Right: Bombed Maltese church. Many holy buildings were destroyed during the continual air raids. Here the Rev Papas manages to rescue a much-treasured icon of the Blessed Virgin from the rubble of the Church of Our Lady of Damascus, built in 1576 and completely destroyed on 13 April 1942. *IWM — GM 503*

Above: The indomitable Mabel Strickland, owner and editor-in-chief of the *Times of Malta*, chats to Brigadier Marshal at the opening of Malta's new aerodrome on 10 November 1942.
IWM — GM 1822

Left: This overturned Austin K2 ambulance was caught up in an air raid whilst going along Old Bakery Street, Valletta.
NWMA Malta — 1822

Opposite bottom: Doing their bit for the war effort. Despite spending long hours working underground in the Fighter Control Operations Room, safely guiding the defending pilots, these girls then practise their dance routines on the rooftops. Can you spot Christina?
IWM — GM 2576

Chapter 12

'Pedestal' – The All-Important Convoy

The End of the Beginning — 'Here's to 1942!'

On New Year's Day 1942 Prime Minister Winston Churchill was travelling by train between Ottawa and Washington, on his way to confer with President Roosevelt. He called all his staff, and the newspaper correspondents who were accompanying him, into the dining-car of the train and raising his glass to everyone he said: 'Here's to 1942, here's to a year of toil — a year of struggle and peril, and a long step forward towards victory. May we all come through safe and with honour.' As he rightly surmised, 1942 would prove to be probably the most important year of the war for the Allies, as it would see a major shift in fortunes between the two sides. No longer would the Axis achieve victory after victory on all fronts, especially in the Middle East. By the autumn the Allies would have victory in North Africa, Churchill calling it 'a remarkable and definite victory' in his famous 'end of the beginning' speech of 10 November 1942. However, between those two dates, there would have to be a lot of 'hard pounding', nowhere more so than in the Central Mediterranean and in particular, around the tiny island of Malta.

Malta was still, as the Italians put it, 'the rock on which our hopes in the Mediterranean foundered', but it was running short of everything it needed to maintain a constant and real threat to the Axis supply routes to North Africa. It was essential that the very staff of life — the food supplies and the domestic fuel, got through to succour the civilian and military defenders of the island, as well as all the military supplies they needed to go on doing their job properly. We have already talked about the Malta convoys in general; now it is time to deal with the convoy that was unquestionably the last-ditch attempt to relieve the island. It had to succeed or Malta was doomed. It had three names: Operation 'Pedestal', the Santa Marija convoy, and Convoy WS 5.21, but probably the first of the three is the most well known. In Malta, however, it is probably best known as 'Il Convoy ta Santa Marija', as its arrival coincided with the Feast of the Assumption on 15 August. It would consist of 14 merchantmen and be protected by one of the largest escort forces ever provided by the Royal Navy (some 59 warships), including two battleships and three aircraft carriers, and also by considerable numbers of Royal Air Force aircraft. This was a formidable force without a doubt; however, so was the opposition ranged against it, which included both surface vessels and submarines, together with massive numbers of shore-based aircraft operating from airfields on Sicily and Sardinia. The most vulnerable part of the journey was, therefore, the final section of some 400 miles which at an average 13 knots (always provided that the merchant ships could make that speed) would take the convoy some 30 hours.

Thanks to the incredible bravery of all those concerned — both on board the merchant ships and those who protected them by sea and air — the convoy got through, despite suffering terrible losses.

Almost two-thirds of the merchant ships were sunk along with many of the escort vessels. Although it still had some months to run, the siege of Malta was, to all intents and purposes, lifted when the five remaining battered merchantmen limped into Valletta harbour, including the barely afloat tanker, the SS *Ohio*. Here are some of the reminiscences of those who were on that convoy, beginning with a report made by an American sailor, Ensign Gerhart S. Suppiger, Jnr, who was the commander of the US Navy armed guard on the SS *Santa Elisa*, which was a US Army transport ship, owned by the Grace Line and registered at Wilmington, Delaware. The master of the vessel was initially a Captain V. Cernesco, who was replaced due to health problems before the journey began by newly promoted Captain T. R. Thomson.

The armed guard comprised an officer, a coxswain, a seaman signaller and seven USN/USNR ratings; the weapons they initially had to man were four 20mm Oerlikon AA guns mounted midships, two .30 calibre Browning machine guns and one 4in low-angle gun. Suppiger was clearly well on top of his job and goes on to list various faults and missing items of kit (eg none of the gun crew had life-jackets), but he managed to ensure that all these problems and deficiencies were rectified before sailing. The ship was then loaded with a cargo of US Army equipment, including tanks, scout cars, trucks, jeeps and food supplies, leaving Halifax, Nova Scotia, on 24 May 1942, and heading out into the Atlantic in a convoy to Belfast, where they arrived safely on 5 June. Whilst in Belfast, the navy gun crew, plus six of the ship's crew attended a gunnery course. They would then move over to Newport, Monmouthshire, where they remained for nearly seven weeks, during which time they unloaded and loaded cargo and changed their berth six times! Eventually they were told that the ship had been allocated to a United Nations shipping pool and that they would be loaded with a cargo of British Army stores. Also, whilst at Newport, they were given additional armament: a Bofors 40mm AA gun (installed on a forward gun position with which the ship was equipped); two 20mm Oerlikons (also installed on the forward gun position); two .30 calibre Marlin machine guns (mounted on the forward resister house); PAC projectors (installed on the top of the bridge — whether these were similar to the fearsome Harvey Rocket Projectiles which G. R. Myers talks about in Chapter 10 I know not!); 300lb depth charges and fittings, etc. In addition they were joined by a sergeant, a bombardier and eight British Gunners.

After a number of minor moves, they eventually sailed from Greenock to join a convoy of 12 cargo ships, two tankers, plus a massive protection force which Suppiger lists as being the battleships *Rodney* and *Nelson*, the aircraft carriers *Argus*, *Eagle*, *Furious*,[1] *Indomitable* and *Victorious*, accompanied by eight cruisers, 20 to 30 destroyers and a screen of British submarines. They then set off around the northern coast of Ireland, out into the Atlantic for some 300 miles before turning southwards, reaching the Strait of

Above: 'Pedestal'. The convoy enters the Mediterranean, with the aircraft carriers *Eagle*, *Victorious* and *Indomitable* providing a powerful force of 72 Fleet Air Arm fighter planes, from eight interceptor squadrons, embarked on the three carriers. They were initially mainly equipped with the Fairey Fulmar two-seater fighter/reconnaissance aircraft. *NWMA Malta — 1790*

Above: However, a crash programme of replacement was put into effect before departure, whereby most squadrons had their Fulmars replaced by Sea Hurricanes, seen here on *Victorious*, behind which are *Indomitable* and then *Eagle*, with their escorting cruisers. *NWMA Malta — 1724*

Gibraltar on 10 August and entering the Mediterranean. Until then the journey had been trouble free, but they would not be left alone much longer. To quote from Suppiger's account:

At 0900 [11 August] we had our first aircraft attack consisting of five Ju88s and at 0930 an attack by seven Ju88s. (The statistics which I quote hereafter were taken from the official log of HMS Penn, a British destroyer which was part of the escort fleet and rescued me after my ship was sunk.) At this time one cargo ship was sunk by bombs. At 1030, HMS Eagle was hit by three torpedoes. She sank in seven minutes and I learned later that 900 members of her crew were rescued. A few of her planes were in the air at the time, but most of them were on the flight deck at the time and slid into the sea when the ship listed before going down. We remained at action stations for two hours but there were no more attacks. I later learned that several Axis submarines had been lying in wait for the convoy. A German submarine that helped to sink the Eagle was sunk by depth charges and an Italian submarine was rammed and sunk by a British destroyer. Stuka dive-bombers appeared for the first time. There were also some Ju88s in the air, that dropped about twenty parachutes with aerial mines attached but no ships hit these mines. During this evening attack, one destroyer was hit and damaged by bombs and two more merchant ships were sunk by dive-bombers. With this last attack at nightfall there was a tremendous display of tracers from the guns of all ships.'

Ensign Suppiger also noticed that their ship seemed to be being singled out for special attention and decided that they were aiming at the black and white checkerboard deck of an RAF crash boat they were carrying as deck cargo. At his suggestion this was covered and thereafter their ship was not singled out for special attention.

'12 August. We had several aircraft attacks throughout the day and did not leave action stations. Stuka dive-bombers, Ju88s, Heinkels and Italian torpedo-carrying planes all took part in these engagements. At 1145 four Ju88s flew across our bow from port to starboard. Our Bofors commenced firing and hit one plane at about 1500 yards range; this aircraft was hit in the tail and started smoking. A minute later it crashed into the sea about five miles off our starboard quarter. At 1600 HMS Victorious was hit on her flight deck by three bombs. Fire broke out on board, enveloping the ship in smoke and flame. Most of the escort vessels stood by her while the merchant ships, two cruisers and a few destroyers proceeded on towards Malta. We learned later that this battle fleet had received word that the Italian fleet had left their bases in Italy to intercept the British fleet. Thus all the escort vessels except those that had gone on with the merchant ships had turned towards Gibraltar to meet the Italian fleet. At this time many people on board expressed sorrow that the large escort vessels had left us because it was evident that most of the protection we had left to us was from fighter planes based on carriers. Our hopes rose, however, when we heard that Spitfires from Malta were flying out to intercept the Axis bombers.

After the main body of the escort vessels had left, we were engaged again by enemy bombers and also attacked again by submarines. At this time HMS Manchester, a British cruiser, was hit and sunk by torpedo. This day we also saw the first appearance of Italian torpedo-carrying planes. They approached the ships from a distance, coming in at nightfall very low off the water. During one attack I saw a dozen fly in from the port side skimming the water, but a barrage caused them to turn off. I only saw one manage to drop its torpedo. This was at a cruiser off our port bow

and missed apparently because he dropped it out of range. During one torpedo plane attack this evening a plane, which had turned off before dropping its torpedo but came close to our ship, was fired upon by W. Hodgkiss, AB. He was stationed at a .30 calibre Browning machine gun on the port side aft. He hit the plane in the tail and it was smoking as it passed. At approximately 2000 one more freighter was sunk by dive-bombers and a stick of bombs straddled our ship drenching many people on board with water. At 2100 came the most concentrated attack of all. Three more merchant ships were sunk by bombs. One ship astern of us was hit and burst into flames. We thought this to be the other US ship, the Almeria Lykes. On the other two which were sunk there were only five survivors. During this attack a Ju88 dropped a stick of bombs on us, again straddling the ship. We shot down another enemy plane during this attack. Second Mate Fred Larson stationed at a 20mm Oerlikon gun amidships shot down a plane at about 1,000 yards range. It crashed into the sea on our starboard beam about a ship's length off.

'During this big engagement all the merchant ships and escort vessels spread out. By then nightfall had come. Suddenly a large merchant ship came along our starboard side and its captain shouted to us: 'Steer course 120 degrees'. This ship was proceeding about five knots faster than we, and then unexpectedly, for some unexplainable reason, cut across our bow. We had to give 'Hard Left Rudder' and 'Full Speed Astern' to avoid hitting her. Ten minutes later another ship cut across our port bow and we again narrowly missed a collision. On both occasions all gun crew ran aft and we missed these ships by less than twenty feet.

'We were proceeding on a course of about 090 and were abeam of Cape Bon (Tunisia) about five miles to the south of us. A large beacon on Cape Bon was flashing on us revealing our ship in the sea. Also there was a ship which had been torpedoed flaming astern of us lighting us up. At this time we could also see white flashes on the other side of Cape Bon, which we took to be shore batteries firing on ships in the convoy ahead. Earlier that evening we received a message to be on the look out for Italian 'E' Boats stationed around Cape Bon and waiting for the convoy to pass. At that time I went down to the chart room to look at our position. Soon thereafter Cpt Thomson and Lt Comdr Baines entered the chart room. They decided to head west out into the open sea towards Pantelleria, instead of around Cape Bon and south as was our designated course. This would take us out of range of 'E' boats and coastal batteries, but would take us into what we knew to be a minefield near Pantelleria. We decided to risk the minefield instead of the others.

'I then went aft and mustered my naval crew. I told them some of the guns needed cleaning and repairing and more ammunition needed to be brought up out of the magazines. After that I went down into the after magazine and supervised the carrying of the additional ammunition topsides. Then I went to the forward gun position to inspect conditions there. I was told by Sgt Jones that we had about 400 rounds of Bofors ammunition left and that one of the 20mm Oerlikon guns wasn't working properly. After leaving there I went to the top bridge and supervised preparations including loading ammunition for an engagement we knew we would receive at daybreak. I instructed my gunners to carefully inspect all the machine guns and make sure they were in operating condition. Then I went down to the radio shack to smoke a cigarette.

'While there one of the British signal ratings, on Comdr Baines' order, broke radio silence and made two attempts to get in contact with the cruiser guide ship for orders, but there was no answer. Soon after one of the ship's engineers and two of my

gunners came to me with one of the 20mm gun barrels. It had become overheated from firing and the spring lock had softened. It prevented the barrel from staying in the locked position when the gun was being fired. They reported to me that two other barrels were in a similar condition due to concentrated firing. I instructed them to see if they could find a new spring or make a spring that would fit in the barrel. After that I inspected all the guns and gun positions again and saw that everything was in as good operating condition as possible. I wanted everyone stationed at guns to be on the look out for 'E' Boats.

'13 August 1942. At about 0330 I remained on the top bridge for a while, then about 0500 went down to the central communication system in the wheelhouse again to give a warning to keep a sharp look out for 'E' Boats. Very shortly after that a lookout aft sighted the wake of some fast moving launch. The gun crew stationed there loaded a 4in gun but did not fire at the launch because the gun could not be depressed enough. At the same time lookouts stationed on the top bridge saw its wake and heard the roar of its engines. The general alarm was sounded. Then we opened fire on it with our port 20mm guns. It fired back at us with a machine gun but we continued firing and it stopped firing. During this action I saw a flash over No 3 hatch. I called Chief Mate Englund's attention to it and he said it might be a fire and would send the ship's boatswain to investigate. (Later on I learned that the flash had been caused by an HE round from one of our own guns which had hit the rigging.)

'Then at approximately 0505 there was a terrific flash and explosion forward. Instantly a large amount of water came up over the ship and into the wheelhouse where I was standing. The ship took a starboard list of about twenty-five degrees. I heard someone say: "We're hit, let's get off before she explodes." Everything was lit up and on fire. I glanced out of the wheelhouse window and saw that coal bags which were stacked on No 2 hatch were burning fiercely. I didn't attempt to go out of the starboard wing of the wheelhouse because we had a starboard list and the water was still rushing in there, and I couldn't get out of the port wing of the wheelhouse because flames blocked the passage. I followed the helmsman T. Kirkwood, AB, and Jr Third Mate Henry Logan out of the alleyway from the wheelhouse and went to the port side of the boat deck. There was no "Abandon Ship" signal on the general alarm, nor "Abandon Ship" signal given on the ship's whistle, but I observed that the ship was burning fiercely, was listing to starboard badly and that No 2 and No 4 lifeboats were fully loaded and had been lowered half way down the ship's side. I jumped into the after end of No 2 lifeboat. There was some difficulty being encountered in lowering the lifeboat because the davits had not been swung all the way out. Also because of the starboard list the boats were scraping the port side of the ship. Then I heard someone say: "Is the plug in? Can't find the plug." I handed my flashlight to 1st Asst Engineer J. Simpson who was forward of me, to look for the plug.

'After a short while the aft end of the boat I was in hit the water, but the forward end was up at about a thirty-five degree angle and for some reason could not be lowered any more. I heard the order: "Release the falls", and attempted to release the after fall but had to force it loose with my 45 automatic. The forward fall was not released. At this time the overboard discharge was rapidly flooding the boat and with the help of some others I attempted to push the boat with an oar away from the flow of water. The boat wouldn't move and was being flooded. Then some people jumped out of that boat into No 4 boat which had been successfully launched astern of us. I jumped out and attempted to reach No 4 boat but could not leap far enough and

fell into the water. The ship was still making slight headway. I drifted along the side of the ship and could see the propeller still revolving ahead of me. There was burning gasoline in the water all around. I swam as hard as I could to avoid hitting the propeller and succeeded in missing it by about two feet. Then I drifted about 1,000 yards astern of the ship and could see three lifeboats in the water moving away from where I was. I shouted as loud as I could and in about an hour's time No 4 lifeboat, which contained Captain Thomson, made its way towards the direction of my voice and picked me up.

'They next picked up three other survivors who were in the water and after about forty-five minutes a British destroyer, HMS Penn, came up and rescued all who were in the lifeboat. All Confidential and Secret papers went down with the ship. After we were taken aboard this destroyer about 0730 a wave of dive-bombers flew over. HMS Penn circled about our sinking ship to fight off dive-bombers, but one bomb struck No 5 hold and she went down by the stern, sinking in about seven minutes. Then this destroyer picked up other survivors in the water. After that our destroyer caught up with the rear of the remaining ships in the convoy. The end ship was an American-built tanker, the British ship SS Ohio. This tanker had been torpedoed the night before but was still capable of making about four knots. We stood by the tanker. Soon there was another air attack and another merchant ship was hit, exploding violently. There were no survivors. With the next air attack a bomb dropped through the tanker's engine room skylight, disabling its engines. The tanker's crew abandoned ship. After circling the tanker for another short period of time, the captain of our destroyer decided that he would take the tanker into tow and attempt to bring it to Malta. After a dark night (13 August) a line was made fast from the destroyer to the tanker and several unsuccessful attempts were made to tow her. Survivors on board the destroyer helped to handle the tow line. This line parted once — the tanker's steering gear had been disabled and the load was too great for the destroyer — but our destroyer remained tied up to the tanker. The only other ship in sight was a destroyer circling a disabled merchant vessel about three miles distant. All through the night we attempted to tow the Ohio in 'E' boat and submarine infested waters. (I learned that night from one of the Penn's officers that her submarine sound detector device was not operating.)

'14 August 1942. Shortly after dawn a British destroyer relieved the destroyer which was standing by the merchant ship. We secured a line to the stern of the tanker from our destroyer, whilst the destroyer that had been standing by the merchant ship secured a line to the bow of the tanker to make another attempt to tow her. By this method the captain of our destroyer thought he would be able to steer the tanker. Some members of my gun crew including Coxswain Parker and S2C Hess, some of the tanker's gunners and some of the other survivors volunteered to go aboard this tanker, whose guns could still be manned. There were no aircraft attacks that day but we had action stations on several occasions. By this time Spitfires had flown out from Malta which was approximately seventy miles distant, to intercept enemy bombers.

'The method of towing the tanker was not satisfactory; lines were not holding and no headway was being made. That evening our destroyer and the other destroyer both made fast along the tanker to try to tow her by this method. Some tugs had come out from Malta to aid in the towing. A line was made fast from the bow of the tanker to one old, side-wheel tug. This method of towing was working more satisfactorily and the tanker and two destroyers were making more speed than the tug was capable of making. We were catching up with the tug and the tug could not release the towline. Then the tug secured to the towline swung around the starboard side of the tanker, the side on which our destroyer was made fast. This tug was rapidly creeping around to our destroyer from the starboard side; for some reason the line could not be released. Suddenly the tug crashed into the after end of our destroyer, breaking a hole twenty-five feet long, five feet high and one foot above the waterline in the position of the destroyer's ward-room. Fortunately we were able to see it approaching in time to move and no one was injured. After that the tug succeeded in releasing its line, then a large minesweeper made fast to the bow of the tanker. We towed all that night. In addition to the ship's company aboard the Penn, there were survivors of our ship and a sunken British ship. Because Penn's crew were at action stations continuously we had only tinned beef and biscuits to eat. But naturally we did not expect more and this ordeal would not have been so harrowing if we had had something to occupy our minds, instead of remaining huddled on the Penn's deck.

'15 August 1942. At 1000 hours we arrived at Valletta, Malta harbor. As we passed into the harbor the people of Malta and gun crews stationed high up on its fortifications cheered the ships. A band played "God Save the King" and then "The Star Spangled Banner". The crew and officers of the Penn deserve special merit. They stayed in their action stations, gallantly defending the convoy and tanker continuously for over a week and at all times were calm and uncomplaining. We survivors were landed at the Naval Dockyards of Malta and immediately taken into a cave where the Admiralty Offices and Workshops are located. I saw to it that three of my USN gun crew (S2C Hayden, S2C Howard and S2C Ussey), were given medical treatment for they had received burns about the face, arms and neck after our ship had been hit and they jumped overboard into flaming gasoline. They had, of course, received first aid treatment on the destroyer and in Malta they were sent to the 9th General Hospital for further treatment. (An RN medical officer reported to me that these men had received second degree burns and would require hospitalisation) . . . We had not been in Malta twenty minutes when the island suffered another air raid. At the Naval Dockyards all survivors were given a change of clothes, allowed to bathe and given a hot meal.'

Ensign Suppiger then goes on to explain all that happened to him and his gun crew in Malta and the adventures they had before returning to the United States. His factual, unemotional account still gets across the high drama of the convoy and the grim determination of all to complete their mission.

Sinking of the *Eagle*

In his account Suppiger also mentions the sinking of various escort vessels, amongst them the aircraft carrier *Eagle* on 11 August 1942. One of the pilots from the carrier, Lieutenant-Commander Brabner, commanding 801 Squadron, Fleet Air Arm, recalled the sinking of his 'aerodrome' as he put it. At the time he and other members of his squadron were airborne on patrol. He recalled that it was a beautiful, hot day and he was looking forward to quenching his thirst when the patrol was completed. However, it was not to be:

'It was a bit hazy when the submarine got our ship, we couldn't see properly what was happening but she suddenly listed over to port and began to settle, the aircraft on the flight deck slipping along the deck and falling into the water. We also couldn't see some two hundred members of the crew assembling on the bulge, then taking off their shoes and socks and leaving them in neat

rows before taking to the water! There we were in the air, with no aerodrome to go back to and no immediate prospect of that long-awaited drink!' [2]

Fortunately they were able to land on other carriers, join in with other squadrons and continue their job of defending the convoy. The next few days would prove to be some of the busiest ever experienced by these Fleet Air Arm pilots.

Eagle had been hit by *U73*, its commander, Kapitänleutnant Helmut Rosenbaum, having skilfully avoided the screen of destroyers protecting the carrier and her 20 Sea Hurricanes (16 aircraft of 801 Sqn and four of 813 Sqn). He had fired four torpedoes into her some 65 miles south of Majorca, the vessel going down in just eight minutes, with considerable loss of life. Rosenbaum was awarded the Knight's Cross for this exploit.

HMS *Victorious*

Whilst Lieutenant-Commander Brabner saw the sinking of his aircraft carrier from thousands of feet above the deck, James Forbes was actually on the flight deck of *Victorious* when it was bombed — but fortunately not hit. He was a pilot in 832 Squadron, but as the squadron's torpedo bombers were not needed at that time, the crews were employed elsewhere in the ship. He was helping one of the Oerlikon gunners on the starboard side of the flight deck. As he recalled in the July 2000 edition of the George Cross Island Association National Newsletter (No 42):

'I may say that all I was permitted to do was to help with the spotting of enemy aircraft. I had quite a good view of the whole scene; our position being about half way between the "Island" and the stern of the ship. Our gunsight was actually built over the side of the ship so I was able to peer over the flight deck behind me to port as well as having a good view to starboard. Prior to the attack by the fighter bombers, a bomb dropped from high level fell into the water beside me and I got splashed. To return to the attacks by the two fighter bombers which everyone mistakenly assumed were Hurricanes. I saw them approaching from the port side and saw the bomb which was dropped by the aircraft on our left, hit the flight deck and bounce. I watched in fascination as it went over my head and fell into the water behind me. I remember thinking at the time, that if it had exploded while it was in the air I was a goner! I banged the gunner on the back and yelled "FIRE!" However, by the time he had fired a few rounds the fighter was fast disappearing and anyway our fire was too close to the other ships to continue.'

Operation 'Bellows'

Furious, of course, was not sunk in this or any subsequent air or submarine attacks, and managed to get close enough to Malta (about 580 miles) for its Spitfires to fly off, 37 of them reaching the island safely, the only one that developed trouble (with its newly fitted propeller) managing to land safely on the *Indomitable*. *Furious*, its task completed, then returned to Gibraltar, giving rise to an incorrect enemy assumption that it had been badly damaged.

Heroes of the *Ohio*

It is almost invidious to pick out any one ship that typifies the bravery of the crews — both Royal Navy and Merchant Navy — who sailed to Malta in the 'Pedestal' convoy. However, the ship that became a living symbol of this heroism, for all Malta convoys, was the battered tanker, the SS *Ohio*, belonging to the Eagle Oil & Shipping Company of London. Torpedoed, dive-bombed for three days, and set on fire, with the help of the Royal Navy she struggled

Above: A tragic loss occurred early, on 11 August 1942, when HMS *Eagle* was hit by four torpedoes from the submarine *U73* and sank in eight minutes, 65 miles south of Majorca. Here survivors are being picked up by one of the escorting destroyers. *IWM — MH 31402*

Above: The *Melbourne Star* enters Valletta harbour on 13 August 1942. Her cargo included 1,350 tons of high-octane spirit, 700 tons of kerosene and 1,450 tons of HE shells — a lethal mixture. *NWMA Malta — 7088*

Above: Barely afloat, its decks awash, the tanker *Ohio* reaches Malta lashed between two destroyers, HMS *Penn* and HMS *Ledbury*. Captain Dudley Mason, Master of the *Ohio* was later awarded the George Cross for his skill and courage. *IWM — A 11263*

Above: The tanker *Ohio* enters Grand Harbour. Having been hit six times, once set on fire, and with its steering gear smashed so it had to be lashed to a destroyer for the last part of the journey, the *Ohio* was one of just five merchant ships of the Pedestal convoy to reach Malta on 15 August 1942. *IWM — GM 1480*

into Malta with her precious cargo. On 4 September 1942 her master, Captain Dudley Mason was awarded the George Cross, his citation reading:

'During the passage to Malta of an important convoy Captain Mason's ship suffered most violent onslaught. She was a focus of attack and was torpedoed early one night. Although gravely damaged, her engines kept going and the Master made a magnificent passage by hand steering without a compass. The ship's gunners helped bring down one of the attacking aircraft. The vessel was hit again before morning, but though she did not sink, her engine room was wrecked. She was then towed. The unwieldy condition of the vessel and persistent enemy attacks made progress slow, and it was uncertain whether she would remain afloat. The next day progress somehow continued and the ship reached Malta after a further night at sea.

'The violence of the enemy could not deter the Master from his purpose. Throughout he showed skill and courage of the highest order and it was due to his determination that, in spite of the most persistent enemy opposition, the vessel and her valuable cargo, eventually reached Malta and was safely berthed.'

Captain Mason made a special point of writing to congratulate the seven Royal Navy gunners who had helped protect his ship during the convoy:

'I cannot speak too highly of the seven Royal Naval Gunners (DEMS ratings) under Gunlayer Piling who accompanied the vessel on this voyage. Following torpedo attack they manned the guns, withstanding practically 48 hours of continuous bombing.' [3]

A Permanent Display

Artefacts from ships that survived the convoy form a permanent exhibition in Malta's National War Museum. These include the helm and name-board from the tanker *Ohio*, the ship's bell from the *Port Chalmers* and a silver medal of a Gozo boat that was presented to the crew of the *Port Chalmers* by the Maltese, together with a relief map showing the convoy's route and numerous photographs of the ships and other items.

Notes

1. *Furious* was not strictly part of the escort force, being loaded with 38 Spitfire Mk VBs, destined for Malta, so it went along for the ride and the protection that the escorts provided.
2. Extract from Imperial War Museum tape No 2418.
3. As quoted in Appendix Seven of *'Pedestal' — The Malta Convoy of August 1942* by Peter C. Smith.

Appendix I
Operation 'Pedestal' — Ships Involved

Commander of Escort Force: Vice-Admiral Sir E. Neville Syfret
Convoy Commodore (Merchant Ships): Commodore A. G. Venables

Merchant Ships

SS *Almeria Lykes* (7,773 tons) US ship — sunk 13 August
SS *Brisbane Star* (12,791 tons) — damaged 12 August*
SS *Clan Ferguson* (7,347 tons) — sunk 12 August
SS *Deucalion* (7,516 tons) — sunk 12 August
SS *Dorset* (10,624 tons) — sunk 13 August
SS *Empire Hope* (12,688 tons) — sunk 12 August
SS *Glenorchy* (8,982 tons) — sunk 13 August
SS *Melbourne Star* (12, 806 tons)*
SS *Ohio* (9,514 tons) — tanker — damaged on both 12 and 13 August*
SS *Port Chalmers* (8,535 tons)*
SS *Rochester Castle* (7,795 tons) — damaged 13 August*
SS *Santa Elisa* (8,379 tons) US ship — sunk 13 August
SS *Waimarama* (12,843 tons) — sunk 13 August
SS *Wairangi* (12,400 tons) — sunk 13 August

Those starred * reached Malta with a total of 55,000 tons of supplies.

Escort Vessels

NB: Not all were with the convoy throughout.

Battleships

Nelson, Rodney

Aircraft carriers (with number of aircraft embarked)

Eagle — sunk 11 August (20 Sea Hurricanes);
Indomitable — damaged 12 August (24 Sea Hurricanes, 14 Albacores and 10 Martlets);
Victorious (16 Fulmars, 14 Albacores and 6 Sea Hurricanes);
Furious (not really part of escort as it was taking part in Operation 'Bellows' (see Appendix II of Chapter 10), the movement of aircraft to Malta for which it carried 38 Spitfire VBs);
Argus — attached for Operation 'Berserk'. (This was a one-off exercise held between 5 and 8 August to take advantage of the numbers of aircraft carriers present to practise operating together within a destroyer screen and with AA cruisers allocated for close protection. They practised in particular manoeuvring, AA protection and refuelling operations.)

Cruisers

Cairo — sunk 12 August, *Charybdis* (AA cruiser), *Kenya* — damaged 13 August, *Manchester* — sunk 13 August, *Nigeria* — damaged 13 August, *Phoebe* (AA cruiser), *Sirius* (AA cruiser)

Destroyers

Antelope, Ashanti, Badsworth, Bramham, Bicester, Derwent, Eskimo, Foresight — sunk 12 August, *Fury, Icarus, Intrepid, Ithuriel, Laforey, Ledbury, Lightning, Lookout, Matchless, Pathfinder, Penn, Quentin, Somali, Tartar, Vansittart, Westcott, Wilton, Wishart, Wrestler, Zetland*

Others

13 x Corvettes
Malta Escort Force (17th Mine-sweeping Flotilla and 3rd Motor Launch Flotilla)
3 x Fleet Oilers
9 x Submarines on patrol (10th Submarine Flotilla (Malta))
Tugs

Above: With damage to her bow, the heavily laden *Brisbane Star* is cheered into port by Maltese civilians and sailors. At one stage in the journey, the *Brisbane Star* was boarded by officers of a Vichy French patrol boat from Monastir Bay, who ordered it into Tunisia and internment. However, Captain Riley used his Irish blarney (and whiskey) on them and was eventually allowed to proceed.
IWM — GM 1439

Right: The end of 'Pedestal'. The *Rochester Castle* unloads its precious cargo of flour, coal, medical supplies, ammunition and army equipment.
NWMA Malta — 7269

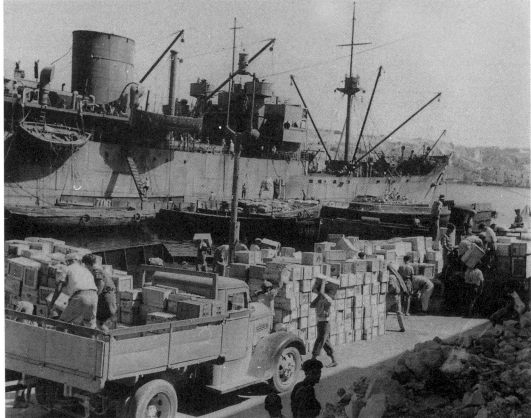

Chapter 13

George Cross Island

In March 1942 the *Daily Telegraph* published a piece about the bravery of the Maltese people, that was then quoted in a radio broadcast by the BBC. It included words to the effect that the writers thought Great Britain's highest military honour for bravery, namely the Victoria Cross, should be awarded to communities as well as to individuals. Furthermore they added that if this were to be the case, then the first community to be granted such an honour should be the garrison and people of Malta who 'have not flinched under the ordeal of unrelenting Nazi attacks'. The bare facts of the scale of the Second Great Siege speak for themselves. For example, 35,000 houses on Malta were destroyed in some 3,000 air raids, during which approximately 14,000 tons of bombs were dropped. To put these figures into perspective, during March and April 1942 alone, twice as many bombs were dropped on Malta as were dropped on the whole of the United Kingdom in the entire year of the Battle of Britain.

The *Daily Telegraph* staff hoisted the Maltese flag above their offices in Fleet Street, whilst many broadcasters went out of their way to praise the bravery of the Maltese people. For example, Commander Anthony Kimmins, a well-known naval commentator, in a broadcast about the award of the VC to submarine commander David Wanklyn after his exploits commanding HMS *Upholder*, explained how during a party in a Maltese bar on the night of his award, Wanklyn had been mobbed and toasted by all present. In his reply Wanklyn had said: 'It [his VC] belongs to the island.' Kimmins went on to say that this epitomised the pride that the people of Malta had always shown in the activities of the naval vessels which were operating from Malta and the fact that for their part the Navy realised that their successes were more than partly due to the endurance of the civilian population of the island.

However, it was left to King George VI to set the royal seal of approval on these aspirations, by awarding the George Cross to Malta. On 15 April 1942 he wrote to the Governor: 'To honour her brave people I award the George Cross to the Island Fortress of Malta to bear witness to a heroism and devotion that will long be famous in history.'

How the George Cross arrived in Malta

Having awarded the George Cross to the island, the King then charged Lord Gort, the Governor Designate, to convey the medal to the people of Malta, when he took over the office of governor in May that year. Original accounts of what happened are somewhat vague, and nowhere do they say that Gort actually did as his sovereign commanded and convey the honour himself. The details can now be made clear, thanks to Frank Rixon BEM, of the George Cross Island Association, who kindly gave me permission to publish an article he had just received, when I visited him in late 2002. The writer of the article, Chevalier Squadron Leader (Rtd) Victor Betty KSJ, was the actual 'medal carrier' and he wrote:

'The story behind the arrival of the George Cross in Malta is one of administrative error understandable in a time of stress. The transport communication route between the UK and Malta at the time was from RAF Hendon, via Portreath and Gibraltar to Luqa. The only aircraft with the necessary range was the Lockheed Hudson and this was used as a transport aircraft. It was small and uncomfortable and had little capacity to keep it beyond the range of the German Focke-Wulf Condors, that patrolled the Western Approaches and the Bay of Biscay. Wisely it was decided to transport the newly appointed Governor and his staff in a Catalina flying boat from Southampton. This was a much safer route and proved a more suitable and more comfortable aircraft. The Catalina was then perhaps the longest range aircraft in service in the RAF.

'There appears to have been a lack of communication somewhere in the administrative chain. An assumption had been made that Lord Gort would travel by the usual land based route from RAF Hendon and the George Cross, together with the Citation, was sent to Hendon. When the error was discovered, the highly classified package was rushed to Southampton. It arrived too late, the captain of the Catalina, bound by the needs of safety and the hours of darkness, was compelled to take off less the arrival of the important George Cross. The captain of the Catalina had no option. The safe arrival of the new Governor in Malta was his priority. The George Cross was left behind. Lord Gort travelled to Malta without the decoration awarded to the island and entrusted to him by King George VI. One can only sympathise with Lord Gort's embarrassment. Lord Gort arrived [on 7 August] at night in Kalafrana, the only seaplane base available in those days.

'It is recorded that General Sir William Dobbie, the retiring Governor of Malta, asked Lord Gort if he could see the George Cross, Lord Gort refused. The George Cross had been awarded to the Island under the Governorship of General Dobbie. The retiring governor made an understandable error. He recorded in his memoirs: "he had it in his pocket". Unknown to General Dobbie, the George Cross was not in Lord Gort's possession. One can appreciate Lord Gort's embarrassment. He was a man of high integrity. Newspapers and radio jumped to the conclusion that he had indeed been able to discharge His Majesty's Royal Command. The error became a myth and was perpetuated.

'To remedy the matter of the failure to deliver the important package to the flying boat at Southampton on time, the Air Ministry sent it to Malta by the first available "safe hand of officer". It so occurred that the task was entrusted to a young Flying Officer, Victor Betty, who was returning from detachment at RAF Abbotsinch where he had been helping to prepare and test Spitfire aircraft for loading onto the US carrier Wasp, for transport to Malta. The aircraft arrived to reinforce the Island around 8 May 1942. On completion of this duty Flying Officer Betty was ordered to report to the Air Ministry, London. He was entrusted with the safe conduct of the George Cross to Malta. He travelled from RAF Hendon, via Portreath, Cornwall and Gibraltar. He arrived at RAF Luqa at about 0200 hours on May 9th (circa). He was tired, dirty and not in a very good mood, to be met by an immaculate Army subaltern from the Governor's staff requesting to accept custody of the George Cross. This brash young subaltern at first refused to sign the receipt. He was met by the ultimatum — "No receipt, no George Cross". He signed.

Flying Officer Betty was only a convenient courier, a "Johnnie on the Spot". The real responsibility lay with the pilot of the Lockheed Hudson reconnaissance aircraft converted for passenger carrying. The pilot was Flying Officer Honeman, Flying Officer Betty and he had met in Iraq when he was a Sergeant Pilot in the famous 84 Squadron in 1936. However, Flying Officer Betty actually carried the famous award to Malta. This is a matter of fact.'

This account has now been confirmed in the George Cross Island National Newsletter (No 51 of March 2003). It also says that a very heavy air raid was in progress when Victor Betty arrived at Luqa and that there was an intense AA barrage going on, which meant that the runways were littered with shell splinters and pieces of shrapnel, any of which would easily burst the tyres of an aircraft landing there. However, they simply had to land because they had only sufficient fuel left for another 20 minutes' flying. So, having told his passengers to strap in securely, the intrepid pilot went in to land, ignoring a barrage of Very lights telling him to abort, and managed to make a safe touchdown.

The precious medal thus arrived in the George Cross Island, not in a Sunderland flying boat with Lord Gort but rather 'wrapped in the courier's pyjamas, in his attaché case on his knees!'

The Presentation

The public ceremony at which the award was made took place at Palace Square on Sunday, 13 September 1942. It was decided not to allow news of the ceremony to be broadcast to the outside world until it had taken place for obvious security reasons. The ceremony was an impressive affair, with detachments from the Navy, Army and Air Force, together with the Police, Special Constabulary and Civil Defence Organisations all lining the square. Police Commissioner Joseph Axisa brought out the case containing the George Cross, and handed it to Lord Gort. Addressing the watching crowds, Lord Gort said:

'On my appointment as Governor of Malta, I was entrusted to carry the George Cross to this Island Fortress. By the command of the King, I now present to the People of Malta and her Dependencies the decoration which His Majesty has awarded to them in recognition of the gallant service which they have already rendered in the fight for freedom.

'How you have withstood for many months the most concentrated bombing attacks in the history of the world is the admiration of all civilised people. Your homes and your historic buildings have been destroyed and only their ruins remain as monuments to the hate of a barbarous foe. The Axis Powers have tried again and again to break your spirit but your confidence in the final triumph of the United Nations remains undimmed.

'What Malta has withstood in the past, without flinching, Malta is determined to endure until the day when the second siege is raised. Battle-scarred George Cross Malta, the sentinel of Empire in the Mediterranean, meanwhile stands firm, undaunted and undismayed, awaiting the time when she can call: "Pass Friend, all is well in the Island Fortress."

'Now it is my proud duty to hand over the George Cross to the People of Malta for safe-keeping.'

Right: The King's hand-written citation to the brave people of Malta.
NWMA Malta — 2837

Above: Presentation of the George Cross, 13 September 1942. The Governor, Lord Gort VC, hands over the case containing the George Cross and the Citation to Sir George Borg. *IWM — GM 1765*

BUCKINGHAM PALACE

The Governor
Malta.

To honour her brave people
I award the George Cross to the
Island Fortress of Malta to bear
witness to a heroism and devotion
that will long be famous in history.

George R.I.

April 15th 1942.

Having given his address, Lord Gort closed by reading the Citation.

The case, containing both the decoration and the citation, was then presented to His Honour Sir George Borg, the Chief Justice, who gave an address on behalf of the people of Malta. The case was then placed on a plinth in the centre of the square, where men of the 1st Battalion The King's Own Malta Regiment, mounted guard, whilst the crowd filed past to view the insignia and the unique document. It has subsequently been viewed by many distinguished visitors to Malta, including both King George VI, when he visited the island on 20 June 1943 and presented a Field Marshal's baton to Lord Gort, and his daughter when, as Princess Elizabeth, she visited Malta in 1949.

The George Cross and its citation are now proudly on show in a special exhibition in the National War Museum in Valletta.

Left:
After the address, the case is placed on a plinth in the centre of the square, with soldiers of the 1st Battalion, King's Own Malta Regiment, mounting guard, as the crowd files past to look at its contents.
NWMA Malta — 4941

Right: Sir George Borg, the Chief Justice of Malta, receives the case from the Governor and then delivers an address to the crowds of spectators in Palace Square, Valletta. *NWMA Malta — 5001*

Below: The George Cross front and reverse, showing the simple inscription. The George Cross was instituted in September 1940 as a reward for heroism for civilians, both men and women. It is also awarded to members of the armed forces, when the situation does not warrant a military award. Between 1940 and 1947, some 105 George Crosses were awarded.
NWMA Malta 01822 and 01824

Chapter 14
The Tide Turns

The Siege Ends

'Officially' the Siege of Malta finished at the end of December 1942, when Operation 'Portcullis', a convoy of five merchantmen with an escort comprising one cruiser, 18 destroyers and one minelayer, brought 55,000 tons of essential supplies to Malta, without loss. That was the very first time since 1941 that a Malta convoy had managed to complete the journey unscathed. As 'Laddie' Lucas says in his book *Malta — The Thorn in Rommel's Side*: 'Hunger slowly begins to recede. Belts eased a notch for Christmas. Issue of four candles and eight nightlights to every family. Battle officially ends.' Naturally some Maltese did not appreciate the fact that instead of turkey they would get a slight increase in the 'luxury item' they received in lieu of turkey, namely beans! However, the 'brightening' of the Christmas week with the issue of the candles and nightlights that 'Laddie' Lucas mentions, was regarded by the civilian population as being the 'Joke of the War'.

The garrison also noticed a considerable difference both in enemy activity and supplies getting through. The arrival of the 'Portcullis' ships had led to the soldiers' rations being increased by 1oz of oatmeal four times a week, 1oz of bread extra daily and ⅔oz of butter daily instead of margarine! However, by the middle of February, a further 23 merchant ships had arrived and rations had become quite good, for example:

'Bread 12oz, four issues of Bully Beef, two of M&V, one of steak and kidney weekly. One of the most popular additions was that of 1½oz of butter daily, also ascorbic tablets supposedly equal to the juice of five oranges. As a result of this improved diet, the incidence of boils and open sores etc, began to decrease.[1]

Now it was time for Malta to hit back wherever it could, on land, sea and in the air because although the worst of the siege was undoubtedly over, the war had some years still to run and it would not even see an end in North Africa until May 1943. Therefore, it would be somewhat premature to think that everything changed quickly at the end of 1942. Nevertheless, more aircraft were now stationed in Malta and were able to harass enemy convoys to North Africa far more effectively, whilst targets in Sicily and Tripolitania were regularly struck. One such pilot was the future Air Marshal Sir Ivor Broom KCB, CBE, DSO, DFC, who served with a Blenheim squadron and had this to say during a taped interview for the Imperial War Museum:

'Our main role was to attack shipping taking supplies to Rommel in North Africa, all daylight. And we'd go out searching for shipping and if we couldn't find any ships, and we were down by the North African coast, then we would go inland to find a target of opportunity, on the Tripoli–Benghazi road area. And we'd attack the target of opportunity and then back to Malta. This was all at low level, 50 feet stuff we're talking about all the time.

'One interesting fact I think might be worth me telling you. The squadron was asked to attack some very important big ship in a Sicilian harbour. The harbour was so well defended that it was decided it had to be done at night, a moonlight night. And so they picked the two most experienced crews in the squadron to do it

and I was one. Now my total night flying was seven and a half hours, which included my training on Airspeed Oxfords . . . I hadn't flown at night since my conversion training six months earlier. We went in low level again, in the moonlight, pilot release. All this bombing at low level was done at pilot release, not [by] navigator, or bomb aimer, [but by] pilot release. We attacked this ship . . . this big ship in the Sicilian harbour — at night with seven and a half hours total night flying! I remember the CO of the squadron saying to me during the briefing: "Would you like to do a couple of circuits and landings" — we called them "circuits and bumps in those days" — "before you set course, so you've had a look at what Malta looks like at night with virtually no lighting?" And before I could answer my air gunner said: 'Not ruddy likely! Let's do the op between the circuit and the bumps!" And so off we went, and it was a very successful trip.'[2]

When quizzed about the interdiction of shipping bound for North Africa and whether the problems were the same as the problems he had encountered earlier in his service when attacking shipping off the Dutch coast, Broom said:

'Almost the same. But the escort vessels were not usually flakships — because the flakships were just little coastal ships which were

Below: After the arrival of the critical 'Pedestal' convoy, the food situation eased slightly but rations were still tightly controlled. Here men of the 1st Battalion, Hampshire Regiment, check rations in the cookhouse. *NWMA Malta — 14249*

Right:
Blenheims were dispatched from Malta to take the battle to the enemy and attack their convoys both at sea and, as seen here, on land in North Africa. *IWM — CM 1501*

Opposite below:
Prior to Operation 'Husky', the invasion of Sicily on 10 July 1943, landing craft were prepared in Malta. These are in No 4 Dock, Valletta. *NWMA Malta — 6199*

Below:
Malta Special Service Troops carried out offensive action against the Kerkenna islands, after practising commando-type training at Manoel Island. *IWM — GM 3039*

bristling with guns — they tended to have more naval support for the ships going to Tripoli. So really the opposition was stronger when escorted, but there were times when ships were not escorted. I'm speaking from memory now, but I believe I am right in saying — and I did check this many years ago and so I believe it is accurate — we sunk or damaged 24 ships during my time with the squadron, and we lost 24 crews during that time. And I suppose in war, you'd probably say that is not bad arithmetic, but it's pretty colossal.

'I was a sergeant pilot when I went to Malta. We lost virtually all the officers and were left with a squadron leader who was due to go home; his tour had expired. He was made acting wing commander until the new one came out. I was commissioned in Malta. One night I moved from the Sergeants' Mess to the Officers' Mess, that was my commissioning. I went down to Luqa and bought myself a forage cap from Gieves and a few inches of pilot officer braid, took off the sergeant stripes and sewed on/pinned on, the pilot officer braid. It didn't make much difference except that I didn't see so much of my friends because we were now living in separate places. I shared a room with a Canadian and when I moved in he said, jokingly, "Well you're my third room mate this week, I hope you're going to stay a bit longer than the others!"'

Offensive Action for the Infantry

The British infantry battalions on the island continued to carry out field training exercises, in case they were called upon to defend the island, despite the fact that the possibility of an attack had now faded considerably. Now they would be called upon to undertake some offensive action. A special unit was formed, known as the Malta Special Service Troop, which practised commando-type training at Manoel Island. This force was given the task of carrying out offensive action against the Kerkenna islands of Rhabi and Chergui, off the east coast of Tunisia, quite near to Sousse. The Malta Special Service Troop consisted of 10 officers and 86 men from the Buffs, Cheshires, Royal West Kents, Royal Irish Fusiliers, Durham Light Infantry and the Royal Signals. They embarked in naval craft at Marsamxett harbour on 4 April 1943, sailed in secret to Tripoli where they spent a few days checking their equipment and making final preparations, then they assaulted the islands on 13 April, landing without any opposition. They were disappointed to find that the Italian garrison had already been withdrawn, so they captured the islands without a shot being fired. The force then returned to Malta on the 19th.

This successful action would be followed, later on that year, by operations against the Aegean Islands, to be carried out by men of 234 (Malta) Infantry Brigade, between 15 and 18 September 1943. The brigade at that time comprised 1 DLI, 2 RIF and 2 RWK, and it would be despatched to the area from Malta at Churchill's behest. However, it would not be anything like the Kerkenna walkover. The idea was a good one in principle, because the occupation of the Dodecanese, in particular of Rhodes, the largest of the islands, not only denied the enemy the continued use of airfields and bases from which they had in the past done considerable damage in the Eastern Mediterranean, but also opened the possibility of bringing Turkey into the war as an ally. This would make available new air bases from which Greece, Romania and Bulgaria could be bombed. Other advantages would be Allied control over the Dardanelles and the Bosporus, a shorter supply route to Russia, and the maintenance, nay increase, of the threat to the enemy's sensitive flank.

However, the Allies did not have the necessary naval, air or ground forces to carry out this action at the critical moment, namely when Italy collapsed, although two British commando officers

(Majors Lord Jellicoe and Dalby) were parachuted into Rhodes to try to persuade the large (30,000-strong) Italian garrison to round up the 7,000-strong German element on the island. Instead the Germans took the initiative and attacked their erstwhile Allies. The Italians gave in, leaving the Germans in charge, which was a much more difficult nut to crack for the Malta Infantry Brigade, especially as it was woefully short of relevant operational experience. It was therefore decided to reduce the scope of the operation and to concentrate on the islands of Cos, Leros, Samos, Simi, Stampalia and Icaria. 1 DLI was assigned to Cos, probably the second most important island after Rhodes, because it contained an airstrip at Antimachia. One company was airlifted there early on 16 September 1943, followed by most of the rest of the battalion, to join the Commando and Special Boat Squadron personnel who were already operating there. By the end of September the garrison amounted to some 1,400 men. There were also small numbers of Commandos/LRDG/SBS operating on Leros, Samos, Simi and some of the other smaller islands.

Turning to the DLI History:

'The Germans reacted with promptitude and vigour that came as a complete surprise. Their aircraft started bombing from the first moment and the bombing steadily increased until the airfield at Antimachia was neutralised. As a result, though C Company remained there, A and B were withdrawn to a position in some olive groves about five miles west of Cos port, where they assisted in the preparation of a new landing ground, whilst C was posted in the outskirts of the town. Although the garrison had twenty-

Above: Additional landing strips were built to accommodate US aircraft — like this Lockheed P38 Lightning single-seat long-range fighter that would support operations against Sicily and Italy. In the centre of this group of American pilots is RAF Wing Commander Adrian 'Warby' Warburton, who had already earned fame as a reconnaissance pilot in Malta. *IWM — GM 3139*

four Bofors guns, the battalion had at its disposal only its own small arms and rifles.'

Unfortunately, events were from then on dogged by bad luck. It was known that the enemy had been assembling a fleet of landing craft at Piraeus and in various harbours on Crete for an amphibious operation. Then on the evening of 2 October, an enemy convoy was sighted off Naxos and it was wrongly assumed it was heading for Rhodes. At almost the same time, all available destroyers had to return to port to refuel, whilst the two submarines which had been ordered to intercept the enemy convoy off Cos failed to arrive in time. The garrison commander on Cos added to the problems, as he wrongly thought that the enemy were heading for Rhodes, so was caught on the hop when they started to land on Cos in the early hours of 3 October.

'Landing on the north side of the island under [the protection of] a heavy air bombardment with about 2,000 troops, the Germans advanced rapidly inland and cut the Cos/Antimachia road, whilst a strong force of parachutists, flown in from Greece, were dropped on the airstrip. D Company, isolated, fought hard, until almost all had been killed, wounded or taken prisoner (although some managed to escape into the hills). The other companies, under Lt-Col Kirby, who had hurried from his sick-bed to take command, had been placed in position astride the main road, where an obstinate pitched battle between the Battalion and the enemy raged all day. Attacking frontally and feeling for the flanks, the enemy gradually made his superior strength felt. B Company, north of the road, was overrun after stubborn resistance. C Company lost a platoon early on. A Company, to

the south of the road, became cut off and received orders to retire to the outskirts of Cos. By this time the Battalion, though it had clearly inflicted heavy casualties, was reduced to less than 200 effectives and had to be withdrawn to form a rough perimeter around the approaches to the town. There, fighting continued all night. An attempt was made to organise a counter-attack, but an unlucky salvo of mortar bombs fell on the assembly point, wounding the CO, OC HQ Company plus another company commander, and killing the Quartermaster. Further organised resistance was impossible.' [3]

That night the battalion received orders to split up the remaining men into parties of a dozen or so, who were then to make their way into the hills and rendezvous at Kargliou. About 60 managed to do this successfully, but they were without food and, although the locals helped them as far as they could, their situation soon became desperate. Nevertheless, many of them succeeded in escaping in a caique on the 13th, reached Kastellorizon and thence made it to Cyprus. By the end of the month all that remained of the battalion were nine officers and some 120 NCOs and men. The Allies had thus lost a costly battle — one estimate was some five battalions, plus various naval craft and aircraft. The Dodecanese would remain in German hands, with some commando activity to keep them 'stirred up' during 1944-45, until they surrendered between 1 and 9 May 1945.

HQ for the Assault on Sicily

Following the surrender of the Axis in North Africa, preparations began on Malta for the invasion of Sicily. Ships, aircraft and war supplies of all types began to arrive. Naturally it was impossible to disguise all this activity and there was an increasing number of air attacks on Malta. However, the air defence was now almost impenetrable and very few enemy aircraft ever managed to get through. The senior commanders, both American and British, agreed that Malta presented the ideal location for an advanced HQ. As Eisenhower wrote in *Crusade in Europe*, his autobiographical account of the war years:

'Because of the existence of splendid naval communications at Malta that place was chosen as our headquarters for the initial stages of the operation . . . General Alexander, Admiral Cunningham and I all went to Malta a day or so before the attack was scheduled, to be in position to take any action that might prove necessary. We were the guests of Field Marshal Lord Gort, Governor of the island.'

Eisenhower then goes on to compliment the island and its inhabitants:

'Malta then presented a picture far different to the one of a few months earlier, when it was still the target for a hostile air force that had little effective opposition. Malta had taken a fearful beating but the spirit of its defenders had never been shaken. As Allied air and naval support approached them through the conquest of North Africa, they rose magnificently to the occasion. By the time we found need for Malta's facilities its airfields were in excellent condition and its garrison was burning to get into the fight.' [4]

Prior to the assault on the main island of Sicily — Operation 'Husky' — timed for 10 July 1943, it was decided to capture the nearby islands of Pantelleria, Lampedusa, Linosa and Lampione. The first of these had long been a major threat to Malta convoys, and was known to be garrisoned by some 12,000 men, with 15 battalions of coastal guns, formidable anti-aircraft defences, together with pillboxes and other defensive works. However, Italian morale was very low and, once they had been pounded by Allied bombing and naval gunfire, they quickly surrendered, on 11 June, before any Allied troops could land. White flags also appeared on Lampedusa, Linosa and Lampione, thus completing a total surrender on 13 June.

One can imagine how busy the Lascaris underground War Headquarters was at this time as Allied staffs worked on finalising their

Below: Operation 'Husky' inevitably led to battle casualties needing hospital treatment, so hospital ships began to frequent Grand Harbour, bringing the wounded who would then be taken to the island's hospitals.
NWMA Malta — 1709

plans for the coming invasion. A major problem now arose over a shortage of airstrips on Malta from which to support the invasion forces, so it was decided to build one swiftly on Gozo. Once approval had been sought and terms agreed to by the local farmers (who would naturally receive compensation for their 'lost' fields), American construction engineers arrived to carry out the job, assisted by local labourers, working around the clock. Work having been started on 8 June, both runways were completed by the 20th and the entire project, including taxiways, dispersal facilities and accommodation for 78 aircraft, was completed and ready for operations by the 22nd, the first American-piloted Spitfires of 31st Fighter Group landing the next day.

Eisenhower's Message to Malta

General Eisenhower would crystallise his feelings for Malta in a message that was printed on the front pages of the local newspapers on 5 August 1943. It read:

'The epic of Malta is symbolic of the experience of the United Nations in this war. Malta has passed successively through the stages of woeful unpreparedness, tenacious endurance, intensive preparation and the initiation of a fierce offensive. It is resolutely determined to maintain a rising crescendo of attack until the whole task is complete. For this inspiring example, the United Nations will forever be indebted to Field Marshal Lord Gort, the fighting services under his command and to every citizen of the heroic Island.'

The King visits Malta

Having made his memorable decision to award the George Cross to Malta, it was only a matter of time before the King would come to see the island and its brave people for himself. This would happen in June 1943 and would be shrouded in secrecy beforehand for obvious reasons. One can imagine the excitement when, at 5.00am on 20 June 1943, the Rediffusion Relay System, the local network over which important announcements were made to the local population, announced the impending arrival. During the siege, the network had often been interrupted due to power failures or damaged cables, but those days were now thankfully past, the last effective enemy air raid having taken place on 23 February 1943. Soon every vantage point around the Grand Harbour was crammed with excited people waiting to catch the first glimpse of the King's arrival. Flags and portraits of the royal family were to be seen all over Malta as the excitement grew to a crescendo.

Then, at last, the cruiser HMS *Aurora*, escorted by four destroyers, approached the breakwater. King George VI, dressed in immaculate white naval uniform, could be seen standing on a specially erected platform on the cruiser's bridge, saluting. He remained at the salute until the vessel dropped anchor in Dockyard Creek. Then, for the next 12 hours on that lovely hot summer's day, the crowds roared their welcome on every possible occasion, fully appreciating the dangers which their sovereign had had to accept in order to reach their still embattled island. The King recorded the visit in his diary:

'On Sunday at 8.15am I was on the bridge as we came into the Grand Harbour. A lovely sunny morning. A wonderful sight. Every bastion and every view point lined with people who cheered as we entered. It was a very moving moment for me. I had made up my mind that I would take a risk and get to Malta and I had got there and by sea. Mussolini had called the Mediterranean Sea his Italian Lake a short time ago.'

Above:
King George VI made a totally unexpected visit to Malta on 20 June 1943. Here, accompanied by Lord Gort, he talks to the Lieutenant-Governor, HE David Campbell.
IWM — GM 3381

Right:
The Maltese people enthusiastically welcomed the King when he toured the island, accompanied by Lord Gort.
IWM — GM 3394

The King goes on to outline how Lord Gort came aboard, how they had then landed and driven through cheering crowds to the Palace in Valletta, where he met the Council and presented Lord Gort with his Field Marshal's baton. Then he had seen the George Cross which he had given to Malta the previous April, before touring the dockyards, the RAF airfields and all the rest. King George comments that all the flowers which were thrown into the car had a 'quite detrimental effect' on his white uniform.

It was an unforgettable day for everyone. The King described it as being 'the real gem of my tour' and when the Lieutenant-Governor, David Campbell, bade him farewell, saying that he had made the people of Malta very happy, King George had replied: 'But I have been the happiest man in Malta today!'

The Italian Surrender

'In the meantime negotiations for the Italian surrender had been dragging along. They were very intricate.' So wrote General Eisenhower in *Crusade in Europe* and he goes on to explain why; namely, because they involved the still strong Italian fleet, the remnants of the Italian air force and their ground forces located throughout Italy and in the Balkans. The situation was made all the more complicated by the fact that the Germans still dominated most of Italy. It was eventually decided that the official Italian surrender would be on the evening of 8 September 1943 — the same date as that chosen for the Allied assault on mainland Italy. From a Maltese point of view it was already an historic day as it was the anniversary of the end of the first Great Siege of 1565, when the Turks had left Malta, after being routed by the Maltese together with the Knights of St John: 'Behind them they left a devastated island, and the slopes behind Birgu and Senglea blackened with their dead,' wrote one historian. In four months the hitherto invincible fleet and army of Sultan Suleyman had been defeated by this tiny island.

Soon another defeated battle fleet would be seen by the Maltese, namely the Italian, which, under the surrender terms, was scheduled to sail from La Spezia and Taranto, shadowed by the British battleships *Warspite* and *Valiant*, plus the 8th Destroyer Flotilla. The journey to Malta would not be without incident — the flagship *Roma*, a *Littorio* Class battleship, was sunk on 9 September by a force of German Dornier 217 bombers using radio-controlled bombs. The *Roma* was hit twice: the first bomb struck amidships, passed through the ship and exploded under the bottom; the second struck abreast of the bridge, went forward and exploded in the forward magazine. There were over 1,200 killed out of the 1,800 crew, including the Italian C-in-C, Admiral Carlo Bergamini.

The first Italian ships arrived on 10 September, and by the next day four battleships, six cruisers and six destroyers had dropped anchor at Malta — a moment to savour for the Maltese. As one can imagine, the celebrations went on for some days, and, as Lord Gort said in his speech to the crowds:

'Who would have foretold on 8th September last year that the bells of the Three Unconquered Cities would ring again, as of old, in commemoration of the great victory of 1565 . . . and would continue their joyous peals to celebrate the downfall of Italy — the Italy who had so recently and so arrogantly boasted that Malta had been 'rubbed out'. Again, who would have dared to predict that the news would flash round the world on 11th

Right: Another unforgettable day was 10 September 1943, when a major portion of the Italian Fleet arrived in Malta to surrender. Some of the crew of the Italian battleship *Caio Duilio* are seen here assembled beneath her 32cm (12.6in) guns. By the end of the month, 76 Italian naval units had surrendered at Malta. IWM — NA 6594)

September 1943, announcing that the great Italian Fleet would be at anchor off the shores of our unconquered Island Fortress.'

Admiral of the Fleet Sir Andrew Cunningham simply but proudly signalled the Admiralty that day:

'Be pleased to inform Their Lordships that the Italian battle fleet is now anchored under the guns of Malta.'

Some days later, on 29 September 1943, Marshal Pietro Badoglio came to Malta in an Italian cruiser to sign the unconditional surrender. He was met by Eisenhower, Lord Gort and other senior Allied officers. He tried to negotiate the clause concerning unconditional surrender, but meekly signed, when the Allied commanders refused to hold any discussions.

Churchill and Roosevelt visit Malta

Finally on the list of VVIP wartime visitors to Malta came two of the three most important Allied war leaders, British Prime Minister Winston Churchill, and American President Franklin Delano Roosevelt. Both had long expressed a wish to visit Malta so that they could see, at first hand, how its brave citizens had suffered. Their visits took place in November and December 1943. Churchill came first on a two-day visit over 17–19 November. He had left England on 12 November, on board HMS *Renown* on a journey that would keep him away from the UK for some two months. His son, Major Randolph Churchill, was with him, plus a very special aide-de-camp, namely his daughter Sarah, then serving in the Air Force. After an uneventful voyage across the Bay of Biscay, they stopped for a few hours at Algiers (Winston talked here with General Georges about the French situation in Africa) then as darkness fell 'we resumed our course for Malta which we reached on the 17th. Here I found Generals Eisenhower and Alexander and other impor-

Above: Another famous visitor to Malta was British Prime Minister Winston Churchill, who toured the dockyards amid great enthusiasm on 19 November 1943, accompanied by Lord Gort, Rear-Admiral MacKenzie and Vice-Admiral Hamilton. *IWM — GM 3999*

tant personages.'[5] At the end of the war in Tunisia Churchill had suggested to the King that both Eisenhower and Alexander should be presented with the North African ribbon, bearing both the 1st and 8th Army numerals on it — thus making it unique. The King had agreed, so Churchill had the pleasure and honour of investing the generals with this unusual accolade. 'They were both taken by surprise and seemed highly gratified when I pinned the ribbons on their coats.'

Unfortunately Churchill was ill with a cold and a high temperature for almost the entire time he was in Malta. Nevertheless, despite having to remain in bed, he continued, in true Churchillian style, to conduct business unceasingly. However, just before he left, he was fortunately well enough to make a final tour of the battered dockyard where, as he put it: 'the whole of the people and workmen gathered with great enthusiasm. At midnight on November 19 we sailed again on our voyage to Alexandria.'

Churchill was on his way to Cairo to meet with FDR and General Chang Kai-shek, the Chinese leader, before going on to Teheran for a conference with Roosevelt and Stalin. Roosevelt would save his trip to Malta until after the Teheran Conference, arriving by aircraft (a Douglas DC-54 Skymaster) on 8 December, with an escort of 20 Lightnings and Spitfires. He was met by a number of VIPs, including Generals Eisenhower, Spaatz, Bedell Smith and Wilson, and of course Lord Gort. To get from the aircraft he used General Eisenhower's Jeep, nicknamed 'Husky' after the operation for the invasion of Sicily. The Jeep was later presented to the island and is now on show in the National War Museum. In addition to making a speech, Roosevelt presented a scroll — a citation from the American people (see photograph opposite). FDR made the point in his speech to the islanders that

he had deliberately dated the scroll 7 December, rather than the 8th, because that day was the second anniversary of the American entry into the war. 'We will proceed until that war is won, but more than that,' said FDR, 'we will stand shoulder to shoulder with the British Empire and our other Allies in making it a victory worth while.'

Whilst on his way back to his aircraft, Roosevelt let it be known that he would like to tour the harbour area, so he transferred to the Governor's car for a lengthy tour and did not leave the island until later that afternoon.

A Second Visit

This would not be the only wartime visit made to Malta by the two great leaders. They would both come to the island between 30 January and 2 February 1945 along with their Combined Chiefs of Staff to hold talks in advance of the Yalta meeting with Stalin. Churchill arrived by air at Luqa just before dawn on 30 January, whilst Roosevelt sailed into Valletta on board the cruiser USS *Quincy* on 2 February. The two leaders held talks on the cruiser, then Roosevelt toured the island, visiting Mdina, Ghajn Tuffieha and Valletta. These meetings were top secret and so was their departure, when, on the night of 2/3 February, several transport planes took off at 10 minute intervals from Luqa. As there were about 700 VIPs and staff to move, including Churchill and Roosevelt, it must have been quite a night.

Many Other VIPs

Of course there were many other VIPs who visited Malta during and after the siege, and in his book *Malta: Blitzed but not Beaten* the late Philip Vella lists some of them as being: the Polish Premier General Wladyslaw Sikorski; South African Prime Minister Jan Smuts; Chief of the French Armed Forces General Henri Giraud; British Foreign Secretary Anthony Eden and many others, all of whom were united in praise for the bravery and steadfastness of the Maltese people.

Left: President of the United States of America, Franklin D. Roosevelt, flew in to Malta on 8 December 1943. He is seen here inspecting a Guard of Honour from a Jeep which is now on show at the National War Museum.
NWMA Malta — 9281

Below: Roosevelt presented Malta with a citation from the American people, which he deliberately dated 7 December, rather than the 8th because it was the anniversary of the Japanese attack on Pearl Harbor in 1941. *NWMA — 12639*

A Presentation to Lord Gort

As a token of their admiration, devotion, gratitude and love for their Governor, the people of Malta presented him with a Sword of Honour on Sunday, 12 March 1944. Made by the Wilkinson Sword Company, it bore the following inscription:

> *'Presented by the Band and Allied Clubs in Malta and Ghawdex, interpreters of the People's admiration, gratitude, devotion and love to HE Field Marshal The Viscount Gort VC, their Leader and Governor during the Second Siege of Malta.'*

The silver scabbard carried on it an embossed silver gilt cross-guard. The obverse featured a Field Marshal's badge with the Arms of Malta on the reverse. The ivory grip was held by four Tudor roses and a laurel wreath eyelet for the gold bullion sword knot. In addition to the inscription, the blade carried a floral design and the George Cross on one side and the Arms of Lord Gort and the Royal cipher on the reverse. Lord Gort was feted again on 5 August 1944, when he left to become High Commissioner and C-in-C Palestine. He was replaced by Lieutenant-General Sir Edmond Schreiber KCB.

Notes
1. Robert A. Bonner: *The Ardwick Boys went to Malta.*
2. IWM Department of Sound Records, Accession No 10981/3.
3. S. G. P. Ward: *Faithful, The Story of the Durham Light Infantry.*
4. Dwight D. Eisenhower: *Crusade in Europe.*
5. W. S. Churchill: *Closing the Ring.*

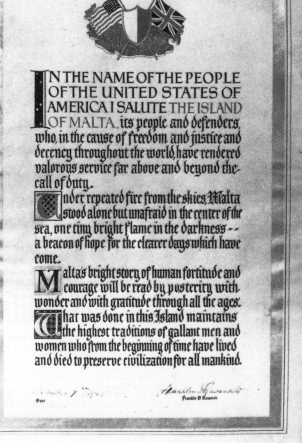

IN THE NAME OF THE PEOPLE OF THE UNITED STATES OF AMERICA I SALUTE THE ISLAND OF MALTA, its people and defenders, who, in the cause of freedom and justice and decency throughout the world, have rendered valorous service far above and beyond the call of duty.

Under repeated fire from the skies Malta stood alone but unafraid in the center of the sea, one tiny bright flame in the darkness -- a beacon of hope for the clearer days which have come.

Malta's bright story of human fortitude and courage will be read by posterity with wonder and with gratitude through all the ages. What was done in this Island maintains the highest traditions of gallant men and women who from the beginning of time have lived and died to preserve civilization for all mankind.

Chapter 15

Malta Today — What Remains to be Seen

A Voyage of Rediscovery

'A large illuminated sign over the Terminal Building proclaimed: "Welcome to Malta" and with this in mind I followed the file of passengers towards Passport Control. This was obviously new and had replaced the battered Nissen huts of the 1940s.

'A 30-minute taxi ride took me to the small, unpretentious hotel, previously booked, where I was welcomed with smiles and a "Hope you enjoy your stay" — a marked contrast to the reception by surly French and indifferent Spaniards on previous visits abroad.

'Early the next day I went for my first walk-about. Nothing appeared to have changed. The same elderly buildings and I swear the same, original small buses, chugging about. Some incredible feats of engineering must have kept them on the road. The main street of Valletta, Kingsway, now renamed Republic Street, also appeared unchanged, although a large ugly scar was all that remained of the once beautiful Opera House. Slowly walking along I noticed a large banner over a row of shops, in large letters it read: "Come back again Brits because we love you".

'Next the Cinema, now rebuilt, once reduced to smoking rubble during an air raid in 1942, with dozens of Servicemen killed or injured. There was, however, as I recall, a comic sequel. Two days after the bombing of the cinema four sailors were dragged from the ruins, still alive and roaring drunk. They had been trapped in the bar, remarkably untouched and had passed their vigil to some purpose. In spite of other preoccupations, the entire garrison rocked with laughter.

'I peeped round the corner and down Strait Street, "The Gut", now empty and desolate. The "Egyptian Queen", the "Lucky Wheel" — Memories! Echoes from the past when, inside, the Devons, Dorsets, West Kents, Irish, Manchesters, Buffs, Cheshires, HMS Manchester, Kelly, Kandahar, Penelope, and RAF chaps, would often hear soft siren voices: "Buy me a sherry Soldier/Sailor/Airman!" All gone but not forgotten.

'Everywhere I went smiles greeted me. The invariable question: "You English?" I reply "Yes". "You been here before?" I reply: "Yes, during the war." The smiles become broader. If it was a bar, the first drinks were always on the house.

'The days pass quickly. I sat on the rocks and looked out to sea. The memory of some German air crew paddling ashore in a rubber dinghy and being thrown back into the water by a crowd of enraged locals, until rescued by a platoon of soldiers came to mind, as did the minute bread ration and the unchanging diet of tinned stew or corned beef. No wonder that we were always hungry.

'The final day and perhaps the most important. A bus ride and a long hot walk brought me to the high walled British Forces Cemetery near Rabat, surrounded by tall poplars. The interior was immaculate, long lines of white headstones, studded here and there with flowering shrubs, and my objective was achieved, the memories flooding back . . . The sun shone and if these boys had to rest, then this peaceful place was as good as any and better than most.

'A forty-three-year ghost was finally exorcised.' [1]

The George Cross Island Association

Whilst Mr Britnell, whose memories of a postwar trip to Malta I have just quoted, made his pilgrimage to Malta on his own, there are regular organised visits arranged by the George Cross Island Association, with Malta Direct Travel.[2] Before briefly describing what is included in one of their itineraries, a few words about the Association which was founded by the late Fred Plenty, RN, who enlisted the help of his wartime skipper, Captain E. A. S. Bailey CBE, DSC. Having gathered a small nucleus around them, they launched the Association in July 1987, Fred being voted Life Vice-President and Founder. Numbers grew fast and by January 1988 had reached over 300, drawn from the three armed services together with the Merchant Navy, both British and Maltese, nursing and civil defence personnel. During their first reunion in Malta, they were received by the President of Malta and senior members of the Government, who were guests at a closing dinner.

Above: Crest of the George Cross Island Association.

Above: 'Faith', the one remaining Gloster Sea Gladiator of the three which had so gallantly defended Malta at the start of the bombing, was partly restored and presented to the people of Malta by Air Vice-Marshal Sir Keith Park on 3 September 1943, in Palace Square, Valletta. *NWMA Malta — 6993*

During their visit there were several memorial church services, visits to war cemeteries, wreath-laying ceremonies and visits to the Lascaris War Rooms, the Malta War Museum and other places of interest. The Malta Branch of the British Legion gave an excellent buffet lunch, followed by the film *Malta Convoy*, which is based on the arrival of the remnants of the Pedestal convoy in August 1942, the tanker *Ohio* being the last to arrive in Grand Harbour — strapped securely between two destroyers — and protected by the garrison's Spitfires and anti-aircraft guns.

Today the Association numbers 2,500 and in October 1993 at the AGM it was decided to give full membership to all members of HM forces who have served or are serving in Malta to ensure that the association continues. In the UK it is presently divided into six regions — Anglia, Midland, North East and Scotland, North West, South East, and West, together with a branch on Malta GC.

On 29 May 1992 the then President, Admiral of the Fleet Lord Lewin KG, GCB, LVO, DSC, was present when Her Majesty The Queen, together with the then President of Malta, His Excellency Doctor Tabone, formally dedicated a 12-tonne bronze memorial bell overlooking Grand Harbour (see below). The bell rings daily at noon for three minutes.

The association has now been honoured by HRH Prince Philip, The Duke of Edinburgh KG, KT, who agreed to become its patron. Prince Philip served in Malta and was also present when the Siege Bell was inaugurated. Patron of the Malta branch is HE Professor Guido de Marco GCMG, KUOM, President of Malta. The current President of the association is Dr Censu Tabone GCB, KUOM.

A Typical Itinerary

The George Cross Island Association visit to Malta in April 2003 was for 14 days and included optional events for each day such as visits to museums and war cemeteries, wreath-laying and commemoration services, cocktail parties and dinners, band displays and social evenings, so there are well organised, varied events to attend which are ideal for those veterans who served on the island during wartime.

The Malta League

The Malta League was set up in London in 1942 by a group of eight Maltese including Dr Richard Castillo (elected as Chairman) and barrister John Colombos who was Master of the Middle Temple and a world authority on international and maritime law. The first AGM was held in the Old Kensington Town Hall on 3 October 1942 and the then Mayor of Kensington, who was greatly interested in the project, welcomed each guest on arrival at the launch. The highpoint of the evening was the unexpected arrival of the ex-governor, General Sir William Dobbie and Lady Dobbie. In his address, he praised the courage and fortitude of the Maltese people through the harsh conditions of the recent siege. At that meeting, the title 'The Malta League' was adopted and a 16-member committee elected under the chairmanship of Dr Castillo. Over the years one of their main roles has been raising money for the Malta Relief Fund, whilst regular meetings/social events have been held, including special gala dinners, concerts and receptions at the Royal Overseas Club in St James and other similar London venues.

Under the chairmanship of Mrs Rosalie Rivett, the Malta League now exists to underpin Anglo-Maltese friendship, holding various annual events, at which any monies raised are donated to a suitable Maltese charity. The last major events were held to celebrate their Diamond Jubilee in October 2002. Their website at www.themaltaleague.org.uk gives further information.

Above: The now fabric-covered fuselage of *'Faith'* on show in the National War Museum. Eventually it is hoped that wings will be fitted and that the aircraft will go on display in the new Malta Aviation Museum. Note the signature of its original pilot — George Burges. *NWMA Malta*

Above: General view of the Main Hall at the National War Museum, Valletta. At the front is an Italian *barchino esplosivo* (MTM) flanked by German torpedoes. *NWMA Malta — 16316*

Museums and Attractions

National War Museum

Lower Fort St Elmo, Valletta; tel: 222430. The George Cross, together with many other displays showing Malta's wartime role, can be seen in the National War Museum, which covers both World War 1 and World War 2. These include such large exhibits as the Jeep used by General Eisenhower when he was planning the invasion of Sicily, the Gloster Gladiator fighter 'Faith' and an Italian MTM (E-boat) as used in the attempt to sink ships in Grand Harbour in July 1941. There is also a 45-minute film, using archive footage, to be seen in the Hostel de Verdelin.

Malta Aviation Museum

Huts 161/2, Crafts Village; tel: 416095. Located at the former RAF base of Ta Qali is the aviation museum which includes amongst its exhibits Hurricanes and Spitfires used in the defence of Malta and restored by volunteers. Eventually it will also house 'Faith'. A new hangar is being constructed to hold more aircraft.

Lascaris War Rooms

Lascaris Bastion, Valletta; tel: 234996. Originally the Bastion was part of the Valletta defences during the Great Siege of 1565, whilst the rooms were used for storage and possibly to house slaves. In 1939 work started to turn them into a command and control centre and they were ready for use in early 1940 and were used throughout the war. After some false starts in the 1970s and 80s, the War Rooms, now run by the Maltese Government, were finally opened in 1995 after many months of hard work. They now show careful re-creations taken from various stages of the war, using carefully crafted replicas and mannequins in uniform or period dress.

Malta George Cross — 'The Wartime Experience'

Palace Square, Valletta; tel: 247891. In a building facing the side of the Main Guard, this 45-minute multi-vision show illustrates the story of Malta during World War 2. Alternating with this show is the 'Valletta Experience' a nostalgic trip through the history of the town.

Memorials

The War Memorial

Designed by Louis Naudi and consisting of five superimposed crosses made of hard Gozo stone, the War Memorial was unveiled on 11 November 1938 by the then Governor, General Sir Charles Bonham-Carter, to commemorate the lives of those Maltese who died during World War 1. The names of 592 Maltese who paid the supreme sacrifice are inscribed on three sides in bronze letters, the fourth side bears a plinth on which is inscribed the message sent by King George V recording Malta's part in the Great War. Soon after the end of World War 2 it was decided that the Memorial should commemorate the dead of both wars, so the original panels at the base were replaced by tablets reproducing Malta's armorial bearings, together with the text of the tributes paid to Malta by King George V, King George VI and President Franklin D. Roosevelt. The new tablets were unveiled on 8 December 1949 by the then Princess Elizabeth.

The Commonwealth Air Forces Memorial

This striking memorial was the result of recommendations made to the Air Council for a memorial to all those members of the Air Forces of the British Commonwealth and Empire, who, while serving in or in association with the Royal Air Force on Malta, lost their lives and have no known graves. The 15-metre high column is of travertine marble from Tivoli, near Rome, and is incised with a light reticulated pattern and surmounted by a gilded bronze eagle 2.35m high. Around the base are the names of 2,301 airmen from the RAF, RCAF, Newfoundland forces, RAAF, RNZAF, SAAF and the civil airline BOAC. A Latin epigram translates: 'An Island resolute of purpose remembers resolute men.' The memorial was unveiled by Queen Elizabeth II on 3 May 1954.

The Siege Bell Memorial

Probably the most evocative of all the memorials, the Siege Bell Memorial extends over a long site on the bastion adjacent to the Lower Barracca Garden and overlooking the entrance to the Grand Harbour. It consists of a neo-classical cupola with a bell inside it and a recumbent figure on a catafalque.[3] It is a tribute to the 7,000 servicemen, merchant seamen and civilians who died in the defence of the island during World War 2. It was inspired by the

Below: The striking War Memorial, that consists of five superimposed crosses of Gozo stone. It commemorates all those Maltese who died in both World Wars. *Harry Gratland*

Right:
One of the displays within the Lascaris War Rooms is the Fighter Control Room, with plotters at work on the plotting table.
NWMA Malta — 15745

Left:
Equally as striking as the War Memorial is the Commonwealth Air Forces Memorial with its gilded bronze eagle, which was unveiled by the Queen on 3 May 1954. *FOTOFORCE Malta — 19*

Below:
The catafalque, with its recumbent figure, and Grand Harbour stretching away below. *Harry Gratland*

Above: As striking as the catafalque is the Siege Bell Memorial, overlooking Grand Harbour, which is probably the most evocative of all memorials. This is the neo–classical cupola, with a bell inside it. *Harry Gratland*

George Cross Island Association and designed by Professor Michael Sandle. The Government of Malta looks after the maintenance of the Memorial. As already mentioned, it was inaugurated by the Queen on the 50th Anniversary of the award of the George Cross to Malta.

A Corner of a Foreign Field

The Commonwealth War Graves Commission lists six principal cemeteries that it is responsible for, covering both World Wars. These are:

Addolorata Cemetery

It lies on the outskirts of the village of Paola some 4.5km from Valletta and a bus service runs in its vicinity. It is open daily.

Mtarfa Military Cemetery

In the hills, some 11km from Valletta lies the former capital of Mdina and about 1km to the northeast is the Mtarfa Cemetery. There is a bus service but it only goes to the village of Rabat, about 1.2km away. There are 262 1939–45 burials.

Capuccini Naval Cemetery, Kalkara

About 2km southeast of Rinella, a bay and hamlet opposite Valletta across the mouth of Grand Harbour and on the outskirts of the village of Kalkara. A bus service runs close to the cemetery, which contains the largest number of 1939–45 burials in Malta.

Marsa Jewish Cemetery and Marsa Muslim Cemetery

Some 4.5km from Valletta is Marsa, a village on Marsa Creek, which is a continuation inland of Grand Harbour. Follow the signs to the airport within the vicinity of the sports club. A bus service is available.

Pembroke Military Cemetery, St Andrew's

Just off the northeast coastal road that runs from Msida through St Andrew's to St Paul's Bay, between St Andrew's and what was originally St Patrick's Barracks. It is some 2.5km from St Julian's Bay and 8km from St Paul's Bay. A bus service runs close by from Valletta and St Paul's Bay. There are 318 1939–45 burials; 53 servicemen whose graves are in other parts of Malta are also commemorated by name on marble plaques let in to the Cross of Sacrifice.

Pieta Military Cemetery

Pieta is a village and a creek at the head of Marsamxett harbour near the base of the peninsula on which Valletta stands. The cemetery is 1.5km from Valletta on the main road to Sliema. A bus service runs close by. There are 180 1939–45 burials and the largest number of World War 1 burials (1,304).

A Solemn Pledge

When the Queen (then Princess Elizabeth) unveiled the new tablets on the Floriana War Memorial, she said: 'It is most fitting that those tributes should be recorded on your Cenotaph, which commemorates those whose supreme sacrifice deserves all honour and glory.' The Prime Minister of Malta, Dr (later Sir Paul) Boffa, replied: 'Recalling with pride the role Malta has played in the cause of Freedom, it is highly befitting that on this day we pay tribute to the Service and the Civilian men and women of Malta who, fighting side by side with fellow members of the British Commonwealth, have paid with their lives that we may live and continue to enjoy our heritage; we solemnly pledge ourselves never to forget their sacrifice.'

Above: A view of part of the Pieta Military Cemetery. *Commonwealth War Graves Commission — COL 13553(14A)*

741212 SERGEANT
D. K. ASHTON
PILOT
ROYAL AIR FORCE
26TH NOVEMBER 1940 · AGE 25

Above: A close-up of the beautiful carving of RAF, RAAF and RCAF badges on the gravestones. *FOTOFORCE Malta — 7*

Notes
1. G. G. Britnell, late 90th General Hospital, RAMC, taken from *Malta Remembered* Volume No 5.
2. Malta Direct Travel is the trading name of Holiday Malta Co Ltd.
3. A catafalque is a temporary raised platform on which a body lies in state before or during a funeral.

Bibliography

Books

Agius, John A., and Galea, Frederick R.: *Lest We Forget*, Malta Aviation Museum Foundation, 1999.

Becker, Cajus: *The Luftwaffe Diaries*, Gerard Stalling Verlag, 1964.

Beurling, George, and Roberts, Leslie: *Malta Spitfire — The Diary of a Fighter Pilot*, OUP, 1943.

Boffa, Charles J.: *The Second Great Siege — Malta 1940–43*, Progress Press, 1992.

Boffa, Charles J.: *The Illustrious Blitz. Malta in Wartime 1940–1941*, Progress Press, 1995.

Bonner, Robert A.: *The Ardwick Boys went to Malta*, Fleur de Lys Publishing, 1992.

Brown, David: *Warship Losses of World War Two*, Arms & Armour, Revised 1996

Cameron, Ian: *Red Duster, White Ensign. The Story of Malta and the Malta Convoys*, Frederick Muller, 1959.

Chaplin, H. D.: *The Queen's Own Royal West Kent Regiment 1920–1950*, Michael Joseph, 1954.

Churchill, Winston: *The Second World War*, Volume III, 'The Grand Alliance', Volume IV, 'The Hinge of Fate'; Volume V 'Closing the Ring', Cassell, 1950, 1951 and 1952.

Connell, John: *Auchinleck*, a critical biography, Cassell, 1959.

Cooper, Bryan: *The Battle of the Torpedo Boats*, Macdonald, 1970.

Eisenhower, Dwight D.: *Crusade in Europe*, William Heinemann, 1948.

Galea, Frederick R. (ed): *A Brief History of Spitfire IX EN199*, Malta Aviation Museum Foundation, 1995.

Galea, Frederick R. (ed): *Call-Out*, Bieb Bieb, Malta, 2002.

Greene, Jack, and Massignani, Alessandro: *The Naval War in the Mediterranean 1940–1943*, Chatham Publishing, 1998.

Guedalla, Philip: *Middle East 1940–1942, A Study in Air Power*, Hodder & Stoughton, 1944.

Herrmann, Hajo: *Eagle's Wings, The Autobiography of a Luftwaffe Pilot*, Airlife, 1991.

Jones, R. V.: *Most Secret War*, Hamish Hamilton, 1978.

Kesselring, Albert: *The Memoirs of Field Marshal Kesselring*, William Kimber, 1953.

Laffin, John, *British VCs of World War 2*, Sutton, 1997.

Lucas, 'Laddie': *Malta: The Thorn in Rommel's Side*, Stanley Paul, 1992.

Luke, Harry: *Malta, An Account and an Appreciation*, George G. Harrap, 1949.

Shores, Christopher, and Cull, Brian; with Malizia, Nicola: *Malta: The Hurricane Years 1940–1941*, Grub Street, 1987.

Shores, Christopher, and Cull, Brian; with Malizia, Nicola: *Malta: The Spitfire Year 1942*, Grub Street, 1991.

Smith, Peter C., and Walker, Edwin: *The Battles of the Malta Striking Forces*, Ian Allan, 1974.

Smith, Peter C.: *Pedestal — The Malta Convoy of August 1942*, William Kimber, 1970.

Trevor-Roper, H. R.: *Hitler's Table Talk 1941–44*, Weidenfeld & Nicolson, 1953.

Vella, Philip: *Malta: Blitzed but not Beaten*, Progress Press, 1985.

Ward, S. G. P.: *Faithful, The Story of the Durham Light Infantry*, Thomas Nelson & Sons, 1963.

Warren, C. E. T., and Benson, James: *Above us the Waves*, George G. Harrap, 1953.

Official Publications

The Air Battle of Malta, HMSO, 1944

The Epic of Malta, Odhams Press, 1943

US World War 2 German Military Studies: Volume 7, Part IV — 'The OKW War Diary Series', Garland Publishing, 1979. Volume 14, Part VI — 'The Mediterranean Theater continued', Garland Publishing, 1979.

Periodicals, Magazines, etc

The National War Museum, Malta GC, Official Guide.

Battlefields Review Issue No 18

After the Battle Number 10: Malta GC

Malta at War Volume 1, Issues 1, 2 and 3

George Cross Island Association National Newsletters

Malta Remembered Volumes 1-6, edited by Frank Rixon BEM, George Cross Island Association. Contains events and stories as told by the veterans of Malta GC.

Index

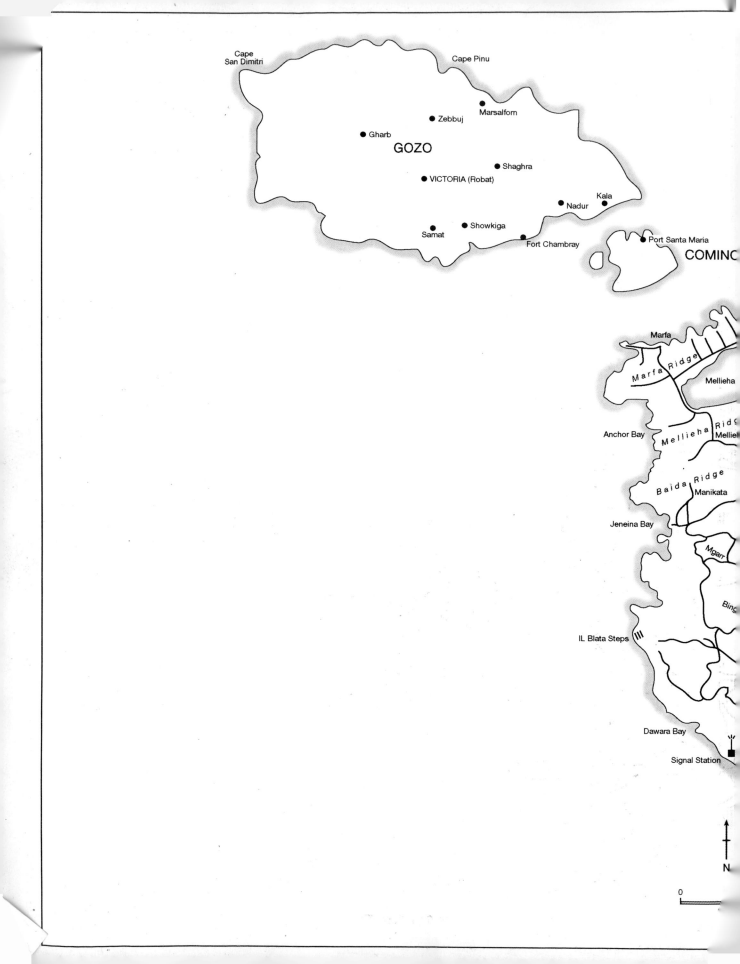

Cape
San Dimitri

Cape Pinu

● Marsalforn

● Zebbuj

● Gharb

GOZO

● Shaghra

● VICTORIA (Robat)

Kala
●

● Nadur

● Showkiga

Samat

Fort Chambray

● Port Santa Maria

COMINO

Marfa

Marfa Ridge

Mellieha

Anchor Bay

Mellieha Ridge

Mellieh

Baida Ridge

Manikata

Jeneina Bay

Mgarr

Bing

IL Blata Steps

Dawara Bay

Signal Station

N

0